P9-CQZ-770

Contents

93219

Illustrations

Maps

Plans

Tables

Ancient Greece

Ancient Greece

From Prehistoric to

Hellenistic Times

■

THOMAS R. MARTIN

Yale University Press   New Haven & London

Designed by James J. Johnson and set
in Gill Sans and Joanna types by Tseng
Information Systems, Inc., Durham,
North Carolina.
Printed in the United States of America
by Edwards Brothers, Inc., Ann Arbor,
Michigan.

Library of Congress Cataloging-in-Publication Data

Martin, Thomas R., 1947–
Ancient Greece : from prehistoric to
Hellenistic times / Thomas R. Martin.
p.   cm.
Includes bibliographical references
and index.
ISBN 0-300-06767-4 (cloth: alk. paper)
ISBN 0-300-06956-1 (pbk.: alk. paper)

1. Greece—History—To 146 B.C. I. Title.
DF77.M3   1996
938—dc20   95–26690

A catalogue record for this book is
available from the British Library.

The paper in this book meets the
guidelines for permanence and durability
of the Committee on Production
Guidelines for Book Longevity of the
Council on Library Resources.

10   9   8   7   6   5   4   3   2

Figures

Introduction

This book offers an overview of the history of ancient Greece, beginning with Greece's place in the prehistory of Europe and ending with the period following the death of Alexander the Great in 323 B.C. until the coming of the Romans in the second century B.C. The narrative forms part of my earlier work writing the "Historical Overview" that appears among the electronic databases published in *Perseus: Interactive Sources and Studies on Ancient Greece*, Gregory Crane, editor in chief, versions 1.0 and 2.0 (Yale University Press, 1992 and 1996, respectively). This new edition revises and expands the sections previously included in *Perseus* on Greece of the eighth to the fourth centuries B.C. and completes the survey of ancient Greek history by adding sections on the prehistory of Greece, the Bronze Age, the Dark Age, and the Hellenistic Age.

Although this book is able to stand on its own, I hope that users of *Perseus* will find it useful as a "hard-copy" complement to their computerized materials. For me, the convenience and portability that books allow make them indispensable tools for learning and thinking, and I see an ongoing need for both books and software in the study of ancient Greece. This volume is intended to contribute to the synergy that these different tools can create when used together. This book expands the text of the overview; the software versions provide many more illustrations and direct links to ancient sources. At http://www.perseus.tufts.edu/Secondary/ TRM_Overview/ readers can visit an on-line version.

The narrative has the bell-curve shape of many histories of ancient Greece. That is, more pages are devoted to the middle of the story than to the beginning and the end because I concentrate on the full development of the Greek city-state as a religious, social, political, and economic entity

in the eighth to fourth centuries B.C. Athens receives the most space because the overwhelming preponderance of the evidence surviving from ancient Greece concerns Athens in the Classical period (c. 500–323 B.C.). Since
Greece was home to hundreds of other city-states, many of which differed
in significant ways from Athens, studying the history of Athens cannot be
taken as equivalent to studying the history of Greece. Above all, it will not
do to generalize about what "ancient Greeks" did or thought or said when
the evidence for such generalizations comes solely from Athens (or indeed
from any one place). With this warning in mind, I have tried to include material from as many different places as possible, but I am under no illusion
of having provided as much coverage of non-Athenian history as others
may like to see. The compensation for the distortion in coverage is that the
history of Athens is interesting in its own right and significant beyond its
own time.

Many topics receive only brief treatment, and some that deserved better
are scarcely mentioned, if at all. The compensation for such compression
and omission is whatever brevity the text can claim. It takes the form of a
chronological narrative because this seems the optimal way to present complex material. Therefore, I have tried to integrate political, social, and cultural history into the text throughout rather than presenting long stretches
of political history followed by an agglomeration of separate sections on
different topics.

Perhaps an overview of the overview will be helpful to give readers
some idea of the periodization of Greek history that this book employs.
Unlike some Greek histories, mine begins with a section on the late Stone
Age because this prehistory provides deep background on the material and
social conditions of later Greek life that is essential for understanding Greek
history in the broader context of Europe and the Mediterranean region.
The following sections on the Bronze Age describe the civilization of the
Minoans on the island of Crete and its successor, that of the Mycenaeans on
the mainland. The prosperous monarchies of these civilizations ended in a
mysterious episode of destruction, which leads to the period usually still
referred to as the Greek Dark Age (c. 1000–c. 750 B.C.). The scale and duration
of the poverty and depopulation that occurred in this Dark Age are increasingly controversial, but there can be no doubt that remarkable changes in
the basic conditions of Greek life came about in this period, opening the
way to the Archaic Age (c. 750–c. 500 B.C.). Most strikingly, the late Dark Age
and the Archaic Age saw the development of the city-state (polis) as a new and
eventually widespread form of political, social, and religious organization.

Next comes the famous Classical Age of Greece in the fifth and fourth
centuries B.C. Focusing primarily on Athens, this part of the overview con-

cerns the cultural achievements and military struggles that made Classical Greece so well known and so influential in later centuries. It also pays special attention to the enduring philosophical legacies of Socrates, Plato, and Aristotle and to the startling transformation of the kingdom of Macedonia into the greatest power in the Greek world, overshadowing the city-states militarily while seeking to emulate them culturally. This part of the story comes to a climax with the career of the legendary Macedonian conqueror Alexander the Great (died 323 B.C.). The overview ends by surveying the Hellenistic period after Alexander's death, when monarchies, this time emerging from Alexander's fragmented empire, once again came to dominate Greek history, even though the traditional city-states remained vital and even, in some cases, independent. Thus the history of the ancient Greeks comes full circle, from the monarchies of the Mycenaeans in the late Bronze Age to the monarchies of Greece after Alexander.

Timelines, maps, plans, and photographs are provided to help readers situate themselves chronologically, geographically, and visually. Like the narrative, these materials are limited because of the importance of keeping the book brief. This overview is meant to be supplemented by other sources of information, from ancient authors to modern discussions of special issues, appropriate to the interests and curiosity of its readers. Lists of selected readings on a variety of topics are therefore also provided as suggested starting points for going beyond the purposely limited boundaries of this book. More detailed surveys of ancient Greek history are recommended there for those who would like a fuller narrative. I hope that this design will make use of the book more flexible: after a relatively modest investment of time, readers can determine for themselves what topics they would like to pursue in greater depth.

Writing history means making observations and forming interpretations, and these activities inevitably influence one another almost all the time. At important points I discuss interpretations that are problematic or controversial, but my commitment to brevity requires that at many other places nothing can be said about the complex interrelationship of observation, interpretation, and controversy surrounding issues that in a longer text might deserve such treatment. Since reading history should imitate writing history as an active process rather than a passive absorption of data, I hope that readers of this book will be challenged to convert their dissatisfaction with the book's omissions and imperfections into energy for researching questions they have been provoked to ask. Pausanias, the author of a famous guide to Greek sites written in the second century after Christ, by which time the period covered by this book was already ancient history, adroitly summed up the challenge ever facing those of us fascinated by this subject:

"Most things in the history of Greece have become a matter of dispute" (*Description of Greece* 4.2.3).

Acknowledgments

The many members of the team working on *Perseus* 2.0 contributed to this overview in ways both direct and indirect. The support of Gregory Crane, editor in chief of *Perseus*, has been important from the beginning. My colleague in the Classics Department at the College of the Holy Cross, Blaise Nagy, deserves special thanks for using earlier versions of this overview in his very popular class on ancient Greek history. His many comments and suggestions helped improve the text and, most important, his enthusiasm encouraged me to produce this version. The various members of the Editorial and Production Departments at Yale University Press, especially Executive Editor Charles Grench and Manuscript Editor Harry Haskell, have cheerfully aided me at every turn. The four anonymous readers of the manuscript for the Press deserve particular recognition for the seriousness, promptness, and positive tone of their comments. Shirley Sui-Nin Sun, who sacrificed her time to do proofreading, and Victoria Baker, who devoted special care to producing the index, both went beyond the call of duty in catching errors. Finally, I want to express my warm thanks to my wife, Ivy Sui-yuen Sun, and our children, Andrea and Alex, for their patient forbearance, which made this work possible.

Readers are encouraged to contact the author via e-mail at tmartin@ holycross.edu to offer suggestions for improving the book.

Abbreviations

ANET   J. B. Pritchard, *Ancient Near Eastern Texts Relating to the Old Testament*, 3d
           ed. with supplement (Princeton, 1969)

Ath. Pol. Aristotle, *Athenaion Politeia* (Constitution of the Athenians)

CAF   T. Kock, *Comicorum Atticorum Fragmenta* (Leipzig, 1880–1888)

D.-K.   H. Diels and W. Kranz, *Die Fragmente der Vorsokratiker*, 10th ed.
           (Berlin, 1960)

FGrH   F. Jacoby et al., *Die Fragmente der griechischen Historiker* (Berlin, 1923–)

GHI   R. Meiggs and D. Lewis, *Greek Historical Inscriptions to the End of the
           Fifth Century B.C.* (Oxford, 1969)

IG   *Inscriptiones Graecae* (Berlin, 1873–)

Lac. Pol. Xenophon, *Lacedaimonion Politeia* (Constitution of the Spartans)

OGIS   W. Dittenberger, *Orientis Graeci Inscriptiones Selectae* (Leipzig,
           1903–1905)

PLF   E. Lobel and D. Page, *Poetarum Lesbiorum Fragmenta* (Oxford, 1955)

PMG   D. Page, *Poetae Melici Graeci* (Oxford, 1962)

West   M. L. West, *Iambi et Elegi Graeci ante Alexandrum cantati* (Oxford,
           1971–1972)

Backgrounds of Ancient Greek History

1

The Physical Environment of Greece

The deepest background of the social, material, and even political history of ancient Greece lies in the physical environment and its effects on the opportunities and the constraints of life in this part of the Mediterranean region. The homeland of the ancient Greeks was located in the regions surrounding the Aegean Sea and in its many islands; this section of the Mediterranean Sea is flanked on the west by the Balkan peninsula (today the territory of the modern nation of Greece) and on the east by the coast of Anatolia (modern Turkey). Greeks also took up residence on the large islands of Crete and Cyprus, on the coast of North Africa, and in southern Italy and on Sicily (an area sometimes referred to by the Latin name "Magna Graecia"), where some of the most famous and prosperous of Greek cities emerged.

Chains of rugged mountains dominate mainland Greece, fencing off plains and valleys in which communities could keep themselves politically separate from one another while still maintaining contacts for trade and diplomacy. These mountains mainly run from northwest to southeast along the Balkan peninsula, with narrow passes connecting Greek territory to Macedonia in the north. The terrain of the islands of the Aegean was also craggy. Only about 20 to 30 percent of the mainland

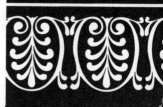

was arable, but some islands, western Anatolia, Magna Graecia, and a few fortunate mainland regions, especially Thessaly in the northeast and Messenia in the southwest, included plains spacious enough to support bounteous crops and large grazing animals. The scarcity of level terrain ruled out the raising of cattle and horses on any large scale in many areas. When Greeks first domesticated animals in the late Stone Age, pigs, sheep, and goats became the most common livestock. By the seventh century B.C. the domestic chicken had been introduced into Greece from the Near East.

Once Greeks learned to farm, they mostly grew barley, which formed the cereal staple of the Greek diet. The generally poor land supported crops of barley far better than of wheat, which made tastier food but needed richer land to flourish. Other major crops were wine grapes and olives. Wine diluted with water was the favorite beverage drunk by Greeks, while olive oil provided a principal source of dietary fat and also served, among many other uses, as a cleaning agent for bathing and a base for perfumes. Meat appeared more rarely in Greek meals than in those of modern Western cultures.

So jagged was the Greek coastline that most settlements lay within forty miles of the sea, providing easy access for fishermen and seagoing merchants. Greek entrepreneurs sailed all over the Mediterranean seeking lucrative trading deals. The ports of Egypt and the eastern Mediterranean coast were favorite destinations. Going to sea with the limited marine technology of the time made bad weather a serious threat to life and limb, and prevailing winds and fierce gales almost ruled out sailing in winter. Even in calm conditions sailors hugged the coast whenever possible and aimed to land every night for safety. As the eighth-century B.C. poet Hesiod remarked, merchants took sail "because an income means life to wretched mortals, but it is a terrible fate to die among the waves" (Works and Days 686–687).

Most Greeks, even if they lived near the sea, never traveled very far from their home. Sea travel nevertheless played a central role in the development of Greek culture because traders and entrepreneurs voyaging from the Near East and Egypt to Greece and vice versa put Greeks into contact with the older civilizations of the eastern Mediterranean region, from which they learned new technologies, religious ideas, and more. Transporting people and goods overland instead of by sea was slow and expensive because rudimentary dirt paths were Greece's only roads. The rivers were practically useless for trade and communication because most of them slowed to a trickle during the many months each year when little or no rain fell. Timber for building houses and ships was the most plentiful natural resource of the mountainous terrain of the mainland, but deforestation had probably already affected many regions by the fifth century. By that time Greeks

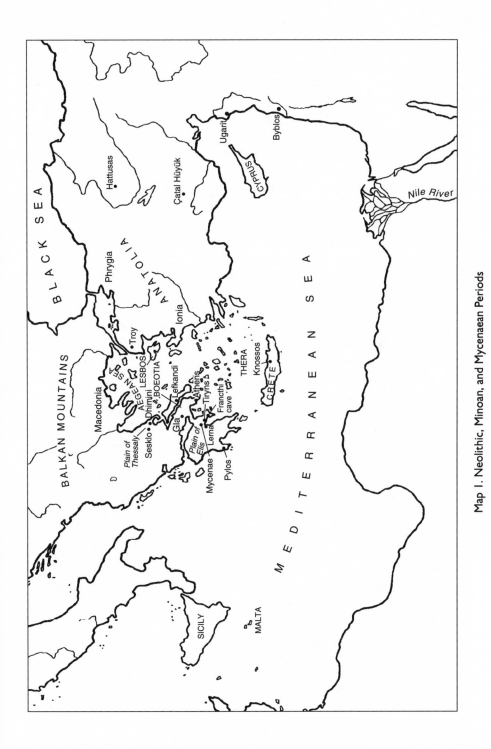

Map I. Neolithic, Minoan, and Mycenaean Periods

were certainly importing lumber from northward regions and paying stiff prices for it. Some deposits of metal ore were scattered throughout Greek territory, as were clays useful for making pots and many other practical objects. Quarries of fine stone such as marble furnished material for expensive buildings and sculpture. The irregular distribution of these resources made some areas considerably wealthier than others. The silver mines in Athenian territory, for example, provided an income that buttressed the exceptional prosperity of Athens's so-called Golden Age in the fifth century B.C.

Modern meteorologists refer to the climate of Greece as Mediterranean, meaning winters drenched with intermittent heavy rain and summers baking with hot, dry weather. Since annual rainfall varied significantly, Greek farmers endured a precarious cycle of boom and bust, fearing both drought and floods. Nevertheless, the Greeks believed their climate was the world's best. "The Greeks occupy a middle position [between hot and cold climates] and correspondingly enjoy both energy and intelligence," commented the fourth-century philosopher and scientist Aristotle, who saw climate as determining political destiny. "For this reason they retain their freedom and have the best of political institutions. In fact, if they could forge political unity among themselves, they could control the rest of the world" (Politics 7.7, 1327b29–33).

As Aristotle implied, throughout their history the ancient Greeks never constituted a nation in the modern sense because their various communities never united politically. On the other hand, Greeks saw themselves as sharing a cultural identity because they spoke dialects of the same language, had similar customs, worshipped the same gods (with local variations in cult), and came together at international religious festivals, such as the celebration of the mysteries of the goddess Demeter at Athens or the athletic games at Olympia in the Peloponnese. Ancient Greece was thus a set of shared ideas and practices rather than a sharply demarcated territorial or national entity. How this sense of Greek cultural identity came to be and how it was maintained over the centuries are difficult questions that must be kept constantly in mind; that its mountainous topography contributed to the political fragmentation of Greece seems clear.

The Human Prehistory of Greece

Greek prehistory (the period before written records) forms part of the prehistory of Europe, which in turn has its beginnings in the movement of early peoples outward from the African continent. The prehistoric human background of Greek history thus begins tens of thousands of years ago, in the latter portion of the Stone Age, so named because the people of the time

c. **45,000–40,000** years ago: *Homo sapiens sapiens* first moves out of Africa into southwestern Asia and Europe.

c. **20,000** years ago: Human habitation begins in the Francthi cave in southeastern Greece.

c. **10,000–8000 B.C.:** Transition from Paleolithic to Neolithic Age: the beginning of agriculture and permanent settlements.

c. **8000 B.C.:** Walled settlement at Jericho in ancient Palestine.

c. **7000–6000 B.C.:** Agriculture and domestication of animals under way in southern and eastern Europe, including Greece.

c. **7000–5000 B.C.:** Settlements of permanent houses being built in fertile plains in Greece.

c. **4000–3000 B.C.:** Copper metallurgy under way in Balkan region.

---

had only stone, in addition to bone and wood, from which to fashion tools and weapons; they had not yet developed the technology to make implements from metals. Most important, at this point human beings did not yet know how to cultivate crops. When people began to develop agricultural technology about ten to twelve thousand years ago, they experienced tremendous changes in their lives and began to affect the natural environment in unprecedented ways.

These transformations slowly opened the way to the growth of cities and the emergence of political states (people living in a definite territory and organized under a system of government and judicial regulations). The people of the ancient Near East first developed these new forms of human organization, which later appeared in Europe. (Early civilizations of this kind also emerged in India, China, and the Americas, whether independently or through some process of mutual influence no one at present knows.) These developments took place in Europe through a complicated process of diffusion from the Near East and independent innovation. The original transformative change in this long process was the invention of agriculture and the spread to more and more prehistoric populations of the technology needed for it.

Before Agriculture

The Stone Age is conventionally subdivided into the Paleolithic (Greek for "Old Stone") and Neolithic ("New Stone") Ages. The end of the Paleolithic and thus the beginning of the Neolithic is usually placed about ten to twelve thousand years ago. During the long Paleolithic period human beings roamed throughout their lives, searching for food in the wild by hunting game, fishing, collecting shellfish, and gathering plants, fruits, and nuts. Living as hunter-gatherers, these early human beings sometimes migrated great distances, presumably following large game animals or searching for more abundant sources of nutritious wild plants. The first human beings in Greece probably migrated there long ago from the African continent via the eastern Mediterranean and Anatolia; a skull found at Petralona in Greece has been dated to at least two hundred thousand years before the present. At least as early as fifty thousand years ago the type of Paleolithic human beings known as Neanderthals (from the finds of their remains in Germany's Neanderthal valley) spread over Macedonia and then into Greece as far south as the plain of Elis in the Peloponnese peninsula. The well-watered plain of Thessaly in northern Greece was particularly popular with hunter-gatherer populations in this period.

People of modern type (Homo sapiens sapiens) began to migrate from Africa into Europe during the last part of the Paleolithic period. This new population eventually replaced completely the earlier populations, such as the Neanderthals; how this happened remains unknown. By this time all humans had already developed spoken language (the invention of writing still lay tens of thousands of years in the future), so it cannot have been the ability to communicate with spoken words that allowed the new type of human to submerge the old. Perhaps the newcomers were better able to cope with natural disasters, such as the tremendous floods that covered the plain of Thessaly for many years beginning about thirty thousand years before the present and forced the populations there to flee to the surrounding hills, where food would have been harder to find.

Archaeological excavation of prehistoric sites combined with information from twentieth-century hunter-gatherers, such as the !Kung San of the Kalahari Desert in southern Africa, allows us to reconstruct some outlines of the life of Paleolithic hunter-gatherers for contrast with later patterns of Greek life. It would be misleading to refer to the prehistoric inhabitants of Greece at this early date as "Greeks" in the same sense in which that term is applied to the population of the region in historical times. There is no evidence to allow us to distinguish clearly among different ethnic groups in prehistoric Europe on the criteria used for populations of later periods, such as language. Regional differences among prehistoric European populations probably existed, but we are not in a position today to identify them confidently. In the Paleolithic Age, therefore, the inhabitants of the territory we call Greece were, as far as we can tell, a subset of the general population of prehistoric Europe. These people banded together in groups numbering in many cases as few as twenty to thirty individuals, who hunted and foraged for food to be shared among one another. Women of childbearing age, who had to nurse their infants, would have found it difficult to forage far from camp and thus, along with smaller children, gathered edible plants and caught small animals close to home base. The plant food gathered by women and children made up most of what the group ate on a daily basis. Men probably did most of the hunting of large animals, expeditions that could take them great distances from camp for long periods. Prehistoric groups thus tended to divide their main labor—finding food—along gender and age lines.

Since the very survival of the group depended on the labor of both men and women, these prehistoric bands perhaps did not strictly allot power and status in their groups by gender and may even have been largely egalitarian, with all adults sharing on a roughly equal basis in making decisions about how the group should be constituted and what its members should do. Such generalizations are risky, of course; modern hunter-gatherers sometimes observe prestige differences according to gender, such as assigning greater value to the meat hunted by men than to the plant food gathered by women. Such distinctions can also be seen as defined by the kind of work one does in the group, however, and gender therefore does not have to have been an originally significant factor in making them. In any case, older people likely enjoyed higher social status in ancient hunter-gatherer populations because their greater age gave them greater knowledge to impart to younger people. It also set them apart as special because disease or accidents killed most people before they had reached thirty years of age.

Ancient hunter-gatherers probably lacked laws, judges, and political organization in the modern sense, which is not to say that they lacked forms of social organization, regulation, and control. Some Paleolithic graves containing weapons, tools, animal figurines, ivory beads, and bracelets in fact suggest that hunter-gatherers recognized social differences among individuals and that an individual's special social status could by marked by the possession of more expensive or elaborate goods. Just as the possession of a quantity of such goods in life had shown that individuals enjoyed superior wealth, power, or status in their groups, so, too, the burial of the goods with the corpse indicated the individual's prestige. Accordingly, it appears that some Paleolithic groups organized themselves not along egalitarian lines but rather in hierarchies, social systems that ranked certain people as more important and more dominant than others. Thus, already in this early period we find traces of the kind of social differentiation (the marking of certain people as wealthier, more respected, or more powerful than others in their group) that characterized later Greek society in the historical period.

If they behaved like the surviving hunter-gatherers of modern times, Paleolithic hunter-gatherer groups tended to stay within territories somehow recognized as their own. Even though they did not build permanent homes, their sense of inhabiting a space of their own nevertheless fore-shadowed the territoriality characteristic of the much later Greek city-states. At the same time, the interest of Paleolithic peoples in trade and contact with other groups also prefigured subsequent patterns of exchange. Prehistoric groups frequently bartered attractive objects and natural resources with each other, which could eventually travel great distances from their point of origin. Such interactions looked forward to the development of inter-national trade, especially in metals, and of exchanges of ideas that forged far-reaching connections among distant peoples in the Mediterranean re-gion in later times and in which Greeks would enthusiastically take part.

Prehistoric human beings had many skills passed down by their ances-tors, from tool making to preparing food with fire. Cooking was an espe-cially important technological innovation, because it converted plants that were indigestible when left raw, such as wild grains, into edible and nutri-tious food. But the interests and curiosity of these peoples extended beyond mere physical survival. Female statuettes (called Venus figurines by mod-ern archaeologists, after the Roman goddess of sexual love) sculpted with extra-large breasts, abdomens, buttocks, and thighs have turned up in Paleo-lithic sites scattered over Europe. Their exaggerated features suggest that the people to whom they belonged maintained beliefs and probably communal rituals about fertility and birth. The care employed in burying the dead — decorating the corpses with pigment of red ochre, flowers, and seashells — further hints at a religious sense concerned with the mystery of death and perhaps belief about the dead retaining some form of power. Religious be-liefs may also be involved in paintings of this period found in Spanish and French caves. The paintings, depicting primarily large animals on the walls of caves, which were then apparently set aside as special places and not used as day-to-day shelters, suggest that the killing of these powerful ani-mals in often dangerous hunts provoked a religious awe among the hunters. Much of Paleolithic religious belief, such as the meaning of the signs (dots, rectangles, and hands) often sketched beside the cave paintings of animals, remains obscure, but it is striking that later Greek religion (like other Medi-terranean religions) made the sacrifice of large animals its most important public ritual.

Hunter-gatherers lived precarious lives dominated by the relentless search for something to eat. Survival was a risky business at best. Only those groups survived that learned to cooperate effectively in securing food and shelter, to profit from technological innovations such as the use of fire and tool making, and to teach their children the knowledge, beliefs, and social traditions that made their society viable. Successful hunter-gatherers passed on to later peoples these traits for survival in a harsh world.

Transformation of Daily Life in the Late Stone Age

Daily life as the ancient Greeks knew it depended on agriculture and the domestication of animals, innovations that gradually took root starting some ten to twelve thousand years ago at the opening of the Neolithic period. The process of gaining this knowledge, which was to change human life radically, extended over several thousand years. Excavations at the site of the Francthi cave in Greece, for example, have revealed the gradual process of adapting to natural change that prehistoric populations underwent as they learned to farm. Hunter-gatherers first showed up in this area near the southeastern Greek seacoast about twenty thousand years before the present. At that time the cave, used for shelter, lay some five to six kilometers from the coast and overlooked a plain verdant with vegetation. Wild horses and cattle grazed there, providing easy hunting. Over about the next twelve thousand years, the sea level gradually rose, perhaps as a result of climatic changes, until only a narrow ribbon of marsh and beach about one kilometer wide separated the cave from the shoreline. With large game animals no longer available nearby, the residents of the Francthi cave now based their diet on seafood and especially wild plants such as lentils, oats, barley, bitter vetch, and pear gathered from nearby valleys and hillsides.

As hunter-gatherer populations, such as the residents of the Francthi cave, came to depend increasingly on plants for their survival, the problem became to develop a reliable supply. The answer, which took thousands of years of repeated trial and error to learn, was to plant part of the seeds from one crop to produce another crop. Knowledge of this revolutionary technology—agriculture—first emerged not in Greece but in the Near East and slowly spread outward. Evidence from the Francthi cave and the plain of Thessaly shows the new technology had reached Greece by around 7000 B.C. How it made its way there is an intriguing puzzle still to be solved. One of perhaps many contributing factors may have been the travels of traders in crafted objects and natural resources, who scoured the Mediterranean in search of materials and markets. They could have brought with them seeds from domesticated strains of barley and wheat, along with knowledge about planting and cultivation. A population unfamiliar with agriculture could have been induced to develop it not only to feed its people but also to create surpluses of wealth that could be traded for things not locally available.

However knowledge of agriculture spread after its invention, Neolithic women had probably played the major role in inventing the technology and the tools needed to practice it, such as digging sticks and grinding stones. After all, women in hunter-gatherer society had developed the greatest knowledge of plants because they were the principal gatherers of this food. In the earliest history of farming women did most of the agricultural labor, while men continued to hunt. During this same transitional period, people also learned to breed and herd animals for food, thus helping replace the meat formerly supplied by the hunting of large mammals, many of which had become extinct. The first animal to be domesticated as a source of meat was the sheep, from about 8500 B.C. in the Near East. (Dogs had been domesticated much earlier but were little used as a meat source.) Domesticated sheep and goats had become common throughout the Near East and southern Europe, including Greece, by about 7000 B.C. In this early stage of domestication, small herds kept close to home were the rule. They could therefore be tended by men, women, and children alike. These early domesticated herds seem to have been used only as a source of meat, not for so-called secondary products like milk and wool for clothing.

The production, instead of just the gathering, of food laid the foundation for other changes that we today take for granted. For example, to farm successfully, people had to live in settled locations, and farming villages formed in the Near East by as early as 10,000 B.C. Permanent communities of farmers, comprising a built environment with a densely settled population, constituted a new stage in human history. Large farming communities appeared earlier in the Near East than in Greece. At Jericho (in modern Israel), for example, a walled settlement large enough to house some two thousand inhabitants had been constructed by 8000 B.C. Sizable Neolithic villages sprang up in Macedonia and further south in Greece in Thessaly and Boeotia during the period 7000–5000 B.C., concentrating in plains suitable for agriculture. The permanent houses of these early settlements were mostly one-room, free-standing dwellings in a rectangular shape up to about twelve meters long. At Sesklo in Thessaly some Neolithic houses had basements and a second story. Greek houses in this period were usually built with a wood frame daubed with clay, but some had stone footings supporting mud bricks (a common building material in the Near East). The inhabitants entered through a single door and baked food in a clay oven attached to the back or side wall. Settlements like those at Sesklo or Dhimini in Thessaly had populations of perhaps several hundred each. At Dhimini a series of low walls encircled the settlement. By the third millennium B.C. large dwellings were being built in Greece, as at Lerna in the Argolid region, where the so-called House of Tiles had a roof of baked tiles covering more than one story of rooms.

The remarkable changes of the late Neolithic period came about as innovative human adaptations to what in anthropological terms would be called the feedback between environmental change and population growth. That is, as agriculture developed (perhaps in a period when the climate became wetter), populations increased, thus further raising the need for production of food, thus leading to further population growth, and so on. The process that led to the innovation of humans producing their food through agriculture instead of simply finding it in the wild clearly underlines the importance of demography—the study of the size, growth, density, distribution, and vital statistics of the human population—in understanding historical change.

Specialization of Labor

An archaeological site in Anatolia, known to us only by its modern Turkish name, Çatal Hüyük (pronounced "Chatal Hooyook," meaning "Fork Mound"), provides the best evidence so far discovered for the new patterns of life that emerged in the Neolithic period. Large for its time (housing perhaps six thousand people by around 6000 B.C.) but otherwise comparable to Greek Neolithic communities, Çatal Hüyük subsisted by raising grains and vegetables in irrigated fields and domesticating animals, along with hunting some game.

Since the community could produce enough food without everyone having to work in the fields or herd cattle, some workers could become craft specialists producing goods for those producing the food. These artisans not only fashioned tools, containers, and ornaments from the traditional materials of wood, bone, hide, and stone but also developed new technological skills by experimenting with the material of the future: metal. Metalworkers at Çatal Hüyük certainly knew how to fashion lead into pendants and to hammer naturally occurring lumps of copper into beads and tubes for jewelry, but traces of slag found on the site further suggest that they were beginning to learn the technique of smelting metal from ore as well. This tricky process—the basis of true metallurgy and the foundation of much modern technology—required temperatures of 700 degrees centigrade. Other workers at Çatal Hüyük specialized in weaving textiles, and the scraps of cloth discovered there are the oldest examples of this craft ever found. Like other early technological innovations, metallurgy and the production of cloth apparently also developed independently in other places where agriculture and settled communities provided a context for such creative divisions of labor.

In addition to craft specialization, trade also played a role in the economy of this early village. Traders brought Çatal Hüyük foreign goods, such as shells from the Mediterranean Sea to wear as ornaments and a special flint from far to the east to shape into ceremonial daggers. In exchange for these goods villagers could trade obsidian, a local volcanic glass valued for its glossy luster and ability to hold a sharp edge. The trading contacts the villagers made with other settlements meant that their world did not consist merely of isolated communities independent of one other.

A consequence of the increasing specialization of labor characteristic of Neolithic settlements such as Çatal Hüyük was the emergence of social and political hierarchy. The need to plan and regulate irrigation, trade, and the exchange of food and goods between farmers and crafts specialists in turn created a need for leaders with greater authority than had been required to maintain peace and order in hunter-gatherer bands. In addition, households that found success in farming, herding, crafts production, or trade made themselves wealthier and thus different from less successful villagers. Such communities no longer existed as socially undifferentiated or egalitarian groups.

For reasons that remain unclear, the greater social equality between men and women postulated for hunter-gatherer society probably also waned by the late Neolithic period. Gradual changes in agriculture and herding over many centuries perhaps contributed to this shift toward the situation characteristic of the historical period, when women in Mediterranean societies lacked social, political, and legal equality with men. Farmers began to employ plows dragged by animals sometime after about 4000 B.C. to cultivate land that was more difficult to sow than the areas cultivated in the earliest period of agriculture. Men apparently operated this new technology, perhaps because plowing required more physical strength than digging with sticks and hoes. Men also took over the tending of the larger herds that had now become more common, with cattle being kept for milk and sheep for wool. Large herds tended to be grazed at a distance from the village because new grasslands had to be found continually. As with hunting in hunter-gatherer populations, men, free from the responsibility of nursing babies, were able to stay away from home to tend to the herds. Women, by contrast, became tied down in the central settlement because they had to raise more children to support agriculture, which was becoming more intensive and therefore required more laborers than had foraging for food or the earliest forms of farming. Women also had to shoulder the responsibility for new labor-intensive tasks processing the secondary products of larger herds. For example, they now processed milk into cheese and yogurt and produced cloth by spinning and weaving wool. It seems possible that men's tasks in this new specialization of labor were assigned greater prestige and thus contributed to the growth of inequality between genders. This form of social differentiation, which became a fundamental ingredient in Greek culture, thus apparently emerged as a contingency of the fundamental changes in human life taking place in the late Neolithic period.

Explaining Technological Change

The issue of how the prehistoric inhabitants of Greece and the rest of Europe learned to use the transformative technologies of the late Stone Age has become more complex as modern scientific technology has provided new information on the chronology of the changes in different areas. In the broadest form, the question is to what extent the prehistoric inhabitants of Europe derived their knowledge of the new technologies from the populations of Mesopotamia and Egypt, who clearly came first in inventing writing, building cities, and forming complex civilizations. For a long time scholars regarded European developments as, for all practical purposes, wholly derived from the Near East through a process of diffusion. That is, traders, farmers, herders, metalworkers, and architects were theorized to have slowly made their way to Europe from the Near East, either peacefully or as violent invaders. They brought with them, on this model, technologies hitherto unknown in the lands they entered, such as agriculture, monumental stone construction, and copper metallurgy. In this way, technological knowledge was gradually diffused from the Near East over Europe.

This explanation of technological change in prehistoric Europe has had to be revised, however, in the light of scientific analytic techniques, refined only as recently as the late 1960s. Radiocarbon dating forced the revision by permitting scientists to give close estimates of the age of prehistoric organic materials from archaeological excavations. Laboratory analysis of the amount of radioactive carbon-14 remaining in materials such as bones, seeds, hides, and wood can now determine with an acceptable margin of error the length of time since the death of the material submitted for testing. Dendrochronology, the chronological evidence obtained from counting the internal rings of long-lived trees, has helped refine the accuracy of radiocarbon dating. These techniques applied to archaeological material from Neolithic Europe have suggested a more complex process of change than previously imagined. It now seems established that farming communities had already developed in Greece and the Balkan mountains immediately to the north as early as the seventh millennium B.C. On this chronology, it is still possible to believe that traders and migrating farmers from the Near East introduced domesticated cereal grains into Greece. The evidence suggests, however, that the domestication of cattle took place in this region of Europe at least as early as in the Near East. In this case, a European population apparently introduced change on its own, by independent local innovation rather than through diffusion.

That independent innovation should always be considered as an explanation of technological or, indeed, cultural change is also implied by what the new dating techniques have shown about the use of large stones (megaliths) to build monumental structures in Neolithic Europe. Before radiocarbon dating, the earliest megalithic stone constructions in history were thought to be the pyramids of Egypt. The many huge prehistoric stone chamber-tombs imbedded in the earth near the western European coast were therefore attributed to traveling Egyptian builders, in accordance with the diffusion theory. Now, however, radiocarbon analysis of materials from the tombs has shown that the earliest of these tombs were constructed before 4000 B.C., more than a thousand years earlier than the pyramids. It is therefore clear that the local Neolithic populations invented techniques for building megalithic monuments without any help from Egyptians. Similarly, the prehistoric population of the Mediterranean island of Malta (south of Sicily) independently constructed substantial temples of stone before 3000 B.C., and their temple complexes rank as the world's earliest freestanding megalithic monuments. Finally, new dating techniques have also revealed that the local population, not visitors from the East, built Stonehenge in what is now southern Britain. They erected this precisely aligned assemblage of mammoth stones between 2100 and 1900 B.C. (or perhaps much earlier), possibly as an observatory to track the movements of the sun and the moon.

Radiocarbon dates further suggest that European metalsmiths developed copper metallurgy independently from Near Eastern metalsmiths because it shows this technology developing in various European locations around the same time as in the Near East. By the fourth millennium B.C., for instance, smiths in the Balkans were casting copper ax heads with the hole for the ax handle in the correct position. The smiths of southeastern Europe started alloying bronze in the same period in the third millennium as their Near Eastern counterparts, learning to add 10 percent of tin to the copper that they were firing. The European Bronze Age (to use the terminology in which periods of history are labeled according to the metal most in use) therefore commenced at approximately the same date as the Near Eastern Bronze Age. This chronology suggests contemporary but independent local innovation, because otherwise we would expect to find evidence that metallurgy had begun much earlier in the Near East than in Europe, to allow the necessary time for the diffusion of the technology all the way from the Near East to Europe.

Thus, the explanation of important changes in prehistoric European history has become more complicated than it was when diffusion alone seemed sufficient to explain these developments. It no longer seems possible to think that the Neolithic population of Europe was wholly dependent on Near Easterners for knowledge of innovative technologies such as megalithic architecture and metallurgy, even if they did learn agriculture from them. Like their neighbors in Europe, the inhabitants of prehistoric Greece participated in the complex process of diffusion and independent invention that brought such remarkable technological and social changes in this period through the interacting effects of contact with others, sometimes very distant others, and local innovation.

2

From Indo-Europeans to Mycenaeans

Greeks Become Greeks

At what point in time does it makes sense to use the term *Greeks* to refer to the inhabitants of the region called Greece? No simple answer will do. The process by which Greeks became Greeks does not lend itself to easy categorization because the concept of identity encompasses not just basic social and material conditions but also ethnic, cultural, and linguistic traditions. So far as the available evidence allows us to determine, the first population in Greece that spoke Greek was the Mycenaeans of the second half of the second millennium B.C. By that date, then, there clearly existed people whom it makes sense to call Greeks. The origins of Greek language and the other components of Greek identity lie much further in the past, of course, but tracing those origins is a matter of speculation. Recent scholarly interest in the deep origins of fundamental components of ancient Greek ethnic and cultural identity has centered on two major questions: the significance of the Indo-European heritage of ancient Greeks in the period c. 4500–2000 B.C., and the nature and ramifications of Greek relations with the older civilizations of the Near East, Egypt in particular, in the second millennium B.C. Even though the details of these processes of cultural interaction remain exceptionally controversial, on a general level it is clear that both these

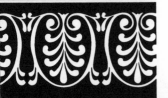

sources of influence affected the construction of Greek identity in fundamental ways.

When we reach the second millennium B.C., it becomes easier to identify
definite sources of influence on early Greek culture. Before the rise of Mycenaean civilization in mainland Greece, Minoan civilization flourished on
the large island of Crete. The Minoans, who did not speak Greek, had grown
rich through complex agriculture and seaborne trade with the peoples of
the eastern Mediterranean and Egypt. The Minoans passed on this tradition
of intercultural contact to the civilization of the Mycenaeans, whom they
greatly influenced before losing their power after the middle of the millennium. The centers of Mycenaean civilization were destroyed in the period
from about 1200 to 1000 B.C. as part of widespread turmoil throughout the
eastern Mediterranean region. The descendants of the Greeks who survived
these catastrophes eventually revived Greek civilization.

Indo-European and Near Eastern Roots

The thorniest question concerning the Indo-European background of
Greek culture is whether groups of peoples collectively labeled Indo-
Europeans migrated into prehistoric Europe over many centuries and radically changed the nature of the society already in place there, of which
indigenous inhabitants of Greece would have been a part. Debate continues over the location of the homeland of the earliest Indo-Europeans,
but the most discussed suggestions are central Asia and Anatolia. The final
phase of Indo-European migration, according to the hypothesis of widespread movement of such people, caused devastation across Europe around
2000 B.C. The Greeks of the historical period are then seen as the descendants of this violent group of invaders.

The notion of an original Indo-European identity is constructed from
the later history of language. Linguists long ago recognized that a single
language had been the earliest ancestor of most of the major ancient and
modern groups of languages of western Europe (including, among others,
Greek, Latin, and English), of the Slavic languages, of Persian (Iranian),
and of various languages spoken on the Indian subcontinent. They therefore bestowed the name Indo-Europeans on the original speakers of this
ancestral language. Since the original language had disappeared by evolving
into its different descendant languages well before the invention of writing, its only traces survive in the words of the later languages derived from
it. Early Indo-European, for example, had a single word for night, which
passed down as Greek *nux* (*nuktos* in the genitive case), Latin *nox*, *noctis*, Vedic
(the type of Sanskrit used in the ancient epic poetry of India) *nakt-*, English
night, Spanish *noche*, French *nuit*, German *Nacht*, Russian *noch*, and so on. That

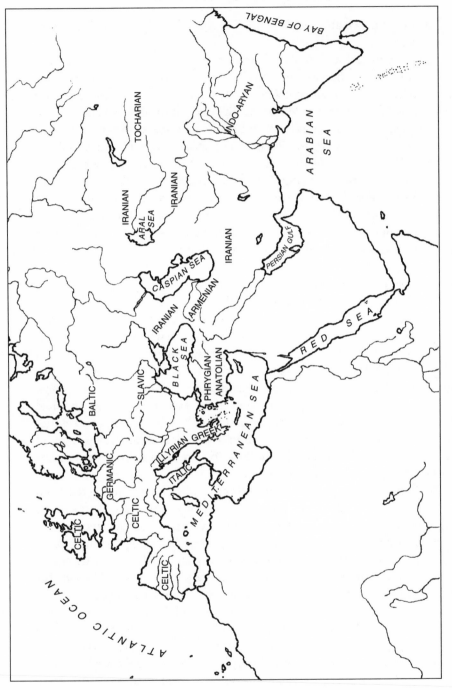

Map 2. Areas of Indo-European Linguistic Groups

---

c. **4500–2000 B.C.**: Movements of Indo-European peoples into Europe?

c. **3000–2000 B.C.**: Development of Mediterranean polyculture.

c. **3000–2500 B.C.**: Bronze metallurgy under way in the Balkans and on the island of Crete.

c. **2200 B.C.**: Earliest Cretan palaces of Minoan civilization.

c. **2000 B.C.**: Violent destruction of many European sites.

c. **1700 B.C.**: Earthquakes destroy early Cretan palaces.

c. **1600–1500 B.C.**: Shaft graves at Mycenae on Greek mainland.

c. **1500–1450 B.C.**: Earliest Mycenaean tholos tombs.

c. **1400 B.C.**: Earliest Mycenaean palaces.

c. **1370 B.C.**: Palace of Knossos on Crete destroyed.

c. **1300–1200 B.C.**: High point of Mycenaean palace culture.

c. **1200 B.C.**: Disturbances across the Aegean region.

c. **1000 B.C.**: Destruction of Mycenaean palace culture complete.

English speakers have two completely dissimilar pronouns to refer to themselves in different grammatical contexts, the words I and me, is a feature inherited from the pronouns of Indo-European.

Words in later languages that descended from the original Indo-European language are thought to offer hints about certain features of the original Indo-European society. For example, the name of the chief Indo-European divinity, a male god, survives in the similar sounds of *Zeus pater* and *Jupiter*, the names given to the chief god in Greek and Latin, respectively. This evidence leads to the surmise that Indo-European society was patriarchal, regarding the father not merely as a parent but as the authority figure over the household. Other words suggest that Indo-European society was also patrilocal (the wife goes to live with the husband's family group) and patrilineal (the line of descent of children being reckoned through their father). Indo-European language also had the notion of king, a detail suggesting a hierarchical and differentiated society rather than an egalitarian one. Finally, Indo-European males are usually seen as warlike and competitive.

The most controversial interpretation of the significance of the Indo-Europeans argues that they invaded Europe in waves and imposed their patriarchal, hierarchical, and martial values on the peoples they found there. On this hypothesis, the indigenous population of prehistoric Europe had been generally egalitarian, peaceful, and matrifocal (centered on women as mothers). These earlier Europeans had worshipped female gods as their principal divinities, the argument further postulates, who were forcibly displaced by the male deities of the Indo-Europeans, such as Zeus for the Greeks. This transformation would have begun about 4500 B.C., with different groups of Indo-Europeans moving into Europe over the following centuries, and culminated in the violent sack of many pre–Indo-European sites around 2000 B.C. The Greeks constituted one linguistically identifiable group descended from these Indo-European ancestors.

Opponents of this version of the Indo-European origins of the Greeks (and others) argue that evidence is lacking to show Indo-Europeans migrating into Europe as distinct groups powerful enough to abolish local social structures and beliefs. It may even be that Indo-European social traditions had never differed significantly from those originally evolved by the non–Indo-European societies of prehistoric Europe. Therefore, historical European social structures characteristic of later Greek history, such as patriarchy and social inequality for women, might have developed from very early indigenous developments. For example, another theory postulates that Paleolithic male hunter-gatherers had pushed human society down the road toward patriarchy by kidnapping women from each other's bands in an attempt to improve their band's ability to reproduce itself and thus survive. Since men as hunters were the members of the band with experience of travel far from base camp, they were the ones to raid other bands. In this way, men would have acquired dominance over women long before the date when Indo-Europeans are supposed to have initiated their invasions of Europe. The indigenous society of Europe would thus have become patriarchal on its own, even though its religion paid great respect to female divinities, as evidenced by the thousands of Venus figurines uncovered in Neolithic European archaeological excavations.

Alternatively, the growth of social inequality between men and women may have been a consequence of the changes accompanying the development of plow agriculture and large-scale herding in late Neolithic Europe described previously. Those who deemphasize the significance of the Indo-Europeans as a source of cultural change argue further against blaming them for the widespread destruction of European sites near the end of the third millennium. Instead, they suggest, exhaustion of the soil, leading to intense competition for land, and internal political turmoil could have motivated the violent clashes that devastated various European settlements around 2000 B.C.

The language of the Greeks, the fundamental component of their identity, indisputably came from Indo-European origins. Much else related to their ethnic and cultural origins must remain controversial, such as the source of the hierarchical and patriarchal structures of their society and of their religion, with its male chief god flanked by powerful female divinities.

No aspect of this question is more discussed at present than the relation between Greece and the Near East, especially Egypt. Some nineteenth-century scholars wished to downplay or deny any significant cultural influence of the Near East on Greece, but that was plainly not the ancient Greek view of the question. Greek intellectuals of the historical period proclaimed that Greeks owed a great deal to the older civilization of Egypt, in particular in religion and art. Recent research agrees with this ancient opinion. Greek sculptors in the Archaic Age chiseled their statues according to a set of proportions established by Egyptian artists. Greek mythology, the stories that Greeks told themselves about their deepest origins and their relations to the gods, was infused with stories and motifs of Near Eastern origin. The clearest evidence of the deep influence of Egyptian culture on Greek is the store of seminal religious ideas that flowed from Egypt to Greece: the geography of the underworld, the weighing of the souls of the dead in scales, the life-giving properties of fire as commemorated in the initiation ceremonies of the international cult of the goddess Demeter of Eleusis (a famous site in Athenian territory), and much more.

These influences are not surprising because archaeology reveals that the population inhabiting Greece had diplomatic and commercial contact with the Near East at least as early as the middle of the second millennium B.C. What cannot be true, however, is the theory that Egyptians invaded and colonized mainland Greece in this period. Egyptian records refer to Greeks as foreigners, not as colonists. Moreover, much of the contact between Greece and the Near East in this early period took place through intermediaries, above all the seafaring inhabitants of the island of Crete. In any case, in thinking about the "cultural debt" of one group to another, it is imperative not to fall into the trap of seeing one group as the passive recipient of ideas or skills or traditions transmitted by a superior group. What one group takes over from another is always adapted and reinterpreted according to the system of values of the group doing the receiving. Everything they receive from others they transform so as to give the innovations functions and meanings suited to their own purposes and cultural traditions. When the Greeks learned from the peoples of the Near East, they made what they learned their own. This is how cultural identity is forged, not by mindless imitation or passive reception. The Greeks themselves constructed their own identity from many sources by putting their own stamp on what they learned from others. The construction of that identity took a long time. It would be pointless to try to fix the beginning of this complex process at any one moment. Rather than look for a nonexistent single origin of Greek identity, we should try to identify as many as possible of the various sources of cultural influence that flowed together over the long run to produce

Greek culture as we find it in later times. The late Bronze Age (the second millennium B.C.) provides crucial evidence for this task.

Bronze Age Civilizations of Europe

The Stone Age communities of Greece have not earned the title of "first civilizations of Europe" because they pale by comparison with the communities that arose in the late Bronze Age. That title is therefore bestowed on the Minoan civilization of Crete and on the Mycenaean civilization of mainland Greece and the islands and coast of the Aegean Sea, a section of the eastern Mediterranean between Greece and Anatolia. The Minoans, who spoke a language still unidentified, built a prosperous civilization before the Greek-speaking Mycenaeans. Both populations had extensive trading contacts with the Near East, advanced agricultural and metallurgical technologies, elaborate architecture, striking art, and a marked taste for luxury. They also inhabited a dangerous world whose perils ultimately overwhelmed all their civilized sophistication.

The Bronze Age was fully under way in Greece by the third millennium B.C., when advanced metallurgy in bronze, lead, silver, and gold developed on the island of Crete, southeast of the mainland peninsula of Greece, and in the Cyclades Islands of the Aegean Sea. These metallurgical advances apparently took place independently of similar developments in the Balkans and the Near East. Devising innovative ways to alloy metals at high temperatures, Aegean smiths created new luxury goods and better tools for agriculture, construction, and warfare. This new technology made metal weaponry much more lethal. A copper weapon had offered relatively few advantages over a stone one, because this soft metal easily lost its shape and edge. Bronze, much stronger and able to hold a razor edge, made feasible the production of durable metal daggers, swords, and spearheads. The earliest Aegean daggers have been found at third-millennium Troy in western Anatolia. The dagger soon became standard equipment for warriors in the Bronze Age and an early entry in the catalogue of weapons that fuel the arms races familiar in human history. Daggers gradually lengthened into swords, increasing the killing efficiency of these new weapons.

Bronze Age smiths could also make daggers and swords that were far more than utilitarian implements for war and hunting. The lavish decorations added to some of them show that these weapons could serve as objects for display and ostentation, highly visible symbols of wealth and status. Such elaborate weapons also marked the division between men and women in society because they signified the masculine roles of hunter and warrior that had emerged long ago in the division of labor of hunter-gatherers. The creation of a new kind of wealth and status represented one of the most important social consequences of the development of metallurgy. The desire to accumulate wealth in the form of various metal objects and to possess those objects as status symbols stimulated demand for metals and for the skilled workers who could fashion them. Greater availability of such objects made even more people want them, further stimulating demand for them across society. This process in turn affected people's expectations about what constituted rewards appropriate for their labor. Now they expected to be able to acquire wealth in metal, not just in foodstuffs, animals, or land. They also prized the products of other specialized crafts perfected in the Near East, such as making jewelry from imported ivory. Growing numbers of crafts specialists in turn swelled Bronze Age Aegean settlements, which nevertheless remained quite small by modern standards. Some of these specialists were itinerant Near Easterners who had traveled west looking for new markets for their skills. They brought with them not only their technological expertise but also a repertory of myths that influenced the peoples with whom they interacted. In this way they became indirect agents of cultural change.

Mediterranean polyculture—the cultivation of olives and grapes, as well as grain, in one agricultural system—also fully evolved in the third millennium B.C., as people began to exploit new plants to expand their diet. The emergence of this system, which still dominates Mediterranean agriculture, had two important consequences: an increase in the food supply, which stimulated population growth, and further diversification and specialization of agriculture. This newly diversified agriculture in turn produced valuable new products: olive oil and wine, both of which required new storage techniques for local use and for trade. The manufacture of great storage jars therefore gained momentum, adding another specialization to the crafts of the period. Specialization in the production of food and goods also meant that the specialists in these fields had no time to grow their own food or fashion the variety of things they needed for everyday life. They had to acquire their food and other goods through exchange.

Society therefore became increasingly interdependent, both economically and socially. In the smaller villages of early Neolithic Greece, reciprocity had probably governed exchanges among the population of self-sufficient farmers. Reciprocal exchange did not aim at economic gain but rather promoted a social value: I give you some of what I produce, and you in return give me some of what you produce. We exchange, not because either of us necessarily needs what the other produces, but to reaffirm our social alliances in a small group. Bronze Age society in the Aegean region eventually reached a level of economic interdependence that went far beyond reciprocity and far surpassed in its complexity the economies that had been characteristic of even larger Neolithic villages such as Çatal Hüyük.

The Palace Society of Minoan Crete

People had inhabited the large, fertile island of Crete for several thousand years before the emergence about 2200–2000 B.C. of the system that has earned the title of the earliest Aegean civilization. This civilization, which was characterized by large architectural complexes today usually labeled "palaces," relied on an interdependent economy based primarily on redistribution. The first, "pre-palace" settlers in Crete presumably immigrated across the sea from nearby Anatolia about 6000 B.C. These Neolithic farming families originally lived in small settlements nestled close to fertile agricultural land, like their contemporaries elsewhere in Europe. In the third millennium B.C., however, the new technological developments in metallurgy and agriculture began to affect society on Crete dramatically. By about 2200 B.C. or somewhat later, sprawling, many-chambered buildings (the so-called palaces) began to appear on Crete, usually near but not on the coast. Today this Cretan society is called "Minoan" after King Minos, the legendary ruler of the island. The palaces housed the rulers and their servants and served as central storage facilities, while the general population clustered around the palaces in houses built one right next to the other, although there were also country houses and modest towns in outlying areas.

Earthquakes leveled the first Cretan palaces about 1700 B.C., but the Minoans rebuilt on an even grander scale in the succeeding centuries. Accounting records preserved on clay tablets reveal how these large structures served as the hub of the island's economy. Probably influenced by Egyptian hieroglyphs, the Minoans at first developed a pictographic script to symbolize objects, for the purpose of keeping such records. This system evolved into a more linear form of writing to express phonetic sounds. Unlike cuneiform or hieroglyphs, this system of writing was a true syllabary, in which characters stood for the sound of the syllables of words. This script, used during the first half of the second millennium, is today called Linear A. Its language remains largely undeciphered, but recent scholarship suggests that it may have been Indo-European. In other ways, such as their religious architecture, the Minoans differed from the population on the Greek mainland. Since Minoan civilization had direct contact with and great influence on the mainland inhabitants, however, it is appropriate to treat it as part of the early history of Greece.

Linear A is sufficiently understood to show that it was used for records in the form of lists: records of goods received and goods paid out, inventories of stored goods, livestock, land holdings, and personnel. With their passion for accounting, the Minoans kept records of everything from chariots to perfumes. The receipts record payments owed, with careful notation of any deficits in the amount actually paid in. The records of disbursements from the palace storerooms cover ritual offerings to the gods, rations to personnel, and raw materials for crafts production, such as metal issued to bronze smiths. None of the tablets records any exchange rate between different categories of goods, such as, for example, a ratio to state how much grain counted as the equivalent of a sheep. Nor do the tablets reveal any use of bullion as money in exchanges. (The invention of coinage lay a thousand years in the future.)

The palace society of Minoan Crete therefore appears to have operated primarily on a redistributive economic system: the central authority told producers how much they had to contribute to the central collection facility and also decided what each member of the society would receive for subsistence and reward. In other words, the palaces did not support a market economy, in which agricultural products and manufactured goods are exchanged through buying and selling. Similar redistributive economic systems based on official monopolies had existed in Mesopotamia for some time, and, like them, the Cretan redistributive arrangement required both ingenuity and a complicated administration. To handle receipt and disbursement of olive oil and wine, for example, the palaces had vast storage areas filled with hundreds of gigantic jars next to storerooms crammed with bowls, cups, and dippers. Scribes meticulously recorded what came in and what went out by writing on clay tablets kept in the palace. This process of economic redistribution applied to craft specialists as well as to food producers, and the palace's administrative officials set specifications for crafts producers' contributions, which amounted to work quotas. Although not everyone is likely to have participated in the redistribution system, it apparently dominated the Cretan economy, minimizing the exchange of goods through markets. People out in the countryside perhaps occasionally sold goods to one another, but the volume of exchange in these small markets never remotely rivaled the scope of the redistributive economic system of the palaces. Overseas trade probably operated as a monopoly through the palace system, too, with little role for independent merchants and traders. Egypt was a favorite destination for Minoan seafarers, who brought back objects for trade and are depicted in Egyptian tomb reliefs as bringing gifts or tribute to Egypt's rulers. Some Minoans evidently stayed on in Egypt as mercenary soldiers or artists, and Minoan-style frescoes (wall paintings on plaster) have been found at Avaris (Tel el-Daba's) there. Minoan Crete was also in contact with the Near East and the island of Cyprus in the eastern Mediterranean, with traders and crafts specialists from those areas probably voyaging westward to Crete as often as the Minoans went eastward.

From all indications, Minoan civilization operated smoothly and peacefully for centuries. For example, contemporary settlements elsewhere around the Aegean Sea and in Anatolia had elaborate defensive walls. The absence of walls around the palaces, towns, and isolated country houses of Minoan Crete is therefore all the more striking and implies that Minoan settlements saw no need to fortify themselves against each other. The remains of the newer palaces, such as the famous one at Knossos on the north side of the island—with its hundreds of rooms in five stories, storage jars holding 240,000 gallons, indoor plumbing, and colorful scenes painted on the walls—have led many to see Minoan society as especially prosperous, peaceful, and happy. The prominence of women in palace frescoes and the numerous figurines of bosomy goddesses found on Cretan sites have even prompted speculation that Minoan society continued to be a female-dominated culture of the kind that, as we have seen, has sometimes been postulated as the indigenous society of prehistoric Europe. But the wealth of weaponry found in the graves of Cretan men shows that martial prowess and display bestowed special status in Minoan society. The weapons strongly suggest that men dominated in the palace society of Minoan Crete, and it is common to speak of "princes" or "kings" as the leaders of the palaces.

Minoan Contact with Mycenaean Greece

The far-flung international trade of Minoan Crete developed extensive overseas contacts for the residents of the palaces, and this network of trade was greatly facilitated by yet another innovation of the third millennium, the longship. The sea travel of Minoans took them not only to Egypt and the other civilizations of the Near East in search of trade goods and pay, but also to the islands of the Aegean and southern Greece. On the Greek mainland they encountered another civilization today called Mycenaean after its most famous archaeological site. Inspired by the Greek poet Homer's tale of the Trojan War, archaeologists have uncovered the Bronze Age site of Mycenae in the Peloponnese (the large peninsula which is southern Greece), with its elaborate citadel on multiple terraces and fortification walls built of large stones meticulously fitted together. The discoveries at Mycenae gained such renown that *Mycenaean* has become the general term for the Bronze Age civilization of mainland Greece in the second millennium B.C., although neither Mycenae nor any other of the settlements of Mycenaean Greece ever ruled Bronze Age Greece as a united state.

The discovery in the nineteenth century of treasure-filled graves at Mycenae thrilled the European world. Constructed as stone-lined shafts, these graves entombed corpses buried with golden jewelry, including heavy necklaces festooned with pendants, gold and silver vessels, bronze weapons decorated with scenes of wild animals inlaid in precious metals, and delicately painted pottery. The first excavator of Mycenae, the businessman-turned-archaeologist Heinrich Schliemann, thought that he had found the grave of King Agamemnon, who commanded the Greeks at Troy in Homer's poem the *Iliad* (which first began to be written down in the eighth century B.C.), but in truth the shaft graves date to the sixteenth century B.C., long before the Trojan War of the twelfth century. The artifacts of the shaft graves point to a warrior culture organized in independent settlements ruled by powerful commanders, who enriched themselves by conducting raiding expeditions near and far, as well as by dominating local farmers. The retrospective story of the Trojan War that the *Iliad* tells symbolizes the aims of this society as reflected in the literature of a later age. The pugnacious heroes of Homer's poem sail far from their homes in Greece to attack the citadel of the Trojans in western Anatolia. Their announced mission is to rescue Helen, the Greek queen whom the son of the king of Troy had lured away from her husband, but they always seem intensely interested in gathering booty by sacking Troy and other places in the neighborhood. The precious objects and symbols of wealth and power found in the graves dating long before the Trojan War show that a society of warriors with goals similar to those of the male heroes of the *Iliad* was in place four centuries earlier than the setting of the poem's story.

The construction of another kind of burial chamber, called *tholos* tombs — spectacular underground domed chambers built in beehive shapes from closely fitted stones — marks the next period in Mycenaean society, beginning in the fifteenth century B.C. The architectural details of the tholos tombs and the style of the burial goods found in them testify to the far-flung contacts that Mycenaean rulers maintained throughout the eastern Mediterranean. Reference to Mycenaean soldiers in Egyptian records indicates that mainland warriors could take up service far from home.

Contact with the civilization of Minoan Crete was tremendously influential for Mycenaean civilization; Minoan artifacts and artistic motifs turn up on the mainland in profusion. The evidence for contact between Minoans and Mycenaeans raises a thorny problem in the explanation of cultural change. Since the art and goods of the Mycenaeans in the middle of the second millennium B.C. display many features clearly reminiscent of Cretan design, the archaeologist who excavated Knossos, Arthur Evans, argued that the Minoans had inspired Mycenaean civilization by sending colonists to the mainland, as they undeniably had to various Aegean islands, such as Thera. This demotion of Mycenaean civilization to secondary status offended the excavators of Mycenae, and a continuing debate emerged over the relationship between the two cultures. They were certainly not identical. They spoke different languages. The Mycenaeans made burnt offerings to the gods; the Minoans did not. The Minoans constructed sanctuaries across the landscape

Table 1. Examples of Words in Linear B Script

I.	⊕ 𝖨	‡ ⊕ 𝖳	∧ 𝖱 𝟓	𝖸 𝗫 𝗬 𝖡	𝗤 𝗠 𝗬 𝖿	𝜙 ⊕ 𝜓	𝖰 𝘫
2.	ka-ko	pa-ka-na	ti-ri-po	i-je-re-ja	qa-si-re-u	tu-ka-te	ko-wo
3.	kha(l)ko(s)	pha(s)gana	tripo(s)	(h)iereia	gwasileu(s)	thugatē(r)	ko(r)wo(s)
4.	khalkos	phasgana	tripous	hiereia	basileus	thugater	kouros
5.	'bronze'	'swords'	'tripod'	'priestess'	'chief'	'daughter'	'boy'

1. The words written in Linear B characters.
2. The words transcribed into syllables (separated by hyphens) using the English alphabet.
3. The words reconstructed into phonetic form (with letters in parentheses that must be supplied by the speaker reading the words).
4. The words as they appear in classical Greek (transliterated into the English alphabet).
5. The words translated into English.

---

in caves, on mountain tops, and in country villas; the mainlanders built no shrines separate from their central dwellings. When in the fourteenth century B.C. the mainlanders started to build palace complexes reminiscent of those on Crete, unlike the Minoans the Mycenaeans designed their palaces around *megarons*, rooms with huge ceremonial hearths and thrones for the rulers. Some palaces had more than one megaron, which could soar two stories high with columns to support a roof above the second-floor balconies of the palace.

The mystery surrounding the relationship between the Minoans and the Mycenaeans deepened with the startling discovery in the palace at Knossos of tablets written in an adaptation of Linear A; the same script occurred on tablets from Mycenaean sites on the mainland and was termed Linear B. Michael Ventris, a young English architect interested in codes, stirred the scholarly world in the 1950s by demonstrating that the language being expressed by Linear B was Greek, not the Minoan language of Linear A. Because the Linear B tablets from Crete dated from before the final destruction of the Knossos palace in about 1370 B.C., they meant that the palace administration had for some time been keeping its records in a foreign language— Greek—rather than in Cretan. Presumably this change in the language used for official record keeping means that Greek-speaking Mycenaeans from the mainland had come to dominate the palaces of Crete, but whether by violent invasion or some kind of peaceful accommodation remains unknown. Certainly the Linear B tablets imply that the mainland had not long, if ever, remained a secondary power to Minoan Crete.

The Zenith of Mycenaean Society

A glimpse at Mycenaean society in its maturity demonstrates the nature of its power. Archaeologists treasure cemeteries, not because of morbid fascination with death but because ancient peoples so often buried goods both special and ordinary with their dead. Bronze Age tombs in Greece tell us that no wealthy Mycenaean male went to the grave without his fighting equipment. The complete suit of Mycenaean bronze armor found in a fourteenth-century B.C. tomb from Dendra in the northeastern Peloponnese shows how extensive first-class individual equipment could be. This dead warrior had worn a complete bronze cuirass (chest guard) of two pieces for front and back, an adjustable skirt of bronze plates, bronze greaves (shin guards), shoulder plates, and a collar. On his head had rested a boar's-tusk helmet with metal cheekpieces. Next to his body lay his leather shield, bronze and clay vessels, and a bronze comb with gold teeth. Originally his bronze swords had lain beside him, but tomb robbers had stolen them before the archaeologists found his resting place. This warrior had spared no cost in availing himself of the best technology in armor and weaponry, and his family thought it appropriate to shoulder the expense of consigning this costly equipment to the ground forever rather than pass it on to the next generation.

Mycenaean warriors dressed like this man could ride into battle in the latest in military hardware—the lightweight, two-wheeled chariot pulled by horses. These revolutionary vehicles, sometimes assumed to have been introduced by Indo-Europeans migrating from Central Asia, first appeared not long after 2000 B.C. in various Mediterranean and Near Eastern societies. The first Aegean representation of such a chariot occurs on a Mycenaean grave marker from about 1500 B.C. Wealthy people evidently craved this dashing new invention not only for war but also as proof of their social status, much like modern people rushing to replace their horse-drawn wagons with cars after the invention of the automobile. It has recently been suggested that the Dendra armor was for a warrior fighting from a chariot, not for an infantryman, on the grounds that a foot soldier would not be able to move freely enough in the metal casing of such a suit. On this provocative and speculative argument, chariots carrying archers provided the principal arm of Mycenaean armies, supplemented by skirmishers fighting on foot, not unlike the tank battles of World War II in which infantrymen crept along into battle in the shadow of a force of tanks as mobile artillery. These supplementary infantrymen escorted the chariot forces, guarded the camps at the rear of the action, chased fugitive enemies after the main clash of battle, and served as attack troops on terrain inaccessible to chariots.

Many of these Mycenaean-era foot soldiers may have been hired mercenaries from abroad.

War was clearly a principal concern of those Mycenaean men who could
afford its expensive paraphernalia. The Mycenaeans spent nothing, by contrast, on the construction of large religious buildings like the giant temples
of the Near East. The nature of Bronze Age mainland religion remains largely
obscure, although the usual view is that the Mycenaeans worshipped primarily the male-dominated pantheon traditionally associated with the martial culture of the Indo-Europeans. The names of numerous deities known
from later Greek religion occur in the Linear B tablets, such as Hera, Zeus,
and Poseidon, as well as the names of divinities unknown in later times. The
name or title potnia, referring to a female divinity as "mistress" or "ruler," is
very common in the tablets, emphasizing the importance of goddesses in
Bronze Age religion.

The development of extensive sea travel in the Bronze Age enabled not
only traders but also warriors to journey far from home. Traders, crafts specialists, and entrepreneurs seeking metals sailed from Egypt and the Near
East to Greece and beyond. Mycenaeans established colonies at various locations along the coast of the Mediterranean. Seaborne Mycenaean warriors
also dominated and probably put an end to the palace society of Minoan
Crete in the fifteenth and fourteenth centuries B.C., presumably in wars over
commercial rivalry in the Mediterranean. By the middle of the fourteenth
century B.C., the Mycenaeans had displaced the Minoans as the most powerful civilization of the Aegean.

The End of Mycenaean Civilization

The Bronze Age development of extensive sea travel for trading and
raiding had put the cultures of the Aegean and the Near East in closer contact than ever before. The wealth that could be won by traders and entrepreneurs, especially those seeking metals, encouraged contacts between the
older civilizations at the eastern end of the Mediterranean and the younger
ones to the west. The civilizations of Mesopotamia and Anatolia particularly
overshadowed those of Crete and Greece in the size of their cities and the
development of extensive written legal codes. Egypt remained an especially
favored destination of Mycenaean voyagers throughout the late Bronze Age
because they valued the exchange of goods and ideas with the prosperous
and complex civilization of that land. By around 1200 B.C., however, the
Mediterranean network of firmly established powers and trading partners
was coming undone. The New Kingdom in Egypt was falling apart; foreign
invaders destroyed the powerful Hittite kingdom in Anatolia; Mesopotamia
underwent a period of political turmoil; and the rich palace societies of

the Aegean all but disintegrated. The causes of the disruption are poorly documented, but the most likely reasons are internal strife between local centers of power and overexploitation of natural resources in overspecialized and centralized economies. These troubles, whose duration we cannot accurately gauge, apparently caused numerous groups of people to leave their homes, seeking new places to live or at least victims to plunder. These movements of peoples throughout the eastern Mediterranean and the Near East further damaged or even destroyed the political stability, economic prosperity, and international contacts of the civilizations of most of these lands, including that of the Mycenaeans. This period of disruption certainly lasted for decades; in some regions it may have gone on much longer. As a rough generalization, it seems accurate to say that the period from roughly 1200 to 1000 B.C. saw numerous catastrophes for Mediterranean civilizations. The consequences for the Mycenaeans were disastrous.

The most informative records of this period are Egyptian and Hittite. They speak of foreign invasions, some from the sea. According to his own account, the pharaoh Ramesses III around 1182 B.C. defeated a fearsome coalition of seaborne invaders from the north who had fought their way to the edge of Egypt: "All at once the peoples were on the move, dispersed in war . . . . No land could repulse their attacks . . . . They extended their grasp over territories as far as the circuit of the earth, their spirits brimming with confidence and believing: 'Our plans will succeed!' . . . The ones who came as far as my border, their seed is no more, their heart and their soul are done for forever and ever . . . . They were dragged in, surrounded, and laid prostrate on the shore, killed, and thrown into piles from tail to head" (ANET, pp. 262–263).

The Egyptian records indicate that many different groups made up these sea peoples, as they are called today. We can surmise that sea peoples originated from Mycenaean Greece, the Aegean islands, Anatolia, Cyprus, and various points in the Near East. They did not constitute a united population in any sense; rather, they should be thought of as independent bands displaced by the various political and economic troubles of their homelands. Some had previously been mercenary soldiers in the armies of once-powerful rulers, whom they eventually turned against in a grab for power and booty. Some came from far away to conduct raids in foreign lands. It may be that one important origin of these catastrophes, which ended the power of Mycenaean civilization, was a relatively sudden reconceptualization of military tactics. That is, previously the preponderance of military might had lain with the chariots carrying archers that the kingdoms of the Bronze Age Mediterranean customarily mustered. These chariot forces had been supplemented by infantrymen, mostly foreign mercenaries. At some point around 1200, the argument goes, these hired foot soldiers realized that they could use their long swords and javelins to defeat the chariot forces in direct battle by swarming in a mass against their vehicle-mounted overlords. Emboldened by this realization of their power and motivated by a lust for booty, the motley bands of mercenaries attacked their erstwhile employers and plundered their wealth. They also conducted raids on other rich targets, which were no longer able to defend themselves with their old tactics dependent on chariots. With no firm organization among themselves, the rebels fatally weakened the civilizations they betrayed and raided but were incapable of or uninterested in putting any new political systems into place to fill the void created by their destruction of the existing ones.

Whether this explanation for the end of the Bronze Age will win widespread assent remains to be seen, if only because one might ask why it took the mercenary infantrymen so long to grasp their advantage over chariots, if such it was, and to put it into play. But one important assumption of this scenario does ring true: what evidence we have for the history of the sea peoples points not to one group spreading destruction across the eastern Mediterranean in a single tidal wave of violence but rather to many disparate bands and conflicts. A chain reaction of attacks and flights in a recurring and expanding cycle put even more bands of raiders on the move.

Some bands of sea peoples were perhaps made up exclusively of men conducting raids, who then expected to return to their homeland. Other groups of warriors and their families may have been looking for a new place to settle, where they could live a more prosperous and secure life than in the disturbed area from which they had voluntarily departed or been driven by other raiders. Any such people in flight could not expect a friendly welcome on foreign shores, and they had to be prepared to fight for new homes. The material damage such marauding bands of raiders would have wreaked would have been made worse by the social disruption their arrival in a new area would also have caused to the societies already in place. However common such migrations may have been—that they were widespread has been both affirmed and denied in modern scholarship—destruction and disruption were ubiquitous in this era. In the end, all this fighting and motion redrew the political map of the Mediterranean, and perhaps its population map as well, although it is unclear how many groups actually resettled permanently at great distances from their original sites in this period. The reasons for all this violent commotion must still be regarded as mysterious in our present state of knowledge, but its dire consequences for Near Eastern and Greek civilization are clear.

The once mighty Hittite kingdom in Anatolia fell about 1200 B.C., when invaders penetrated its borders and its supply lines of raw materials were cut by incessant raids. The capital city, Hattusas, was burned to the ground and never reinhabited, although smaller Neo-Hittite principalities survived for another five hundred years before falling to the armies of the Neo-Assyrian kingdom. The appearance of the sea peoples weakened Egypt's New Kingdom by requiring a great military effort to repel them and by ruining Egypt's international trade in the Mediterranean. Struggles for power between the pharaoh and the priests undermined the centralized authority of the monarchy as well, and by the middle of the eleventh century B.C., Egypt had shrunk to its old territorial core along the banks of the Nile. Egypt's credit was ruined along with its international stature. When an eleventh-century Theban temple official named Wen-Amon traveled to Byblos in Phoenicia to buy cedar for a ceremonial boat, the city's ruler insultingly demanded cash in advance. The Egyptian monarchy continued for centuries after the New Kingdom, but internal struggles for power between pharaohs and priests, combined with frequent attacks from abroad, prevented the reestablishment of centralized authority. Egypt never again assumed the role of an active and aggressive international power that it had enjoyed during much of the Old and New Kingdoms.

The calamities of this time also affected the copper-rich island of Cyprus and the flourishing cities along the eastern coast of the Mediterranean. The Greeks later called these coastal peoples the Phoenicians, apparently from the much sought after reddish-purple dye that they extracted from shellfish. The inhabitants of cities such as Ugarit on the coast of Syria thrived on international maritime commerce and enjoyed a lively polyglot culture. A catastrophic attack of the sea peoples overwhelmed Ugarit, but one of its most brilliant accomplishments lived on. In this crossroads of cultures, the first alphabet had been developed from about 1700 to 1500 B.C., and its later form eventually became the base of the ancient Greek and Roman alphabets and hence of modern Western alphabets. The letters of an alphabet offered a simpler and more flexible system of writing than the other writing systems of the ancient Near East, and an alphabetic system with pictures that stood for only one sound had also begun to be developed in Egypt by 1600–1550 B.C. to write foreign words and names.

The Mycenaeans in mainland Greece had reached their pinnacle of prosperity after 1400 B.C., the period during which the enormous domed tomb at Mycenae called the Treasury of Atreus was constructed. Its elaborately decorated façade and soaring roof testify to the confidence of Mycenae's warrior princes. The last phase of the extensive palace at Pylos on the west coast of the Peloponnese also dates to this time. It was outfitted with everything that wealthy people of the Greek Bronze Age required for comfortable living, including elaborate and colorful wall paintings, storerooms crammed with food, and even a royal bathroom fitted with a built-in tub and intricate plumbing.

Their wealth failed to protect the Mycenaeans from the spreading violence of the late Bronze Age. Ominous signs of the dangers of this period occur in Linear B tablets from Pylos, which record the disposition of troops to guard this unwalled site around 1200 B.C. The palace inhabitants of eastern Greece, such as those at Mycenae and nearby Tiryns, now constructed such massive stone walls for defense that later Greeks thought they must have been built by giants. These fortifications could have served to protect these palaces near the coast against raiders from the sea, who may have been either seafaring Greeks or outsiders. The wall surrounding the palace at Gla in central Greece, however, a settlement located far enough from the coast that foreign pirates presented no threat, confirms that above all the Mycenaeans had to defend themselves against other Mycenaeans or rebellious mercenaries. Never united in one state, the fractious "princes" of Mycenaean Greece by the late thirteenth century B.C. were fighting each other at least as much as they did foreigners. On Crete, inhabitants at the eastern end of the island constructed small, remote settlements in the mountains to serve as refuges from the violence of the era.

Internal conflict among the rulers of Mycenaean Greece, not foreign invasion, offers the most plausible explanation of the destruction of the palaces of the mainland in the period after about 1200 B.C. The destructive consequences of this conflict were probably augmented by major earthquakes in this seismically active region. Near-constant warfare placed great stress on the elaborate economic balance of the redistributive economies of the palaces and hindered recovery from earthquake damage. The eventual failure of the palace economies had a devastating effect on the large part of the Mycenaean population that was now dependent on this system for its subsistence. Peasant farmers, who knew how to grow their own food, could support themselves even when the redistribution of goods and foodstuffs broke down, but the palaces fell into ruins. Warriors left unattached to their old rulers by the fall of the palaces set off to find new places to live or at least plunder, forming roving bands of the kind remembered by the Egyptians as sea peoples. The later Greeks remembered an invasion of Dorians (speakers of the form of Greek characteristic of the northwest mainland) as the reason for the disaster that befell Bronze Age Greece, but the Dorians who did move into southern Greece most likely came in groups too small to cause such damage by themselves. Indeed, small-scale movements of people, not grand invasions, characterized this era, as bands of warriors with no prospects at home emigrated from lands all around the eastern Mediterranean to become pirates for themselves or mercenaries for foreign potentates.

The damage done by the dissolution of the redistributive economies of Mycenaean Greece after 1200 B.C. took centuries to repair fully. Only Athens seems to have escaped wholesale disaster. In fact, the Athenians of the fifth century B.C. prided themselves on their unique status among the peoples of Classical Greece: "sprung from the soil" of their homeland, as they called themselves, they had not been forced to emigrate in the turmoil that engulfed the rest of Greece in the twelfth and eleventh centuries B.C. The nature of the Athenians' boast gives some indication of the sorry fate of many other Greeks in the period c. 1200–1000 B.C. Uprooted from their homes, they wandered abroad in search of new territory to settle. The Ionian Greeks, who in later times inhabited the central coast of western Anatolia, dated their emigration from the mainland to the end of this period. Luxuries of Mycenaean civilization like fine jewelry, knives inlaid with gold, and built-in bathtubs disappeared. To an outside observer, Greek society at the end of the Mycenaean Age might have seemed destined for irreversible economic and social decline, even oblivion. As it happened, however, great changes were in the making that would create the civilization we today think of as Classical Greece.

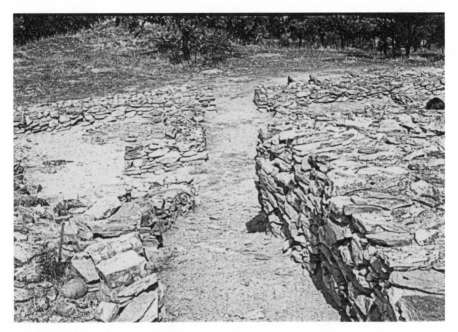

1. This narrow but relatively straight street ran between a row of houses in the neolithic settlement at Dimini. (Courtesy of the Perseus Project)

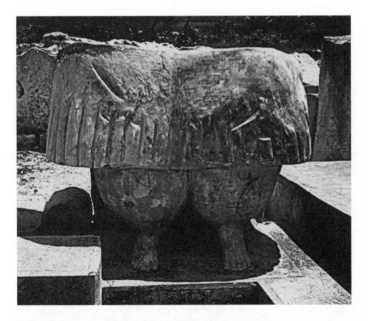

2. This fragmentary female statue from prehistoric Tarxien on the island of Malta shows the prominent endomorphy also characteristic of so-called Venus figurines from the Stone Age. (Photo by author)

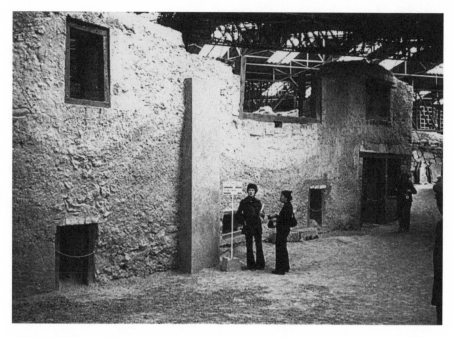

3. These multistory buildings from the Minoan settlement on Thera were buried in the explosion of the volcano in the center of the island. (Photo by author)

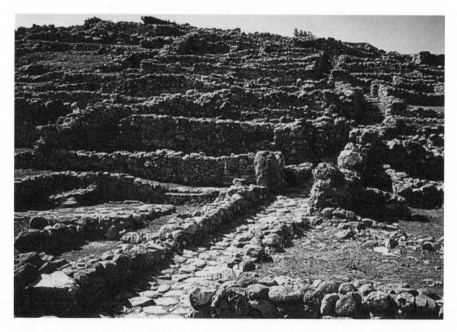

4. The Minoan settlement at Gournia on the island of Crete had closely packed houses separated by a network of streets. (Photo by author)

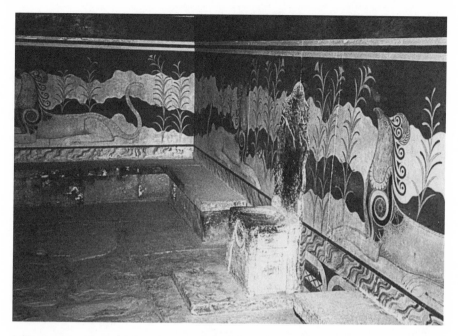

5. The restored frescoes in a throne room of the palace at Knossos on Crete display the vibrancy of Minoan decorative art. (Photo by author)

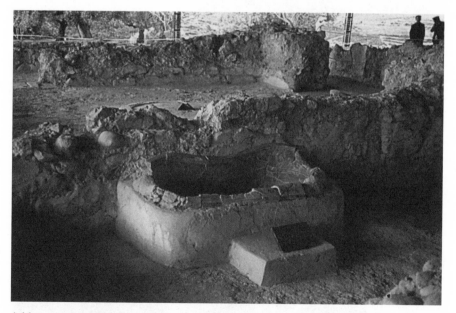

6. Mycenaean palaces featured creature comforts such as this built-in bathtub from the palace complex at Pylos in the western Peloponnese. (Photo by author)

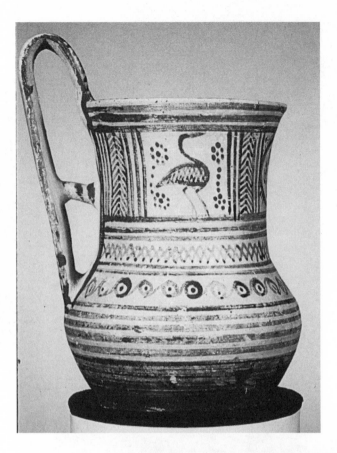

7. This vase shows the type of nonfigural decoration dubbed Geometric by art historians, supplemented by the picture of a bird; the depiction of figures on Greek pottery had ceased with the fall of Mycenaean civilization but was reintroduced in later Geometric art in imitation of Near Eastern models. (Courtesy of the Yale University Art Gallery)

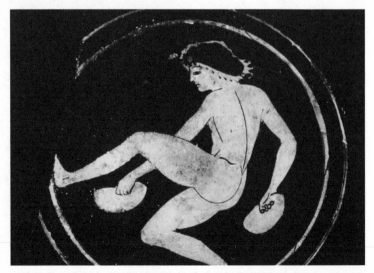

8. Greek athletes performed the broad jump while swinging hand weights forward to increase their momentum; they dropped the weights in the middle of the jump. (Courtesy of the Yale University Art Gallery)

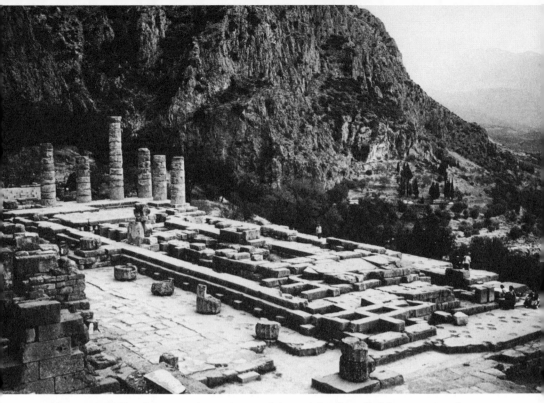

9. The main temple of the oracular sanctuary of the god Apollo at Delphi was situated high on a slope commanding a panoramic view over the deep valley. (Photo by author)

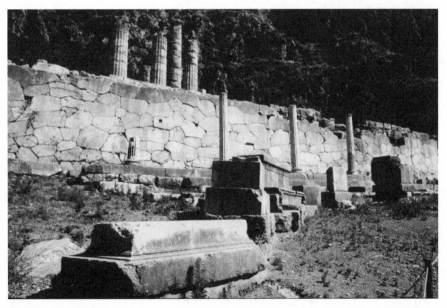

10. Immediately below the temple of Apollo at Delphi, the city-state of Athens built a stoa to display spoils captured in the Persian Wars; the booty served as tokens of gratitude for the god's support and as proof to an international audience of Athenian martial valor in defense of Greece. (Courtesy of the Perseus Project)

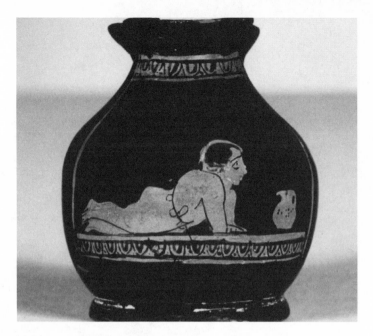

11. The physiognomy of this baby drawn on a vase betrays the tendency of Greek artists to depict children as small-scale adults. (Courtesy of the Yale University Art Gallery)

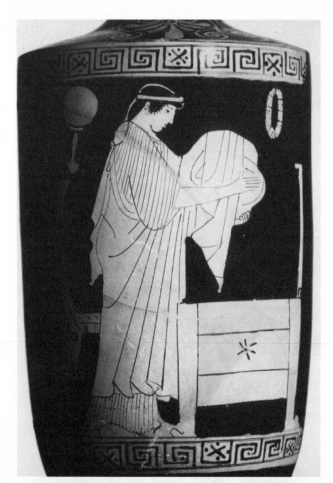

12. This depiction of a woman putting cloth away in a chest reflects the Greek expectation that women were responsible for maintaining and preserving the family's possessions inside the house. (Courtesy of the Yale University Art Gallery)

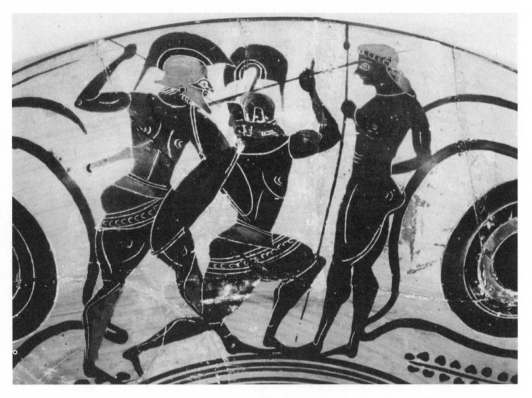

13. Depictions of hoplites overcoming Amazons, mythological women usurping the male role of warrior, illustrated the restoration of the proper order of the world in the Greek view. (Courtesy of the Yale University Art Gallery)

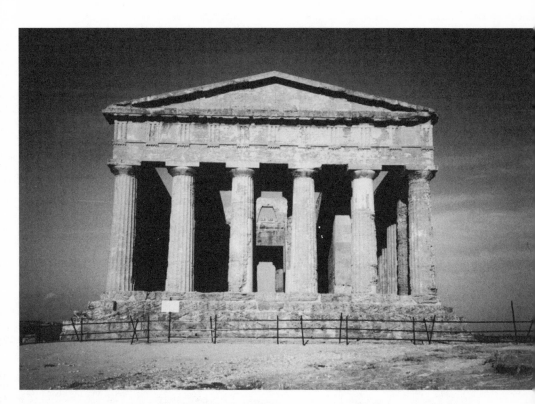

14. Some of the best-preserved temples from the ancient Greek world are found on the island of Sicily, as exemplified by the fifth-century B.C. Temple F at Agrigento (ancient Acragas); its stone architecture was originally covered by white stucco and paint in bright colors. (Photo by author)

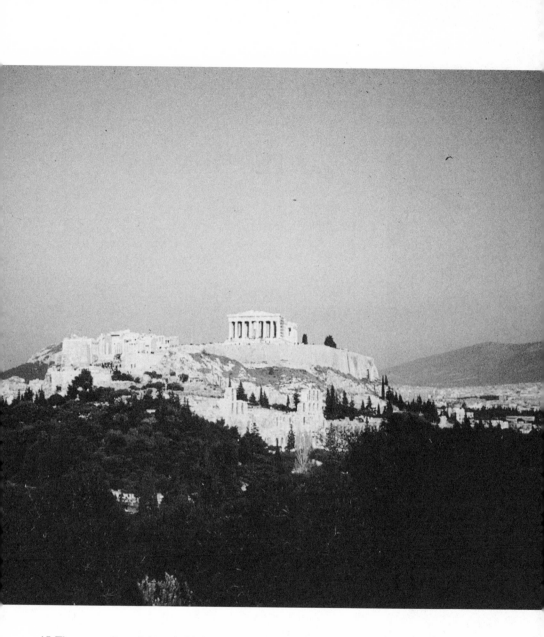

15. The acropolis at Athens held the city-state's most important temples, such as the Parthenon, and other civic buildings; its dramatic prominence showcased their immense size and cost, and thus the community's prosperity in its Golden Age. (Photo by author)

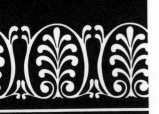

The Dark Age

A Period of Transition

The local conflicts, economic disruptions, and movements of peoples of the period c. 1200–c. 1000 B.C. that destroyed Mycenaean civilization in Greece and weakened or obliterated cities, kingdoms, and civilizations across the Near East brought grinding poverty to many of the populations that managed to survive the widespread violence of these centuries. Enormous difficulties impede our understanding of the history of this troubled period and of the recovery that followed because few literary or documentary sources exist to supplement the incomplete information provided by archaeology. Both because conditions were so grueling for many people and, perhaps more than anything, because the absence of written records from Greece limits us to a dim view of what happened there in these years, it is customary to refer to the era beginning toward the end of the eleventh century as a Dark Age: the fortunes of the people of the time seem generally dark, as does our understanding of the period.

The Near East recovered its strength much sooner than did Greece, ending its Dark Age by around 900 B.C. The end of this period in Greece is conventionally placed some 150 years after that, in the mid-eighth century. We should not imagine, however, that some enormous gulf separated the culture of Bronze Age Greece from that of the Dark Age. Above all, the continuing contact in the Dark Age between Greece and the Near East meant that the survivors of the fall of Mycenaean Greece never lost touch with the technology and the ideas, especially religious traditions, of the inventive peoples to the east. The details of Greek history in the Dark Age may remain difficult to discern, but there is no doubt that in these centuries Greeks laid the foundations for the values, traditions, and new forms of social and political organization that would characterize them in later ages.

Economy and Society in the Early Dark Age

Economic conditions in Greece after the undoing of Mycenaean civilization dramatically exemplified the reduced circumstances of life which many people in the Mediterranean and Near Eastern world had to endure during the worst years of the Dark Age. Mycenaean society had collapsed because the violence of the period after about 1200 B.C. had destroyed the complex economic system on which Mycenaean prosperity had depended. The most startling indication of the severe conditions of life in the early Dark Age is that the Greeks apparently lost their knowledge of writing when Mycenaean civilization was destroyed, although it has recently been suggested that the loss was not total. In any case, the total or near-total loss of the common use of a technology as vital as writing is explicable because the Linear B script used by the Mycenaeans was difficult to master and probably known only by the palace scribes, whose job was to keep the many records required for a centralized economy. These scribes employed writing as a technical skill for recording the flow of goods into the palaces and then out again for redistribution. Once the palaces and the redistributive economy of Mycenaean Greece had fallen apart, with nothing coming in to be recorded and no central authority to keep records, there was no longer a place for scribes or a need for writing. Significantly, however, the oral transmission of the traditions of the past allowed Greek culture to survive this loss by continuing its stories and legends as valuable possessions passed down through time. Storytelling, music, singing, and oral performances of poetry, which surely had been a part of Greek life for longer than we can trace, transmitted the most basic cultural ideas of the Greeks about themselves from generation to generation.

As far as accurate historical knowledge went, however, the Greeks of later periods suffered from a virtual amnesia about the Bronze Age. They knew very little about Mycenaean civilization and its fall, and some of the major things that they thought they knew seem not to have been true. They believed, for example, that, following the collapse of Mycenaean civilization, a Greek-speaking group from the north, called the Dorians, began to

---

c. 1000 B.C.: Almost all important Mycenaean sites except Athens by now destroyed.

c. 1000–900 B.C.: Period of most severe depopulation and reduced agriculture.

900–800 B.C.: Early revival of population and agriculture; iron beginning to be in use for tools and weapons.

c. 800 B.C.: Greek trading contacts with Al Mina in Syria.

776 B.C.: First Olympic Games.

c. 775 B.C.: Euboeans found trading post on Ischia in the Bay of Naples.

c. 750–700 B.C.: Homeric poetry recorded in writing after Greeks learn to write again, using a Phoenician alphabet modified with vowels; Hesiod composes his poetry; oracle of Apollo at Delphi already famous.

---

invade central and southern Greece. Dorians were especially remembered as the ancestors of the Spartans, the most powerful city-state on the mainland before the spectacular rise to prominence of Athens in the fifth century B.C. Strikingly, however, modern archaeology has not discovered any distinctive remains attesting a Dorian invasion, and many scholars reject this ancient idea as a fiction, at least if it is taken to mean a large-scale movement of people all at once. Since the lack of written works dating from the Greek Dark Age, when the Greeks probably could not write, means that the mute evidence uncovered by archaeologists must provide the foundation for reconstructing the history of this transitional period, we have no choice but to put greater credence in the conclusions of archaeology than in what the Greeks themselves believed about Dorians.

Archaeological excavation has shown that the Greeks cultivated much less land and had many fewer settlements in the early Dark Age than at the height of Mycenaean prosperity. No longer did powerful rulers ensconced in fortresses of stone preside over towns and tightly organized territories, with their redistributive economies providing a tolerable standard of living for farmers, herders, and a wide array of craft workers. The number of ships filled with Greek adventurers, raiders, and traders plying the Mediterranean was now minuscule compared to the Mycenaean fleets that had sailed during the late Bronze Age. Developed political states no longer existed in Greece in the early Dark Age, and people eked out their existence as herders, shepherds, and subsistence farmers bunched in tiny settlements as small as twenty people in many cases. Prosperous Mycenaean communities had been many times larger. Indeed, the entire Greek population was far smaller in the early Dark Age than it had been previously. As the population shrank, less land was cultivated, leading to a decline in the production of food. The decreased food supply in turn tended to encourage a further decline in the population. By reinforcing one another, these two processes multiplied their effects.

The withering away of agriculture led more Greeks than ever before to herd animals as a larger part of their living in what remained nevertheless a complex agricultural economy. This increasingly pastoral way of life meant that people became more mobile because they had to be prepared to move their herds to new pastures once they had overgrazed their current location. If they were lucky, they might find a new spot that allowed them to grow a crop of grain if they stayed there long enough. As a result of this less-settled lifestyle, people built only simple huts as their houses and got along with few possessions. Unlike their Mycenaean forebears, Greeks in the early Dark Age no longer had monumental architecture—no palaces with scores of rooms, no fortresses defended by mammoth stone walls. Art also experienced a kind of impoverishment, as Greek potters no longer included pictures of people and animals in the decoration on their painted pottery.

The general level of poverty in the early Greek Dark Age might suggest that many communities were relatively egalitarian in this period, at least as compared with the manifest hierarchy of Mycenaean civilization. Archaeological evidence, however, suggests either that a hierarchical social system survived in some spots or that it had revived as early as the late eleventh century B.C., which is to say not very far into the Dark Age. In any case, indications of social hierarchy in Dark Age Greece are unmistakable in the tenth century B.C. at a site now known as Lefkandi on the island of Euboea, off the eastern coast of the Greek mainland. There excavation has revealed the richly furnished burials of a man and woman, who died about 950 B.C. Their graves contained various luxury items, some characteristic of Near Eastern manufacture, and the dead woman wore elaborate gold ornaments testifying to her exceptional wealth. The couple were buried under a building more than 150 feet long with wooden columns on the exterior. The striking architecture and riches of their graves suggest that these individuals enjoyed high social status during their lives and perhaps received a form of ancestor worship after their death. Such wealthy and powerful people were probably still few in number at this date, but their existence at Lefkandi proves that marked social differentiation had either persisted or once again emerged in at least certain areas of the Greek world. Stresses in this hierarchical organization of Greek society, as we shall see, were to set the stage for the emergence of Greece's influential new political form, the self-governing city-state of free citizens.

Economic Recovery and Technology

Archaeological excavation has revealed that by about 900 B.C. at least small numbers of Greeks in various locations had become wealthy enough to have valuable objects buried with their bodies. This accumulation of conspicuous wealth indicates that a hierarchical arrangement of society was evidently spreading throughout Greece by this time; the families of the few men and women rich enough to have expensive material goods laid beside their mortal remains at their funerals were marking their status at the pinnacle of society by this display. In the earlier part of the Dark Age, the vast majority of dead people could afford no better grave offerings than a few plain clay pots. This social differentiation marked by wealth, which endured even into the grave, corresponded to significant economic changes based on technology that were already under way by the ninth century B.C.

Two burials from Athens illustrate the changes taking place during this period in metallurgical and agricultural technology, advances that would eventually help bring about the end of the Greek Dark Age. The earlier of the two burials, that of a male about 900 B.C., consisted of a pit into which was placed a clay pot to hold the dead man's cremated remains. Surrounding the pot were metal weapons including a long sword, spear heads, and knives. The inclusion of weapons of war in a male grave was a continuation of the burial traditions of the Mycenaean Age, but these arms were forged from iron, not bronze, which had been the primary metal of the earlier period. This difference reflects a significant shift in metallurgy that took place throughout the Mediterranean region during the early centuries of the first millennium B.C.: iron displacing bronze as the principal metal used to make tools and weapons. For this reason, following the habit of characterizing periods of history from the name of the metal most used at the time, the Dark Age can also be referred to as the early Iron Age in Greece.

Greeks probably learned the special metallurgical techniques needed to work iron, such as a very high smelting temperature, from traders searching for metal ores and itinerant workers from Cyprus, Anatolia, and the Near East. Iron eventually replaced bronze in many uses, above all in the production of agricultural tools, swords, and spear points, although bronze remained in use for shields and armor. The use of iron spread because it offered practical advantages over bronze. For one thing, iron ore was relatively easy to procure, making iron tools and weapons less expensive than ones of bronze. Furthermore, iron implements kept their sharp edges longer because properly worked iron was harder than bronze. The popularity of this metallurgical innovation was also accelerated by difficulties in obtaining the tin needed for alloying with copper to produce bronze. International trading routes, which had once brought tin to Greece and the Near East from Anatolia and more distant sources, had been disrupted for a while in the upheaval associated with the widespread turmoil that had affected the eastern Mediterranean region beginning around 1200 B.C. Greeks could mine iron ore in their own territory.

Better and more plentiful farming implements of iron eventually helped to increase the production of food, a development reflected by the evidence of a second burial from Athens. This grave, from about 850 B.C., held the remains of a woman and her treasures, including gold rings and earrings, a necklace of glass beads, and an unusual chest of baked clay. The necklace had been imported from Egypt or Syria or perhaps had been made locally by an itinerant metalworker from there. The technique of the gold jewelry was also that of the Near East. These objects reflected the ongoing contact between Greece and the more prosperous civilizations of that region, a relationship whose cultural influence on Greece increased as the Dark Age came to an end in the next century. The most intriguing object from the burial is the woman's terra cotta storage chest. It was painted with characteristically intricate and regular designs, whose precision has led modern art historians to give the name Geometric to this style of the late Dark Age. On its top were sculpted five beehive-like urns that are miniature models of granaries (structures for storing grain). If these models were important enough to be buried as objects of special value, then actual granaries and the grain they held were obviously valuable commodities in real life.

This deduction in turn means that already by 850 B.C. Greek agriculture had begun to recover from its devastation in the early Dark Age, when herding animals had become more prevalent and cultivation had decreased. Whether the woman was the owner of grain fields we cannot know, but from her sculpted chest we can glimpse the significance of farming for her and her contemporaries. Increased agricultural production in this period accompanied a growth in population. It is impossible to determine whether a rise in population preceded and led to the raising of more grain or, conversely, whether improvements in agricultural technology and the placing of more fields under cultivation spurred a consequent growth in the population by increasing the number of people the land could support. These two developments reinforced one another: as the Greeks produced more food, the better-fed population reproduced faster, and as the population grew, more people could produce more food. The repopulating of Greece in the late Dark Age established the demographic conditions under which the new political forms of Greece were to emerge.

The Social Values of the Greek Elite

People like the wealthy woman buried with the granary model at Athens and the earlier couple from Lefkandi constituted the wealthiest, most prestigious, and most powerful members of the social hierarchy that clearly had become widespread in Greece by the later part of the Greek Dark Age. The term aristocracy, from the Greek meaning "rule of the best," is often employed as shorthand for this elite social group, but the term can be misleading because of its varying connotations. In other times and places the aristocracy has been a legally constituted and formally recognized nobility, the members of which inherited their status by being born into a family officially designated as aristocratic. Greece never had such an official nobility. For this reason, it is more accurate to refer to the leading members of Greek society as an elite rather than as an aristocracy, and that is the usage prevailing in this book. When "aristocracy" and its relatives, such as "aristocrat," do appear in discussions of Greek history, it is imperative to remember that they do not mean what they often mean in, for example, French or English history.

Members of the Greek social elite in this period achieved their status based on a combination of interrelated factors, including conduct, wealth, and birth. Being born into a family that already enjoyed wealth and prestige obviously provided a fundamental criterion for membership in the social elite, but by itself one's lineage did not guarantee general acknowledgment as a member of the "best" in the society. It was essential to adhere to the code of behavior expected of this group and to be wealthy. Furthermore, it was crucial to employ one's wealth appropriately in public contexts: to make displays of status by acquiring fine goods and financing celebrations, to cement relationships with social equals by exchanging gifts and with inferiors by doing them favors, and to pay due homage to the gods by expensive sacrifices, especially of large animals. Therefore, in gaining recognition from others as a member of the elite of the society, the way in which one behaved was at least as important as the family into which one was born. Losing one's wealth or failing to observe the code of behavior expected of the elite could catapult one into social obloquy.

We can only speculate about the various ways in which families might have originally gained their designation as elite and thus become entitled to pass on this wealth and status to those descendants able to maintain them. Some families in the Dark Age might have inherited an elite status as survivors of prominent families of the Mycenaean Age that had somehow managed to hold on to wealth or land during the early Dark Age; some might have made their way into the elite during the Dark Age by amassing wealth and befriending less fortunate people who were willing to acknowledge their benefactors' superior status in return for material help; and some might have acquired superior social status by monopolizing control of essential religious rituals that they perpetuated for others to participate in.

The ideas and traditions of this social elite concerning the organization of their communities and proper behavior for everyone in them—that is, their code of values—represented, like the reappearance of agriculture, basic components of Greece's emerging new political forms. The social values of the Dark Age elite underlie the stories told in the *Iliad* and *Odyssey*, two

Table 2. Examples of Letters from Early Alphabets

I. Proto- Canaanite	2. Early Letter Names and Meanings		3. Phoenician	4. Early Greek	5. Modern English Capitals
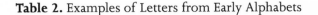	*alp*	oxhead	𐤀	Λ	A
	bêt	house	𐤁	𐌁	B
	gaml	throwstick	𐤂	𐌂	C
	digg	fish	𐤃	Δ	D
	hô(?)	man calling	𐤄	𐌄	E

1. The letters in the Proto-Canaanite alphabet of the second millennium B.C., as written at sites such as Serabit al-Khadim in Sinai.
2. The names of the letters and the words from which they were taken; for example, the letter named *bet* was written to indicate the sound of the letter *b*, which was the first sound in the Canaanite word for "house," *bet*.
3. The same letters as taken over by the Phoenicians for their alphabet.
4. The same letters as taken over by the Greeks for their alphabet.
5. The same letters as written in modern English capitals.

book-length poems that first began to be written down about the middle of the eighth century B.C., at the very end of the Dark Age. The Greeks had relearned the technology of writing as a result of contact with the literate civilizations of the Near East and the alphabet developed there long before. Sometime between about 950 and 750 the Greeks adopted a Phoenician alphabet to represent the sounds of their own language, innovating in a fundamental way by introducing vowels as letters. The Greek version of the alphabet eventually formed the base of the alphabet used for English today. Greeks of the Archaic Age (roughly 750–500 B.C.) swiftly applied their newly acquired skill to write down oral literature, such as these two poems. The Greeks believed that Homer, a blind poet from the region of Anatolia called Ionia (today on the western coast of Turkey), had composed the *Iliad* and *Odyssey*. Homeric poetry, even if it was put into final form by a single author, grew out of centuries of oral performance by countless Greek poets singing of the deeds and values of legendary warriors and their families. Near Eastern poetic tales influenced this oral poetry, which for centuries helped to transmit cultural values from one generation of Greeks to the next. Despite the ancient origins of Homeric poetry, the behavioral code portrayed in its verses primarily reflected values established in the society of Greece of the Dark Age before the rise of political systems based on citizenship.

The main characters in the Homeric poems are unmistakably members of the social elite, who are expected to live up to a demanding code of values. The men are warriors, like the incomparable Achilles of the *Iliad*. This poem tells part of the famous story of the attack by a Greek army on the city of Troy, a stronghold in northwestern Anatolia. Although it is commonly assumed that the Trojans were a different people from the Greeks, the poems themselves provide no definitive answer to the question of their ethnic identity. In the *Iliad*'s representation of the Trojan War, which the Greeks believed occurred about four hundred years before Homer's time, Achilles is "the best of the Greeks" (for instance, *Iliad* 1.244) because he is a "doer of deeds and speaker of words" (*Iliad* 9.443) without equal. Achilles' overriding concern in word and action is with the glorious reputation (*kleos*) that he can win with his "excellence" (the best available translation for Greek *arete*, a word with a range of meanings). Like all members of the social elite, Achilles feared the disgrace that he would feel in the eyes of others if he were seen to fail to live up to the code of excellence. Under this code, failure and wrongdoing produced public shame.

Excellence as a moral value also carried with it a strong notion of obligation and responsibility. The strongest of these duties was the requirement that ties of guest-host friendship (*xenia*) be respected no matter what the situation. In the *Iliad*, for example, the Greek Diomedes is preparing to battle an enemy warrior, Glaucus, when he discovers that Glaucus's grandfather once hosted his own grandfather as a guest while he was traveling abroad in Glaucus's land. This long-past act of hospitality had established ties of friendship and made the men "guest-host friends" of one another, a relationship which still remained valid for the two descendants and had to be respected even in the heat of battle. "Therefore," says Diomedes in the story, "let us not use our spears against each other. . . . There are many other Trojans and their allies for me to kill, the gods willing, and many other Greeks for you to slay if you can" (*Iliad* 6.226–229). To show their excellence in this case, these fighters were obliged to respect morally binding commitments they themselves had no part in making. Thus, the notion of excellence could serve both as a competitive social value and as a cooperative one. That is, in the context of warfare among people with no obligations toward one another, excellence demanded that warriors compete to defeat their enemies and to outshine their friends and allies in their ability to win battles. In the context of relationships such as guest-host friendship, however, excellence required that even enemies put aside martial competitiveness to cooperate in respecting moral obligation established among individuals.

The concentration on excellence as a personal quality distinguishes the code of values not just of warriors in the Homeric poems but also of socially elite women. This essential feature of the elite society portrayed in the *Iliad* and the *Odyssey* comes most prominently to the fore in the character of Penelope, the wife of Odysseus, the hero of the *Odyssey*, and his partner in the most important household of their home community of Ithaca, on an island off the west coast of the Peloponnese. Penelope's excellence requires her to preserve her household and property during her husband's long absence by relying on her intelligence, social status, and intense fidelity to her husband. She is obliged to display great stamina and ingenuity in resisting the attempted depredations of her husband's rivals at home while Odysseus is away for twenty years fighting the Trojan War and then sailing home in a long series of dangerous adventures.

When Odysseus finally returns to Ithaca, he assumes the disguise of a wandering beggar to observe conditions in his household in secret before revealing his true identity and reclaiming his leading position. Penelope displays her commitment to excellence by treating the ragged stranger with the kindness and dignity owed to any and all visitors according to Greek custom, in contrast to the rude treatment that he receives from the female head of the servant corps of the house. Odysseus, still in disguise, therefore greets her with the words of praise that were due a woman who understood the demands of her elite status and could carry them through: "My Lady, no mortal on this boundless earth could find any fault with you; your glorious reputation [*kleos*] reaches to the broad heavens, like that of a king without blame, who respects the gods and upholds justice in his rule over many strong men, and whose dark land sprouts wheat and barley, whose trees bend with the weight of their fruit, whose sheep bear lambs every season, whose sea teems with fish, all the result of his good leadership, and thus his people flourish under his rule" (*Odyssey* 19.107–114).

Although Penelope clearly counts as an exceptional figure of literature, that the *Odyssey* employs in her praise a description also fitting for a man of surpassing virtue and achievement demonstrates that the society of Dark Age Greece expected as much of women as of men and entitled them to the same level of recognition for their achievements or disgrace for their failures. In real life, women of the social elite, like men of the same status, saw their proper role in life as requiring them to develop an exceptional excellence to set themselves apart from others of more ordinary character and status. Under this code, any life was contemptible whose goal was not the pursuit of excellence and the fame that it brought. This code of values of course consigned the great majority of the population to secondary status, from which they had little, if any, hope of escaping unless they could somehow manage to accumulate the wealth that would allow them to participate in the way of life of the elite.

The Olympic Games and Panhellenism

Excellence as a competitive value for Greek males of the social elite showed up clearly in the Olympic Games, a religious festival associated with a large sanctuary of Zeus, king of the gods of the Greeks. The sanctuary was located at Olympia, in the northwestern Peloponnese, where the games were held every four years beginning in 776 B.C. During these great celebrations men wealthy enough to spend the time to become outstanding athletes competed in running events and wrestling as individuals, not as national representatives on teams, as in the modern Olympic Games. The emphasis on physical prowess and fitness, competition, and public recognition by other men as winners corresponded to the ideal of Greek masculine identity as it developed in this period. In a rare departure from the ancient Mediterranean tradition against public nakedness, Greek athletes competed without clothing (hence the word gymnasium, from the Greek word meaning "naked," *gymnos*). Other competitions, such as horse and chariot racing, were added to the Olympic Games later, but the principal event remained a sprint of about two hundred yards called the *stadion* (hence our word *stadium*). Winners originally received no financial prizes, only a garland made from wild olive leaves, but the prestige of victory could bring other rewards as well. Prizes with material value were often awarded in later Greek athletic competitions. Admission to the Olympic Games was free to men; married women were not allowed to attend, on pain of death, but women not yet married could. Women had their own separate festival at Olympia on a different date in honor of Zeus's wife, Hera. Although less is known about the games of Hera, Pausanias (*Description of Greece* 5.16.2) reports that women not yet married competed on the Olympic track in a foot race five-sixths as long as the men's stadion. In later times, international games including the Olympics were dominated by professional athletes, who made good livings from appearance fees and prizes won at various events held all over Greece. The most famous athlete of all was Milo, from Croton in southern Italy. Winner of the Olympic wrestling crown six times beginning in 536 B.C., he was renowned for showy stunts, such as holding his breath until his blood expanded his veins so much that they would snap a cord tied around his head.

The Olympic Games centered on contests among individuals, who prided themselves on their innate distinctiveness from ordinary people, as the fifth-century B.C. poet Pindar made clear in praising a family of victors: "Hiding the nature you are born with is impossible. The seasons rich in their flowers have many times bestowed on you, sons of Alatas [of Corinth], the brightness that victory brings, when you achieved the heights of excellence in the sacred games" (*Olympian Ode* 13). The organization of the festival as an event for all of Greece nevertheless indicates a trend toward communal activity that was under way in Greek society and politics by the mid-eighth century B.C. First of all, the building of a special sanctuary for the worship of Zeus at Olympia provided an architectural focus for public gatherings with a surrounding space for crowds to assemble. The social complement to the creation of this physical environment was the tradition that the Games of Zeus and Hera were panhellenic, that is, open to all Greeks. Moreover, an international truce of several weeks was declared to guarantee safe passage for competitors and spectators traveling to and from Olympia, even if wars were in progress along their way. In short, the arrangements for the Olympic Games demonstrate that in eighth-century B.C. Greece the values of individual activity and pursuit of excellence by one's self were beginning to be channeled into a new context appropriate for a changing society that needed ways for its developing communities to interact with one another peacefully. This assertion of communal in addition to individual interests was another important precondition for the creation of Greece's new political forms.

Religion and Myth

Religion provided the context for almost all communal activity throughout the history of ancient Greece. Sports, as in the Olympic Games held to honor Zeus, took place in the religious context of festivals honoring specific gods. War was conducted according to the signs of divine will that civil and military leaders identified in the sacrifice of animals and in omens derived from occurrences in nature, such as unusual weather. Sacrifices themselves, the central event of Greek religious rituals, were performed before crowds in the open air on public occasions that involved communal feasting afterward on the sacrificed meat. The conceptual basis of Greek religion was found in myth (*mythos*, a Greek word meaning "story" or "tale") about the gods and their relationship to humans. Greek myth was deeply influenced by Near Eastern myth in the Dark Age, as Greeks heard stories from Near Eastern traders passing through in search of metals and markets and tried to understand the drawings and carvings of Near Eastern mythological figures found on imported objects such as furniture, pots, seals, and jewelry. In the eighth century B.C., the Greeks began to record their own versions of these myths in writing, and the poetry of Hesiod preserved from this period (there was at this date not yet any Greek literature in prose) reveals how religious myth, as well as the economic changes and social values of the time, contributed to the feeling of community that underlay the creation of new political structures in Greece.

Hesiod, living in the region of Boeotia in central Greece, employed myth to reveal the divine origin of justice. His long poem the *Theogony* ("The Genealogy of the Gods") details the birth of the race of gods from primordial Chaos ("void" or "vacuum") and Earth, the mother of Sky and numerous other children. Hesiod explained that when Sky began to imprison his siblings, Earth persuaded her fiercest male offspring, Kronos, to overthrow him by violence because "[Sky] first contrived to do shameful things" (166). When Kronos later began to swallow up all his own children, Kronos's wife had their son Zeus overthrow his father by force in retribution for his evil deeds. These vivid stories, which had their origins in Near Eastern myths like those of the Mesopotamian *Epic of Creation*, carried the message that existence, even for gods, entailed struggle, sorrow, and violence. Even more significantly, however, they showed that a concern for justice had also been a component of the divine order of the universe from the beginning.

In his poem *Works and Days*, Hesiod identified Zeus as the fount of justice in all human affairs, a marked contrast to the portrayal of Zeus in Homeric poetry as primarily concerned only with the fate of his favorite warriors in battle. Hesiod presents justice as a divine quality that will assert itself to punish evildoers: "Zeus ordained this law for men, that fishes and wild beasts and birds should eat each other, for they have no justice; but to human beings he has given justice, which is far the best" (276–280). In the Dark Age society of Hesiod's day, men dominated the distribution of justice, exercising direct control over their family members and household servants. Others outside their immediate households would become their followers by acknowledging their status as leaders. A powerful man's followers would grant him a certain amount of authority because, as the followers were roughly equal in wealth and status among themselves, they needed a figure invested with authority to settle disputes and organize defense against raids or other military threats. In anthropological terms, such leaders operated as chiefs of bands. A chief had authority to settle arguments over property and duties, oversaw the distribution of rewards and punishments, and usually headed the religious rituals deemed essential to the security of the group. At the same time, his actual power to coerce recalcitrant or rebellious members of his band was limited. When decisions affecting the entire group had to be made, his leadership depended on being capable of forging a consensus by persuading members of the band about what to do. Hesiod describes how an effective chief exercised leadership: "When wise leaders see their people in the assembly get on the wrong track, they gently set matters right, persuading them with soft words" (*Theogony* 88–90). In short, a chief could only lead his followers where they were willing to go and only by the use of persuasion, not compulsion.

Chiefs were of course not immune to misuse of their status and ability to persuade others to do their will, and it seems likely that friction became increasingly common between leaders and their poorer followers in the late Dark Age. A story from the *Iliad* provides a fictional illustration of the kind of behavior that could have generated such friction in the period during which the city-state began to emerge. When Agamemnon, the arrogantly self-important leader of the Greek army besieging Troy, summoned the troops to announce a decision to prolong the war, now in its tenth year, an ordinary soldier named Thersites spoke up in opposition. Thersites had the right and the opportunity to express his opinion because Agamemnon led the Greeks as a Dark Age chief led a band, which required that all men's opinions be heard with respect in a common assembly. It was thus in front of Agamemnon's assembled followers that Thersites criticized the leader as overweeningly greedy. "Let's leave him here to digest his booty," Thersites shouted to his fellow soldiers in the ranks. Odysseus, another chief, immediately rose to support Agamemnon, saying to Thersites, "If I ever find you being so foolish again, may my head not remain on my body if I don't strip you naked and send you back to your ship crying from the blows I give you." Odysseus thereupon cowed Thersites with a blow to his back, which drew blood (2.211–277).

At the conclusion of this episode, the assembled soldiers are described as approving of Odysseus's inequitable treatment of Thersites, who is portrayed as an unattractive character. For the city-state to be created as a political institution in which all free men had a share, this complacent attitude of the mass of men had to change in the real world. Ordinary men had to insist that they deserved equitable treatment, according to the definition of equity valid in their society, even if members of the social elite were to remain in leadership positions, while they themselves remained as subordinates to the elite leaders in war and their social inferiors in peace.

Hesiod reveals that by the eighth century B.C. a state of heightened tension concerning the implementation of justice in the affairs of everyday life had indeed developed between chiefs and peasants (the free proprietors of small farms, who might own a slave or two, oxen to work their fields, and other movable property of value). Peasants' ownership of property made them the most influential group among the men, ranging from poor to moderately well-off, who made up the bands of followers of elite chiefs in late Dark Age Greece. Assuming the perspective of a peasant farming a smallholding, the poet insisted that the divine origin of justice should be a warning to "bribe-devouring chiefs" who settled disputes among their followers and neighbors "with crooked judgments" (*Works and Days* 263–264). This outrage evidently felt by peasants at receiving unfair treatment in the settlement of disputes served as yet another stimulus for the gradual movement toward new forms of political organization, those of the city-state.

The Archaic Age

4

Developing the City-State

During the Archaic Age the Greeks fully developed the most widespread and influential of their new political forms, the city-state (*polis*). The term *Archaic Age*, meaning the "Old-Fashioned Age" and designating Greek history from approximately 750 to 500 B.C., stems from art history. Scholars of Greek art, employing criteria of aesthetic judgment that are today not so common, judged the style of works from this period as looking more old-fashioned than the more naturalistic art of the following period (the fifth and fourth centuries B.C.), which they saw as producing models of beauty and therefore named the Classical Age. Archaic sculptors, for example, made free-standing figures who stood stiffly, staring straight ahead in imitation of Egyptian statuary. By the Classical Age, sculptors depicted their subjects in more varied and lively poses.

The question of the merits of its statues aside, the Archaic Age saw the gradual culmination of developments in social and political organization in ancient Greece that had begun much earlier in the Dark Age and led to the emergence of the Greek city-state. Organized on the principle of citizenship, the city-state included in its population male citizens, female citizens, their children, resident foreigners, and slaves belonging to individuals as well as to the city-state as a whole. It was thus a complex

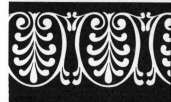

---

before **750 B.C.:** Phoenicians found colonies in western Mediterranean, such as
at Cadiz (in modern Spain).

c. **750 B.C.:** Greek city-states beginning to organize spatially and socially.

c. **750–550 B.C.:** Greek colonies founded all around the Mediterranean region.

c. **700–650 B.C.:** Hoplite armor becoming much more common in Greece.

c. **600** and after: Chattel slavery becomes increasingly common in Greece.

---

community made up of people of very different legal and social statuses.
One of its most remarkable characteristics was the extension of citizenship
and a certain share of political rights to even the poorest free-born local
members of the community. Although poverty could make their lives as
physically deprived as those of slaves, this distinction gave an extra meaning
to the personal freedom that set them apart from the enslaved inhabitants
of the city-state and the foreigners resident there.

The Characteristics of the City-State

Polis, the Greek term from which is derived the modern term "politics,"
is usually translated as "city-state" to emphasize its difference from what we
today normally think of as a city. As in many earlier states in the ancient
Near East, the polis included not just an urban center, often protected by
stout walls in later centuries, but also countryside for some miles around
dotted with various small settlements. Members of a polis, then, could live
both in the town at its center and also in villages or isolated farmhouses
scattered throughout its rural territory. Together these people made up a
community of citizens embodying a political state, and it was this partnership among citizens that represented the distinctive political characteristic
of the polis. Only men had the right to political participation, but women
still counted as members of the community legally, socially, and religiously.
Presiding over the polis as protector and patron was a particular god, as, for
example, Athena at Athens. Different communities could choose the same
deity as their protector; Sparta, Athens's chief rival in the Classical period,
also had Athena as its patron god. The members of a polis constituted a
religious association obliged to honor the state's patron deity as well as the
community's other gods. The community expressed official homage and
respect to the gods through its cults, which were regular sets of public religious activities paid for at public expense and overseen by citizens serving
as priests and priestesses. The central ritual of a city-state's cults was the sacrifice of animals to demonstrate to the gods as divine protectors the respect
and piety of the members of the polis.

A polis was independent of its neighbors and had political unity among its urban and rural settlements of citizens. At this point it is appropriate to signal clearly how controversial is the question of the deepest origins of the Greek polis as a community whose members self-consciously shared a common political identity. Since by the Archaic Age the peoples of Greece had absorbed many innovations in technology, religious thought, and literature from other peoples throughout the eastern Mediterranean region and the Near East, it is possible that they might have been influenced also by earlier political developments elsewhere, as, for example, in the city-kingdoms on Cyprus or the cities of Phoenicia. It is less easy to imagine how political as opposed to cultural precedents might have been transmitted to Greece from the East, however. The stream of Near Eastern traders, crafts specialists, and travelers to Greece in the Dark Age could more easily bring technological, religious, and artistic ideas with them than political systems. One Dark Age condition that certainly did affect the formation of the city-state was the lack of powerful imperial states. The political extinction of Mycenaean civilization had left a vacuum of power that made it possible for small, independent city-states to emerge without being overwhelmed by large states.

What matters most for present purposes in any case is to stress that the Greek city-state was organized politically on the concept of citizenship for all its indigenous free inhabitants. The distinctiveness of citizenship as an organizing concept in this period in Greece was that it assumed in theory certain basic levels of legal equality, essentially the expectation of equal treatment under the law, with the exception that different regulations could apply to women in certain areas of life such as acceptable sexual behavior and the control of property. But the general legal equality that the Greek city-state provided was not dependent on a citizen's wealth. Since pronounced social differentiation between rich and poor had characterized the history of the ancient Near East and Greece of the Mycenaean Age and had once again become common in Greece by the late Dark Age, it is remarkable that a notion of some sort of legal equality, no matter how incomplete it may have been in practice, came to serve as the basis for the reorganization of Greek society in the Archaic Age. The polis based on citizenship remained the preeminent form of political and social organization in Greece from its earliest definite appearance about 750 B.C., when public sanctuaries serving a community are first attested archaeologically, until the beginning of the Roman Empire eight centuries later. The other most common new form of political organization in Greece was the "league" or "federation" (*ethnos*), a flexible form of association over a broad territory which was itself sometimes composed of city-states.

The most famous ancient analyst of Greek politics and society, the phi-

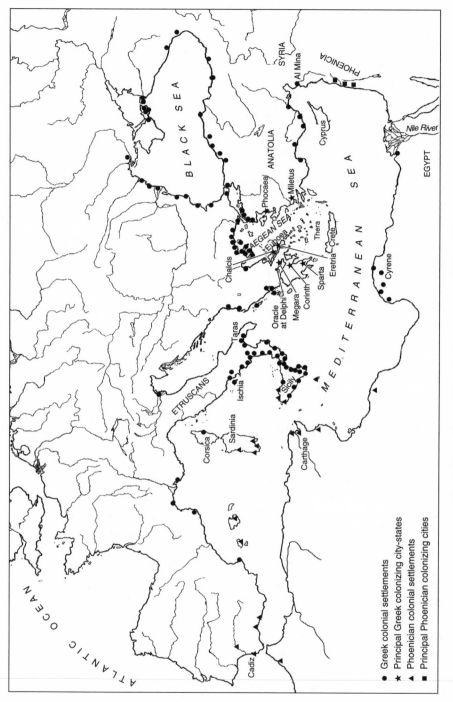

Map 3. Phoenician and Greek Colonization, c. 800–c. 500 B.C.

- Greek colonial settlements
- ★ Principal Greek colonizing city-states
- ▲ Phoenician colonial settlements
- ■ Principal Phoenician colonizing cities

losopher Aristotle (384–322 B.C.), insisted that the emergence of the polis had been the inevitable result of the forces of nature at work. "Humans," he said, "are beings who by nature live in a polis" (*Politics* 1253a2–3). Anyone who existed self-sufficiently outside the community of a polis, Aristotle only half-jokingly maintained, must be either a beast or a god (1253a29). In referring to nature, Aristotle meant the combined effect of social and economic forces. But the geography of Greece also influenced the process by which this novel way of organizing human communities came about. The severely mountainous terrain of the mainland meant that city-states were often physically separated by significant barriers to easy communication, thus reinforcing their tendency to develop politically in isolation and not to cooperate with one another despite shared culture and language. City-states could also exist next to one another with no great impediments to travel between them, as in the plains of Boeotia. A single Greek island could be home to multiple city-states maintaining their independence from one another: the large island of Lesbos in the eastern Aegean Sea was home to five different city-states. Since few city-states controlled enough arable land to grow food sufficient to feed a large body of citizens, polis communities no larger than several hundred to a couple of thousand people were normal even after the population of Greece rose dramatically at the end of the Dark Age. By the fifth century B.C. Athens had grown to perhaps forty thousand adult male citizens and a total population, including slaves and other noncitizens, of several hundred thousand people, but this was a rare exception to the generally small size of Greek city-states. A population as large as that of Classical Athens at its height could be supported only by the regular importation of food from abroad, which had to be financed by trade and other revenues.

Early Colonization

Some Greeks had emigrated from the mainland eastward across the Aegean Sea to settle in Ionia as early as the ninth century B.C. Starting around 750 B.C., however, Greeks began to settle even farther outside the Greek homeland. Within two hundred years of this date, Greeks had established colonies in areas that are today southern France, Spain, Sicily and southern Italy, and along North Africa and the coast of the Black Sea. Eventually the Greek world included hundreds of city-states. A scarcity of arable land certainly gave momentum to emigration from Greece, but the revival of international trade in the Mediterranean in the Archaic era perhaps provided the original stimulus for Greeks to leave their homeland, whose economy was still struggling overall. Some Greeks with commercial interests took up residence in foreign settlements, such as those founded in Spain in this period by the Phoenicians from Palestine; the Phoenicians were active in building commercially motivated settlements throughout the western Mediterranean, usually at spots where they could most easily trade for metals. Within a century of its foundation sometime before 750 B.C., for example, the Phoenician settlement on the site of modern Cadiz in Spain had become a city thriving on economic and cultural interaction with the indigenous Iberian population. The natural resources of Spain included rich veins of metals.

Although it was very common for emigrant Greeks to take up residence in overseas Phoenician communities, they also established trading posts abroad on their own. Traders from the island of Euboea, for instance, had already established commercial contacts by 800 B.C. with a community located on the Syrian coast at a site now called Al Mina. Men wealthy enough to finance risky expeditions by sea ranged far from home in search of metals. Homeric poetry testifies to the basic strategy of this entrepreneurial commodity trading. In the *Odyssey*, the goddess Athena once appears disguised as a metal trader to hide her identity from the son of the poem's hero: "I am here at present," she says to him, "with my ship and crew on our way across the wine-dark sea to foreign lands in search of copper; I am carrying iron now" (1.178–188). By about 775 B.C., Euboeans, who seem to have been particularly active explorers, had also established a settlement for purposes of trade on the island of Ischia, in the Bay of Naples off southern Italy. There they processed iron ore imported from the Etruscans, a thriving population inhabiting central Italy. Archaeologists have documented the expanding overseas communication of the eighth century by finding Greek pottery at more than eighty sites outside the Greek homeland; by contrast, almost no pots have been found that were carried abroad in the tenth century.

Learning from overseas traders, Greeks and non-Greeks alike, of favorable places in which to relocate, Greek colonists set out from their "mother city" (*metropolis*), which organized the expedition by selecting a leader called the "founder" (*ktistes*). Even though they were going to establish an independent city-state at their new location, colonists were expected to retain ties with their metropolis. A colony that sided with its metropolis's enemy in a war, for example, was regarded as disloyal. Sometimes the colonists enjoyed a friendly welcome from the local inhabitants where they settled; sometimes they had to fight to win land for their new community. Since colonizing expeditions were apparently usually all male, wives for the colonists had to be found among the locals, either through peaceful negotiation or by violent kidnappings. The colony's founder was in charge of laying out the settlement properly and parceling out the land, as Homer describes in speaking of the foundation of a fictional colony: "So [the founder] led them away, settling them in [a place called] Scheria, far from the bustle of men. He had a wall constructed around the town center, built houses, erected temples for the gods, and divided the land" (*Odyssey* 6.7–10).

Commercial interests perhaps first induced Greeks to emigrate, but greater numbers of them began to move abroad permanently in the mid-eighth century B.C., probably because the population explosion in the late Dark Age had caused a scarcity of land available for farming, the most desirable form of wealth in Greek culture. The disruptions and depopulation of the Dark Age originally had left much good land unoccupied, and families could send their offspring out to take possession of unclaimed fields. Eventually, however, this supply of free land was exhausted, giving rise in some city-states to tensions caused by competition for land to farm. Emigration helped solve this problem by sending men without land to foreign regions, where they could acquire their own fields in the territory of colonies founded as new city-states.

The foundation of Cyrene (in what is now Libya in North Africa) in about 630 B.C. reveals how contentious the process of colonization could be. The people of the polis of Thera, on an island north of Crete, apparently were unable to support their population. Sending out colonists therefore made sense as a solution to population pressures. A later inscription describing how the expedition was organized under the leadership of the ktistes Battus reveals the urgency of the situation: "Since Apollo of Delphi spontaneously instructed Battus and the Therans to send a colony to Cyrene, the Therans decided to send Battus to North Africa as leader and king and for the Therans to sail as his companions. They are to go on equal and fair terms according to their household and one adult son [from each family] is to be conscripted, [and those who are to be chosen are to be those who are the adults, and of the other Therans only those who are free men are to sail]. And if the colonists succeed in establishing the settlement, men who sail to North Africa later on to join it shall share in citizenship and magistracies and shall be given portions from the land that no one owns. But if they fail to establish the settlement and the Therans are unable to send assistance and the colonists suffer hardship for five years, they shall depart from the land to Thera without fear of punishment, they can return to their own property, and they shall be citizens. And if any man is unwilling to depart for the colony once the polis decides to send him, he shall be liable to the death penalty and his property shall be confiscated. Any man who shelters or hides such a one, whether he is a father helping his son, or a brother aiding his brother, is to suffer the same penalty as the man who refuses to sail. An agreement was sworn on these conditions by those who remained in Thera and those who sailed to found the colony in Cyrene, and they invoked curses against those who break the agreement or fail to keep it, whether they were those who settled in North Africa or those who stayed behind" (GHI, no. 5).

It is evident that the young men of Thera were reluctant to leave their home for the new colony. This poignant document shows, then, that colonization in response to population growth was not always a matter of individual choice. The possibility of acquiring land in a colony on which a man could perhaps grow wealthy had to be weighed carefully against the terrors of being torn from family and friends to voyage over treacherous seas to regions filled with unknown dangers. Greek colonists had reason to be anxious about their future.

In some cases, population growth was not the principal spur to colonization. The foundation of colonies could also serve to rid the metropolis of undesirables whose presence was causing social unrest. The Spartans, for example, colonized Taras (modern Taranto) in southern Italy in 706 B.C. with a group of illegitimate sons whom they could not successfully integrate into their citizen body. Like the young men of Thera, these unfortunate outcasts certainly did not go as colonists by their own choice.

The participation of Greeks in international trade and in colonization increased their contact with the peoples of Anatolia and the Near East. They admired and envied these older civilizations for their wealth, such as the gold of the Phrygian kingdom of Midas, and for their cultural accomplishments, such as the lively pictures of animals on Near Eastern ceramics, the magnificent temples of Egypt, and the alphabets of the Phoenician cities. During the early Dark Age, Greek artists had stopped portraying people or other living creatures in their designs. The pictures they saw on pottery imported from the Near East in the late Dark Age and early Archaic Age influenced them to begin once again to depict figures in their paintings on pots. The style of Near Eastern reliefs and free-standing sculptures also inspired creative imitation in Greek art of the period. When the improving economy of the later Archaic Age allowed Greeks to revive monumental architecture in stone, temples for the worship of the gods emulating Egyptian architectural designs represented the most prominent examples of this new trend in erecting large, expensive buildings. The Greeks began to mint coins in the sixth century B.C., a technology they learned from the Lydians of Anatolia, who had invented coinage in the seventh century. Long after this innovation, however, much economic exchange continued to be made through barter, especially in the Near East. Highly monetized economies took centuries to develop.

Knowledge of writing was the most dramatic contribution of the ancient Near East to Greece as the latter region emerged from its Dark Age. The Greeks probably originally learned the alphabet from the Phoenicians to use it for record keeping in business and trade, as the Phoenicians did so well, but they soon started to employ it to record literature, namely, Homeric poetry. Since the ability to read and write remained unnecessary for most purposes in the predominately agricultural economy of Archaic Greece and there were no schools, few people at first learned the new technology of letters.

Competition for international markets significantly affected the fortunes of larger Greek city-states during this period. Corinth, for example, grew prosperous from its geographical location controlling the narrow isthmus of land connecting northern and southern Greece. Since ships plying the east-west sea lanes of the Mediterranean preferred to avoid the stormy passage around the tip of southern Greece, they commonly offloaded their cargoes for transshipment on a special roadbed built across the isthmus and subsequent reloading on different ships on the other side. Small ships may even have been dragged over the roadbed from one side of the isthmus to the other. Corinth became a bustling center for shipping and earned a large income from sales and harbor taxes. It also earned a reputation and income as the foremost ship-building center of Archaic Greece. By taking advantage of its deposits of fine clay and the expertise of a growing number of potters, Corinth furthermore developed a thriving export trade in pottery painted in vivid colors. It is not altogether certain whether the people in whose possession such pots ended up overseas, such as the Etruscans in central Italy, prized the pots themselves as foreign luxury items or were more interested in whatever may have been shipped inside the pots, such as wine or olive oil. It is clear that Greek painted pots were regularly transported far from their point of manufacture. By the late sixth century B.C., however, Athens began to displace Corinth as the leading Greek exporter of fancy painted pottery, evidently because consumers came to prefer designs featuring the red color for which the chemical composition of its clay was better suited than Corinth's.

The Greeks were always careful to solicit approval from their gods before setting out from home, whether for commercial voyages or colonization. The god most frequently consulted about sending out a colony, as in the case of Cyrene, was Apollo in his sanctuary at Delphi, a hauntingly scenic spot in the mountains of central Greece. The Delphic sanctuary began to be internationally renowned in the eighth century B.C. because it housed an oracular shrine in which a prophetess, the Pythia, spoke the will of Apollo in response to questions from visiting petitioners. The Delphic oracle operated for a limited number of days over nine months of the year, and demand for its services was so high that the operators of the sanctuary rewarded generous contributors with the privilege of jumping to the head of the line. The great majority of visitors to Delphi consulted the oracle about personal matters such as marriage and having children. That Greeks hoping to found a colony felt they had to secure the approval of Apollo of Delphi demonstrates that the oracle was held in high esteem as early as the

700s B.C., a reputation that continued to make the oracle a force in Greek international affairs in the centuries to come.

Forming the City-State

Identifying the reasons for the changes in Greek politics that led to the gradual emergence of the city-state in the Archaic Age remains a knotty problem. The surviving evidence mainly concerns Athens, which was not a typical city-state in significant aspects, particularly in the large size of its population. Much of what we can say about the formation of the early Greek city-state therefore applies solely to Athens. Other city-states certainly emerged under varying conditions and with different results. Nevertheless, it seems possible to draw some general conclusions about the slow process through which city-states began to emerge starting around the middle of the eighth century B.C.

The economic revival of the Archaic Age and the growth in the population of Greece evident by this time certainly gave momentum to the process. Men who managed to acquire substantial property from success in agriculture or commerce could now demand a greater say in political affairs from the social elite, who claimed preeminence based on their wealth, their prestige, and, especially when these first two characteristics were weakened, the glory of their lineage. Theognis of Megara, a sixth-century poet whose verses also reflect earlier conditions, gave voice to the distress of threatened members of the elite at the ever-increasing importance of wealth as the avenue to social and political influence: ". . . men today prize possessions, and noble men marry into 'bad' [that is, formerly nonelite] families and 'bad' men into noble families. Riches have mixed up lines of breeding . . . and the good breeding of the citizens is becoming obscured" (Theognidea 189–190). This cry is more than a little disingenuous because it glosses over the traditional interest of the elite in amassing wealth, but it does reveal the growing tension between those members of society who had been enjoying prominence and those who wished to achieve it through upward mobility.

The increase in population in this era probably came mostly in the ranks of the nonelite. Their families raised more children, who could help to farm more land, so long as it was available for the taking in the aftermath of the depopulation of the early Dark Age. Like the Zeus of Hesiod's Theogony, who acted in response to the injustice of Kronos, the growing number of people with some property to their name apparently reacted against what they saw as unacceptable inequity in the leadership of the elite, whose members evidently tended to behave as if they were petty kings in their local territory and dispensed what seemed "crooked" justice to those with less wealth and power. This concern for equity and fairness on the part of those hoping to improve their lot in life gave a direction to the social and political pressures created by the growth of the population.

For the city-state to be created as a political institution in which all free men had a share, members below the level of the social elite had to insist that they deserved equitable treatment, even if members of the elite were to retain the leadership positions and carry out the policies agreed on by the group. The implementation of the concept of citizenship as the basis for the city-state and the extension of citizen status to all free-born members of the community responded to that demand. Citizenship above all carried certain legal rights, such as access to courts to resolve disputes, protection against enslavement by kidnapping, and participation in the religious and cultural life of the city-state. It also implied participation in politics, although the degree of participation open to the poorest men varied among different city-states. The ability to hold public office, for example, could be limited in some cases to owners of a certain amount of property or wealth. Most prominently, citizen status distinguished free men and women from slaves and metics (foreigners who were officially granted limited legal rights and permission to reside in a city-state that was not their homeland). Thus, even the poor had a distinction setting themselves apart from these groups not endowed with citizenship.

Social and economic inequality among male citizens persisted as part of life in the Greek city-state despite the legal guarantees of citizenship. The incompleteness of the equality that underlay the political structure of the city-state also revealed itself in the status of citizen women. Women became citizens of the city-states in the crucial sense that they had an identity, social status, and local rights denied metics and slaves. The important difference between citizen and noncitizen women was made clear in the Greek language, which included a term meaning "female citizen" (politis, the feminine of polites, "male citizen"), in the existence of certain religious cults reserved for citizen women only, and in legal protection for women against being kidnapped and sold into slavery. Citizen women also had recourse to the courts in disputes over property and other legal wrangles, but they could not represent themselves and had to have men speak for their interests, a requirement that reveals their inequality under the law. The traditional paternalism of Greek society — men acting as "fathers" to regulate the lives of women and safeguard their interests as defined by men — demanded that every woman have an official male guardian (kyrios) to protect her physically and legally. In line with this assumption about the need of women for regulation and protection by men, women were granted no rights to participate in politics. They never attended political assemblies, nor could they vote. They did hold certain civic priesthoods, however, and they had access

along with men to the initiation rights of the popular cult of the goddess
Demeter at Eleusis near Athens. This internationally renowned cult, about
which more will be said later, served in some sense as a safety valve for the
pressures created by the remaining inequalities of life in Greek city-states
because it offered to all regardless of class its promised benefits of protection from evil and a better fate in the afterworld.

The Poor and Citizenship

Despite the limited equality characteristic of the Greek city-state, the
creation of this new form of political organization nevertheless represented
a significant break with the past, and the extension of at least some political rights to the poor stands as one of the most striking developments in
this process of change. Unfortunately, we cannot identify with certainty the
forces that led to the emergence of the city-state as a political institution
in which even poor men had a vote on political matters. The explanation
long favored by many makes a so-called hoplite revolution responsible for
the general widening of political rights in the city-state, but recent research
has undermined the plausibility of this theory. Hoplites were infantrymen
clad in metal body armor, and they constituted the main strike force of the
citizen militias that defended Greek city-states in the period before navies
became important. Hoplites marched into combat shoulder to shoulder in
a rectangular formation called a phalanx, which bristled with the spears of
its arrayed soldiers. Staying in line and working as part of the group was
the secret to successful phalanx tactics. A good hoplite, in the words of
the seventh-century B.C. poet Archilochus, was "a short man firmly placed
upon his legs, with a courageous heart, not to be uprooted from the spot
where he plants his feet" (West, no. 114). Greeks had fought in phalanxes for
a long time, but until the eighth century B.C., only leaders and a relatively
small number of their followers could afford to buy metal weapons, which
the use of iron made more readily available. Presumably these new hoplites,
since they paid for their own equipment and trained hard to learn phalanx
tactics to defend their community, felt they too were entitled to political
rights. According to the theory of a hoplite revolution, these new hoplite-
level men forced the elite to share political power by threatening to refuse
to fight and thereby cripple the community's military defense.

The theory correctly assumes that new hoplites had the power to demand an increased political say for themselves, a development of great significance for the development of the city-state as an institution not solely
under the power of a small circle of the most prominent male citizens. The
theory of a hoplite revolution cannot explain, however, one crucial question: Why were poor men as well as hoplites given the political right of

voting on policy in the city-state? Most men in the new city-states were too poor to qualify as hoplites. Nor had the Greeks yet developed navies, the military service for which poor men would provide the manpower in later times when a fleet was a city-state's most effective weapon. If being able to make a contribution to the city-state's defense as a hoplite was the only prerequisite to the political rights of citizenship, the elite along with the old and new hoplites had no obvious reason to grant poor men the right to vote on important matters. Yet poor men did become politically empowered citizens in many city-states, with some variations on whether a man had to own a certain amount of land to have full political rights or whether eligibility for higher public offices required a certain level of income. In general, however, all male citizens, regardless of their level of wealth, eventually were entitled to attend, speak in, and cast a vote in the communal assemblies in which policy decisions for the city-states were made. That poor men gradually came to participate in the assemblies of the city-states means that they were citizens possessing the basic component of political equality. The hoplite revolution fails as a complete explanation of the development of the city-state above all because it cannot account for the extension of this right to the poor. Furthermore, the emergence of large numbers of men wealthy enough to afford hoplite armor seems to belong to the middle of the seventh century B.C., well after the period when the city-state as an innovative form of political organization was first coming into existence.

No thoroughly satisfactory alternative or complement to the theory of hoplite revolution has yet emerged to explain the origins of the political structure of the Greek city-state. The laboring free poor—the workers in agriculture, trade, and crafts—contributed much to the economic strength of the city-state, but it is hard to see how their value as laborers could have been translated into political rights. The better-off elements in society certainly did not extend the rights of citizenship to the poor out of any romanticized vision of poverty as spiritually noble. As one contemporary put it, "Money is the man; no poor man ever counts as good or honorable" (Alcaeus, PLF, no. 360).

Perhaps an emphasis on the development of hoplite armor and tactics in the Archaic Age misrepresents the reality of Greek warfare in this early period. In the Dark Age few men could have afforded metal body armor, and military tactics presumably reflected this fact, with most soldiers accustomed to leather gear as the best protection available to them. Since the numbers of poorer men far exceeded those of the wealthy, any leader wishing to assemble a significant force would have to have relied on the ranks of poor men. Even poorly armed men probably could have formed a formidable force against better-armed opponents if their numbers were great enough. Lightly-armed combatants in the eighth century—even those only wielding staves, throwing rocks, and employing farming implements as weapons—could have helped their city-state's contingent of hoplites to sway the tide of battle against an opposing force. If it is true that poor men were a significant factor in Dark Age warfare, this importance could have persisted until well into the Archaic Age, as it took a long time for hoplite armor and weapons to become common. And even after more men had become sufficiently prosperous to afford hoplite equipment, they still would have been well outnumbered by the poor. Early hoplite forces, therefore, may have been only the "forefighters" (*promachoi*) spearheading larger forces of less heavily armed troops assembled from poorer men. In this way, the contribution of the poor to the defense of the city-state as part of its only military force at this date—a citizen militia—would have been essential and worthy of citizenship.

Another significant boost to extending political rights to the poor perhaps came from the sole rulers, called tyrants, who seized power for a time in some city-states and whose history will be discussed subsequently. Tyrants could have used grants of citizenship to poor or disenfranchised men as a means of marshaling popular support for their regimes. Another, more speculative possibility is that the upper levels of Greek society had simply become less cohesive as a political group in this period of dramatic change, thereby weakening opposition to the growing idea that it was unjust to exclude the poor from political participation. When the poor agitated for power in the citizen community, on this view, there would have been no united front of members of the elite and hoplites to oppose them, making compromise necessary to prevent destructive civil unrest.

In any case, the hallmark of the politics of the developed Greek city-states was certainly the practice of the citizen men making decisions communally. Members of the social elite continued to be powerfully influential in Greek politics even after city-states had come into existence, but the unprecedented political sway that men not ranking in the elite came to enjoy in city-states constituted the most remarkable feature of the change in the political organization of Greek society in the Archaic Age. This process was gradual, as city-states certainly did not suddenly emerge fully formed around 750 B.C. Three hundred years after that date, for example, the male citizens of Athens were still making major changes in their political institutions to disperse political power more widely among the male citizen body.

Chattel Slavery

The only evidence for slavery in the Dark Age—the language of the poetry of Homer and Hesiod, such as *dmos, doule,* and *douleios*—reveals complex relationships of dependency among free and unfree people. Some people taken prisoner in war seem to be chattel slaves, wholly under the domination of others, who benefit from the captives' labor. Other dependent people in the poems seem more like inferior members of the owners' households. They live under virtually the same conditions as their superiors and enjoy a family life of their own. If the language of this poetry reflects actual conditions in the Dark Age, chattel slavery was not the primary form of dependency in Greece during that period.

The creation of citizenship as a category to define membership in the exclusive group of people constituting a Greek city-state inevitably highlighted the contrast between those included in the category of citizens and those outside it. Freedom from control by others was a necessary precondition to becoming a citizen with full political rights, which in the city-states meant being a free-born adult male. The strongest contrast citizenship produced, therefore, was that between free (*eleutheros*) and unfree or slave (*doulos*). In this way, the development of a clear idea of personal freedom in the formation of the city-state as a new political form may paradoxically have encouraged the complementary development of chattel slavery in the Archaic Age. The rise in economic activity in this period probably also encouraged the importation of slaves by increasing the demand for labor. In any case, slavery as it developed in the Archaic Age reduced unfree persons to a state of absolute dependence; they were the property of their owners. As Aristotle later categorized slaves, they were a "sort of living possession" (*Politics* 1253b32).

Captives taken in war provided an important source of slaves, and relatively few slaves seem to have been born and raised in the households of those for whom they worked. Slaves were also imported from the rough regions to the north and east of Greek territory, where non-Greek people would be seized by pirates or foreign raiders. The local bands in these areas would also capture each other and sell the captives to slave dealers. The dealers would then sell their purchases in Greece at a profit. Herodotus, a Greek historian of the fifth century B.C., reported that some of the Thracians, a group of peoples living to the north of mainland Greece, "sold their children for export" (*History* 5.6). But this report probably meant only that one band of Thracians sold children captured from other bands of Thracians, whom the first group considered different from themselves. The Greeks lumped together all foreigners who did not speak Greek as "barbarians" (*barbaroi*) — people whose speech sounded to Greeks like the repetition of the meaningless sounds "bar, bar." Greeks, like Thracians and other slaveholding peoples, found it easier to enslave people whom they considered different from themselves and whose ethnic and cultural otherness made it easier to disregard their shared humanity. Greeks also enslaved fellow Greeks, however, especially those defeated in war, but these Greek slaves were not members of the same city-state as their masters. Rich families prized Greek slaves with some education because they could be made to serve as tutors for children, for whom there were no publicly financed schools in this period.

Chattel slavery became widespread in Greece only after about 600 B.C. Eventually, slaves became cheap enough that people of moderate means could afford one or two. Nevertheless, even wealthy Greek landowners never acquired gangs of hundreds of slaves like those who maintained Rome's water system under the Roman Empire or worked large plantations in the southern United States before the American Civil War. Maintaining a large number of slaves year around in ancient Greece would have been uneconomical because the cultivation of the crops grown there called for short periods of intense labor punctuated by long stretches of inactivity, during which slaves would have to be fed even while they had no work to do.

By the fifth century B.C., however, the number of slaves in some city-states had grown to as much as one-third of the total population. This percentage still means that most labor was performed by small landowners and their families themselves, sometimes hiring free workers. The special system of slavery in Sparta, as will be explained subsequently, provides a rare exception to this situation. Rich Greeks everywhere regarded working for someone else for wages as disgraceful, but their attitude did not correspond to the realities of life for many poor people, who had to earn a living at any work they could find. Like free workers, chattel slaves did all kinds of labor. Household slaves, often women, had the physically least dangerous existence. They cleaned, cooked, fetched water from public fountains, helped the wife with the weaving, watched the children, accompanied the husband as he did the marketing (as was the Greek custom), and performed other domestic chores. Yet they could not refuse if their masters demanded sexual favors. Slaves who worked in small manufacturing businesses, like those of potters or metalworkers, and slaves working on farms often labored alongside their masters. Rich landowners, however, might appoint a slave supervisor to oversee the work of their other slaves in their fields while they remained in town. The worst conditions of life for slaves obtained for those men leased out to work in the narrow, landslide-prone tunnels of Greece's few silver and gold mines. The conditions of their painful and dangerous job were dark, confined, and back-breaking. Owners could punish their slaves with impunity, even kill them without fear of meaningful sanctions. (A master's murder of a slave was regarded as at least improper and perhaps even illegal in Athens of the Classical period, but the penalty may have been no more than ritual purification.) Beatings severe enough to cripple a working slave and executions of able-bodied slaves were probably infrequent because destroying such property made no economic sense for an owner.

Some slaves enjoyed a measure of independence by working as public slaves (*demosioi*, "belonging to the people") owned by the city-state instead of an individual. They lived on their own and performed specialized tasks. In Athens, for example, public slaves later had the responsibility for certifying the genuineness of the city-state's coinage. They also performed distasteful tasks that required the application of force to citizens, such as serving as the assistants to the citizen magistrates responsible for arresting malefactors. The city's official executioner was also a public slave in Athens. Slaves attached to temples also lived without individual owners because temple slaves belonged to the god of the sanctuary, for which they worked as servants. Female temple slaves at the temple of Aphrodite in Corinth served as sacred prostitutes, whose earnings helped support the sanctuary.

Under the best conditions, household slaves with humane masters might live lives free of violent punishment. They might even be allowed to join their owners' families on excursions and attend religious rituals such as sacrifices. Without the right to a family of their own, however, without property, without legal or political rights, they lived an existence alienated from regular society. In the words of an ancient commentator, chattel slaves lived lives of "work, punishment, and food" (Pseudo-Aristotle, *Oeconomica* 1344a35). Their labor helped maintain the economy of Greek society, but their work rarely benefited themselves. Yet despite the misery of their condition, Greek chattel slaves—outside Sparta—almost never revolted on a large scale, perhaps because they were of too many different origins and nationalities and too scattered to organize themselves for rebellion. Sometimes owners freed their slaves voluntarily, and some promised freedom at a future date to encourage their slaves to work hard in the meantime. Freed slaves did not become citizens in Greek city-states but instead mixed into the population of resident foreigners, the metics. They were expected to continue to help out their former masters when called upon.

Households and Marriage

The emergence of slavery in the city-state on a large scale made households bigger and added new responsibilities for women, especially rich women, whose lives were circumscribed by the responsibility of managing their households. As partners in the maintenance of the family with their husbands, who spent their time outside farming, participating in politics, and meeting their male friends, wives were entrusted with the management of the household (*oikonomia*, whence our word "economics"). They were expected to raise the children, supervise the preservation and preparation of food, keep the family's financial accounts, weave cloth to make clothing, direct the work of the household slaves, and nurse them when they were ill. Households thus depended on women, whose work permitted the family to be economically self-reliant and the male citizens to participate in the public life of the polis.

Poor women worked outside the home, often as small-scale merchants in the public market (*agora*) that occupied the center of every settlement. Only at Sparta did women have the freedom to participate in athletic training along with men. Women played their major role in the public life of the city-state by participating in funerals, state festivals, and religious rituals. Certain festivals were reserved for women only, especially in the cult of the goddess Demeter, whom the Greeks credited with teaching them the indispensable technology of agriculture. As priestesses, women also fulfilled public duties in various official cults; for example, women officiated as priestesses in more than forty such cults in Athens by the fifth century B.C. Women holding these posts often enjoyed considerable prestige, practical benefits such as a salary paid by the state, and greater freedom of movement in public.

Upon marriage, women became the legal wards of their husbands, as they previously had been of their fathers while still unmarried. Marriages were arranged by men. A woman's guardian—her father, or if he were dead, her uncle or her brother—would commonly betroth her to another man's son while she was still a child, perhaps as young as five. The betrothal was an important public event conducted in the presence of witnesses. The guardian on this occasion repeated the phrase that expressed the primary aim of marriage: "I give you this woman for the plowing [procreation] of legitimate children" (Lucian, *Timon* 17). The marriage itself customarily took place when the girl was in her early teens and the groom ten to fifteen years older. Hesiod advised a man to marry a virgin in the fifth year after her puberty, when he himself was "not much younger than thirty and not much older" (*Works and Days* 697–705). A legal marriage consisted of the bride's going to live in the house of her husband. The procession to his house was as close to the modern idea of a wedding ceremony as Greek marriage offered. The woman brought with her a dowry of property (perhaps land yielding an income, if she were wealthy) and personal possessions that formed part of the new household's assets and could be inherited by her children. Her husband was legally obliged to preserve the dowry and to return it in case of a divorce. Procedures for divorce were more concerned with power than law: a husband could expel his wife from his home, while a wife, in theory, could on her own initiative leave her husband to return to the guardianship of her male relatives. Her freedom of action could be constricted, however, if her husband used force to keep her from leaving. Monogamy was the rule in ancient Greece, and a nuclear family structure (that is, husband, wife, and children living together without other relatives in the same house) was common, except at Sparta, although at different stages of life a married couple might have other relatives living with them. Citizen men could have sexual relations without penalty with slaves, foreign concubines, female prostitutes, or willing pre-adult citizen males. Citizen women had no such sexual freedom and adultery carried harsh penalties for wives as well as male adulterers. The only exception was at Sparta when a woman was childless, the aim of the liaison was to produce children, and the husband gave his consent.

More than anything else, a dual concern to regulate marriage and procreation and to maintain family property underlay the placing of the legal rights of Greek women and the conditions of their citizenship under the guardianship of men. The paternalistic attitude of Greek men toward women was rooted in the desire to control human reproduction and, consequently, the distribution of property, a concern that had gained special urgency in the reduced economic circumstances of the Dark Age. Hesiod, for instance, makes this point explicitly in relating the myth of the first woman, named Pandora (*Works and Days* 42–105, *Theogony* 507–616). According to the legend, Zeus, the king of the gods, created Pandora as a punishment for men when Prometheus, a divine being hostile to Zeus, stole fire from Zeus to give it to Prometheus's human friends, who had hitherto lacked that technology. Pandora subsequently loosed "evils and diseases" into the previously trouble-free world of men by removing the lid from the jar or box the gods had filled for her. Hesiod then refers to Pandora's descendants, the female sex, as a "beautiful evil" for men ever after, comparing them to drones who live off the toil of other bees while devising mischief at home. But, he goes on to say, any man who refuses to marry to escape the "troublesome deeds of women" will come to "destructive old age" without any children to care for him. After his death, moreover, his relatives will divide his property among themselves. A man must marry, in other words, so that he can sire children to serve as his support system in his waning years and to preserve his holdings after his death by inheriting them. Women, according to Greek mythology, were for men a necessary evil, but the reality of women's lives in the city-state incorporated social and religious roles of enormous importance.

5

Oligarchy, Tyranny, and Democracy

Diverging Paths of Political Development

Although the Greek city-states differed in size and natural resources, over the course of the Archaic Age they came to share certain fundamental political institutions and social traditions: citizenship, slavery, the legal disadvantages and political exclusion of women, and the continuing predominance of wealthy elites. But city-states developed these shared characteristics in strikingly different ways. Monarchy had died out in Greece with the end of Mycenaean civilization, except for the dual kingship that existed in Sparta as part of its complex oligarchic system rather than as a monarchy in the ordinary sense. In Sparta and some other Greek city-states, only a rather restricted number of men exercised meaningful political power (thus creating a political system called an oligarchy, *oligarchia* in Greek, meaning "rule by the few"). Other city-states experienced periods of domination by the kind of sole ruler who seized power in unconstitutional fashion and whom the Greeks called a tyrant (from the Greek *tyrannos*). Tyranny, passed down from father to son, existed at various times across the breadth of the Greek world, from city-states on the island of Sicily in the west to Samos off the coast of Ionia in the east.

Still other city-states created early forms of democracy (*democratia*, "rule by the people") by giving all male

citizens the power to participate in governing. Assemblies of men with some influence on the king had existed in certain early states in the ancient Near East, but Greek democracy broke new ground with the amount of political power that it invested in its male citizen body. The Athenians established Greece's most renowned democracy, in which the individual freedom of citizens flourished to a degree unprecedented in the ancient world. These diverging paths of political and social development reveal the extent of the challenges faced by the Greeks as they struggled to construct a new way of life during the Archaic Age. In the course of this struggle, they also began to formulate new ways of understanding the physical world, their relations to it, and their relationships with each other.

Early Sparta

The Spartans made oligarchy the political base for a society devoted to military readiness, and the Spartan way of life became famous for its discipline, which showed most prominently in the Spartan infantry, the most powerful military force in Greece during the Archaic Age. Sparta's easily defended location gave it a secure base for developing its might, as it was nestled on a narrow north-south plain between rugged mountain ranges in the southeastern Peloponnese, in a region called Laconia (hence the regional designation of Spartans as Laconians; as Spartans proper, they could also be called Lacedaimonians, from the alternative name Lacedaimon applied to Sparta as a place). Sparta had access to the sea through Gytheon, a harbor situated some twenty-five miles south of its urban center, but this harbor opened onto a dangerous stretch of the Mediterranean whipped by treacherous currents and winds. As a consequence, enemies could not threaten the Spartans by sea, but their relative isolation from the sea also kept the Spartans from becoming adept sailors. Their interests and their strength lay on the land.

The Greeks believed the ancestors of the Spartans were Dorians, who had invaded the Peloponnese from central Greece and defeated the original inhabitants of Laconia around 950 B.C., but no archaeological evidence supports the notion that a "Dorian invasion" actually took place. The inhabitants of Laconia in historical times indeed spoke the Dorian dialect of Greek, but no secure evidence exists to identify their earliest origins. At first the Spartans settled in at least four small villages, two of which apparently dominated the others. These early settlements later cooperated to form the core of what would in the Archaic Age become the polis of the Spartans. The Greeks gave the name "synoecism" ("union of households") to this process of political unification. In this case most people continued to live in their original villages even after one village began to serve as the center of the

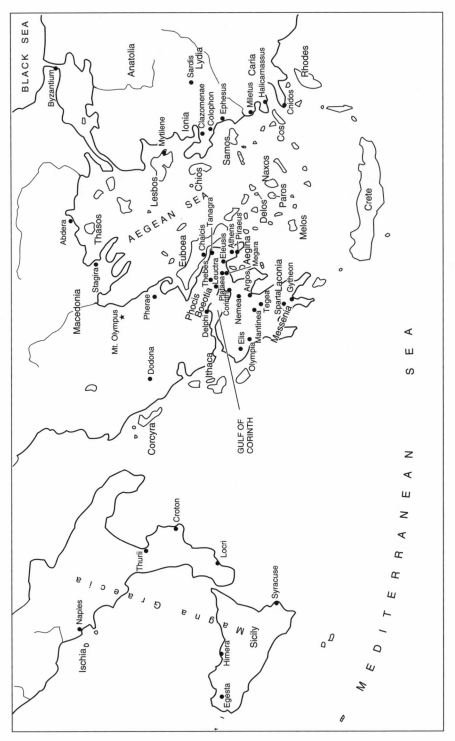

Map 4. Greece, Anatolia, and Magna Graecia

c. **730–710 B.C.**: Spartans invade Messenia in First Messenian War.

c. **657 B.C.**: Cypselus becomes tyrant at Corinth.

c. **640–630 B.C.**: Spartans invade Messenia in Second Messenian War. Athenians may have already developed an early stage of their democracy.

c. **632 B.C.**: Cylon attempts a coup against Athenian democracy.

c. **630 B.C.**: Sappho of Lesbos born.

625 B.C.: Cypselus dies and is succeeded by his son Periander as tyrant of Corinth.

c. **625–545 B.C.**: Lifetime of Thales of Miletus.

621 B.C.: Draco creates code of law for Athenians.

c. **610–540 B.C.**: Lifetime of Anaximander of Miletus.

594 B.C.: Athenians appoint Solon to recodify their laws in an attempt to put an end to social unrest.

c. **580–480 B.C.**: Lifetime of Xenophanes of Colophon.

546 B.C.: Pisistratus becomes tyrant at Athens on his third attempt.

c. **540 B.C.**: Tyranny begins on Samos.

c. **530 B.C.**: Pythagoras emigrates from Samos to southern Italy.

527 B.C.: Pisistratus dies; his sons take over as tyrants of Athens.

510 B.C.: Athens freed from tyranny by Alcmaeonid family and Spartans.

508 B.C.: Cleisthenes begins to reform Athenian democracy.

---

new city-state. (Synoecism could also be accomplished by everyone involved moving to a central location.) This unification in time made Sparta the most powerful community in Laconia, and the Spartans used this power to conquer the other people of the region. We cannot determine the chronology of this extension of Spartan power over Laconia, but its consequences for Spartan life were grave and enduring, as will be explained below.

One apparent result of the compromises required to forge Spartan unity was that the Spartans retained not one but two hereditary military leaders of high prestige, whom they called kings. These kings, who had perhaps originally been the chiefs of the two dominant villages, served as the religious heads of Sparta and commanders of its army. The kings did not enjoy unfettered power to make decisions or set policy, however, because they operated not as pure monarchs but as leaders of the oligarchic institutions that governed the Spartan city-state. Rivalry between the two royal families periodically led to fierce disputes, and the initial custom of having two supreme military commanders also paralyzed the Spartan army when the kings disagreed on strategy in the middle of a military campaign. The

Spartans therefore eventually decided that the army on campaign would be commanded by only one king at a time.

The "few" who made policy in Sparta were a group of twenty-eight men over sixty years old, joined by the two kings. This group of thirty, called the "council of elders" (*gerousia*) formulated proposals that were submitted to an assembly of all free adult males. This assembly had only limited power to amend the proposals put before it; mostly it was expected to approve the council's plans. Rejections were rare because the council retained the right to withdraw a proposal when the reaction to it by the crowd in the assembly presaged a negative vote. "If the people speak crookedly," according to Spartan tradition, "the elders and the leaders of the people shall be withdrawers [of the proposal]" (Plutarch, *Lycurgus* 6). The council could then bring the proposal back on another occasion after there had been time to marshal support for its passage.

A board of five annually elected "overseers" (*ephors*) counterbalanced the influence of the kings and the gerousia. Chosen from the adult male citizens at large, the ephors convened the gerousia and the assembly, and they exercised considerable judicial powers of judgment and punishment. They could even bring charges against a king and imprison him until his trial. The creation of the board of ephors diluted the political power of the oligarchic gerousia and the kings because the job of the ephors was to ensure the supremacy of law. The Athenian Xenophon later reported: "All men rise from their seats in the presence of the king, except for the ephors. The ephors on behalf of the polis and the king on his own behalf swear an oath to each other every month: the king swears that he will exercise his office according to the established laws of the polis, and the polis swears that it will preserve his kingship undisturbed if he abides by his oath" (*Lac. Pol.* 15.6–7).

The Spartans were sticklers for obedience to the law as the guide to proper behavior on matters large and small. When the ephors entered office, for example, they issued an official proclamation to the men of Sparta: "Shave your mustache and obey the laws" (Plutarch, *Agis and Cleomenes* 9). The depth of Spartans' respect for their system of government under law was symbolized by their tradition that Apollo of Delphi had sanctioned it with an oracle called the Rhetra. A Spartan leader named Lycurgus, they said, had instituted the reforms that the Rhetra institutionalized. Even in antiquity historians had no firm information about the dates of Lycurgus's leadership or precisely how he changed Spartan laws. All we can say today is that the Spartans evolved their law-based political system during the period from about 800 to 600 B.C. Unlike other Greeks, the Spartans never had their laws written down. Instead, they preserved their system from generation to generation with a distinctive, highly structured way of life based on a special economic foundation.

Spartan Neighbors and Slaves

The distinctiveness of the Spartan way of life was fundamentally a re-action to their living in the midst of people whom they had conquered in war and enslaved to exploit economically but who outnumbered them greatly. To maintain their superiority over their conquered Laconian neighbors, from whom they derived their subsistence, Spartan men had to turn themselves into a society of soldiers constantly on guard. They accomplished this transformation by a radical restructuring of traditional family life enforced by strict adherence to the laws and customs governing practically all aspects of behavior. Through constant, daily reinforcement of their strict code of values, the Spartans ensured their survival against the enemies they had created by subjugating their neighbors. The seventh-century poet Tyrtaeus, whose verses replete with mythological references exemplify the artfulness of the poetry produced in early Sparta before its military culture began to exclude such literary accomplishments, expressed that code in his ranking of martial courage as the supreme male value: "I would never remember or mention in my work any man for his speed afoot or wrestling skill, not if he was as huge and strong as a Cyclops or could run faster than the North Wind, nor more handsome than Tithonus or richer than Midas or Cinyras, nor more kingly than Pelops, or had speech more honeyed than Adrastus, not even if he possessed every glory—not unless he had the strength of a warrior in full rush" (West, no. 12).

Some of the conquered inhabitants of Laconia continued to live in self-governing communities. Called literally "those who live round about" (*perioikoi*), which might also be translated as "neighbors," these Laconians were required to serve in the Spartan army and pay taxes but lacked citizen rights. Perhaps because they retained their personal freedom and property, however, the perioikoi almost never rebelled against Spartan control. Far different was the fate of the conquered people who had to endure the slavery of *helot* status, a term derived from the Greek term for "capture." Later ancient commentators described the helots as "between slave and free" (Pollux, *Onomasticon* 3.83) because they were not the personal property of individual Spartans but rather slaves belonging to the whole community, which alone could free them. Helots had a semblance of family life because they were expected to produce children to maintain the size of their population, which was compelled to labor as farmers and household slaves as a way of freeing Spartan citizens from any need to do such work. Spartan men in fact wore their hair very long to show they were "gentlemen" rather than laborers, for whom long hair was an inconvenience.

When the arable land of Laconia proved too small to support the full citizen population of Sparta, the Spartans attacked their Greek neighbors in the southwestern part of the Peloponnese, the Messenians. In the First

Messenian War (c. 730–710 B.C.) and then in the Second (c. 640–630 B.C.), the Spartan army captured the territory of Messenia, which amounted to 40 percent of the Peloponnesian peninsula, and reduced the Messenians to the status of helots. With the addition of the tens of thousands of people in Messenia, the total helot population now more than outnumbered that of Sparta, whose male citizens at this time amounted to perhaps between eight and ten thousand. The terrible loss felt by the Messenians at their fate is well portrayed by their legend of King Aristodemus, whom the Messenians remembered as having sacrificed his beloved daughter to the gods of the underworld in an attempt to enlist their aid against the invading Spartans. When his campaign of guerrilla warfare at last failed, Aristodemus is said to have slain himself in despair on her grave. Deprived of their freedom and their polis, the Messenian helots were ever after on the lookout for a chance to revolt against their Spartan overlords.

In their private lives, helots could keep some personal possessions and practice their religion, as could slaves generally in Greece. Publicly, however, helots lived under the threat of officially sanctioned violence. Every year the ephors formally declared a state of war to exist between Sparta and the helots, thereby allowing any Spartan to kill a helot without any civil penalty or fear of offending the gods by unsanctioned murder. By beating the helots frequently, forcing them to get drunk in public as an object lesson to young Spartans, marking them out by having them wear dog-skin caps, and generally treating them with scorn, the Spartans consistently emphasized the otherness of the helots compared to themselves. In this way, the Spartans erected a moral barrier between themselves and the helots to justify their harsh treatment of fellow Greeks.

Their labor made helots valuable to the Spartans. Laconian and Messenian helots alike primarily farmed plots of land belonging to Spartan households, and they were tied to that land in perpetuity. Some helots also worked as household servants. By the fifth century, helots would also accompany Spartan hoplite warriors on the march to carry their heavy gear and armor. In military emergencies, the Spartans would even arm the helots to use them as soldiers, with the promise of freedom as an inducement to valor. The few helots who escaped enslavement in this way were classified as less than full citizens (*neodamodeis*) and existed in a state of social and political limbo, whose details remain obscure. Most helots, however, had no hope of freedom, and their hatred of their masters sometimes induced them to revolt. The historian Xenophon, who knew Sparta well, recorded the feelings of rebellious helots toward the Spartans: "They said they would be glad to eat them raw" (*Hellenica* 3.3.6).

It was the labor of this hostile population, compelled to farm to produce food for free Spartans, that allowed Spartan men to devote themselves to full-time training for hoplite warfare in order to protect themselves from external enemies and to suppress helot rebellions, especially in Messenia. In the words of Tyrtaeus, helots worked "like donkeys exhausted under heavy loads; they lived under the painful necessity of having to give their masters half the food their plowed land bore" (West, no. 6). This compulsory rent of 50 percent of everything produced by the helots working on each free family's land was supposed to amount to seventy measures of barley each year to the male master of the household and twelve to his wife, along with an equivalent amount of fruit and other produce. In all, this food was enough to support six or seven people. Contrasting the freedom of Spartan citizens from ordinary work with the lot of the helots, the later Athenian Critias commented, "Laconia is the home of the freest of the Greeks, and of the most enslaved" (D.-K. 88B37).

The Spartan Way of Life

The entire Spartan way of life was directed toward keeping the Spartan army at tip-top strength. Boys lived at home only until their seventh year, when they were taken away to live in communal barracks with other males until they were thirty. They spent most of their time exercising, hunting, training with weapons, and being acculturated to Spartan values by listening to tales of bravery and heroism at the common meals presided over by older men. The standard of discipline was strict, to prepare young males for the hard life of a soldier on campaign. For example, they were not allowed to speak at will. (Our word "laconic," meaning "of few words," comes from the Greek word "Laconian.") Boys were also purposely underfed so that they would have to develop the skills of stealth by pilfering food. Yet if they were caught, punishment and disgrace followed immediately. One famous Spartan tale taught how seriously boys were supposed to fear such failure: having successfully stolen a fox, which he was hiding under his clothing, a Spartan youth died because he let the panicked animal rip out his insides rather than be detected in the theft. By the Classical period, older boys would be dispatched to live in the wilds for a time as members of the "secret band" whose job it was to murder any helots who seemed likely to foment rebellion. Spartan men who could not survive the tough conditions of their childhood training fell into social disgrace and were not certified as Equals (Homoioi), the official name for adult males entitled to full citizen rights of participation in politics and the respect of the community. Only the sons of the royal family were exempted from this training, the agoge, perhaps to avoid a potential social crisis if a king's son failed to stay the course.

Each Equal had to gain entry to a group that dined together at common meals, in a "common mess" (sussition), each of which had about fifteen members. Applicants were scrutinized by current members of the sussition, any of whom could blackball the prospective member and force him to look for another group to join. Once he passed scrutiny, the new member was admitted on the condition that he contribute a regular amount of barley, cheese, figs, condiments, and wine to the mess from the produce provided by the helots working on his family plot. Some meat was apparently contributed, too, because Spartan cuisine was infamous for a black, bloody broth of pork condemned as practically inedible by other Greeks. Perhaps it was made from the wild boars Spartan men loved to hunt, an activity for which messmates were formally excused from the compulsory communal meals. If any member failed to keep up his contributions, he was expelled from the mess and lost his full citizen rights. The experience of spending so much time in these common messes schooled Sparta's young men in the values of their society. There they learned to call all older men "father" to emphasize that their primary loyalty was to the group and not to their genetic families. There they were chosen to be the special favorites of males older than themselves to build bonds of affection, including physical love, for others at whose side they would have to march into deadly battle. There they learned to take the rough joking of army life for which Sparta was well known. In short, the common mess in many ways served as a boy's school and even his alternate family while he was growing up, and this group of males remained his main social environment once he had reached adulthood. Its function was to mold and maintain his values consistent with the demands of the one honorable occupation for Spartan men: as soldiers obedient to orders. Tyrtaeus enshrined the Spartan male ideal in his poetry: "Know that it is good for the polis and the whole people when a man takes his place in the front row of warriors and stands his ground without flinching" (West, no. 12).

Spartan women were renowned throughout the Greek world for their relative freedom. Other Greeks regarded it as scandalous that Spartan girls exercised with boys and did so wearing minimal clothing. Women at Sparta were supposed to use the freedom from labor provided by the helot system to keep themselves physically fit to bear healthy children and raise them to be strict upholders of Spartan values. A metaphorical formulation of the male ideal for Spartan women appears, for example, in the late seventh century in the poetry of Alcman, who wrote songs for the performances of female and male choruses that were common on Spartan civic and religious occasions. The dazzling leader of a women's chorus, he writes, "stands out as if among a herd of cows someone placed a firmly-built horse with ringing hooves, a prize winner from winged dreams" (PMG, no. 1). Although Sparta deliberately banned ordinary coined money to discourage the accumulation of material goods, women, like men, could own land privately. Daughters probably inherited portions of land and property equal to one-half of what their brothers would get, but they received their portion earlier, at marriage rather than only upon a parent's death. More and more land came into the hands of women in later Spartan history because the male population declined through losses in war, especially during the Classical Age.

With their husbands so rarely at home, Spartan women directed the households, which included servants, daughters, and sons until they left for their communal training. As a result, women at Sparta exercised more power in the household than did women elsewhere in Greece. Until he was thirty, a Spartan husband was not allowed to live with his family, and even newly wed men were expected to pay only short visits to their brides by sneaking into their houses at night. This tradition was only one of the Spartan customs of heterosexual behavior that other Greeks found bizarre. If all parties agreed, a married woman with an infertile husband could have children by a man other than her husband, so pressing was the need to reproduce in this strictly ordered society. The freedom of Spartan women from some of the restrictions imposed on them in other Greek city-states had the same purpose as the men's common messes: the production of manpower for the Spartan army. By the Classical Age, the ongoing problem of producing enough children to keep the Spartan citizen population from shrinking had grown acute. Men were legally required to get married, with bachelors subjected to fines and public ridicule.

All Spartan citizens were expected to put service to their city-state before personal concerns because Sparta's survival was continually threatened by its own economic foundation, the great mass of helots. Since Sparta's well-being depended on the organized exploitation of these enslaved Greeks, its entire political and social system by necessity had as its aim a staunch militarism and a conservatism in values. Change meant danger at Sparta. As part of its population policy, however, Spartan conservatism encompassed sexual behavior seen as overly permissive by other Greeks. The Spartans simultaneously institutionalized a form of equality as the basis for their male social unit, the common mess, while denying true social and political equality to ordinary male citizens by making their government an oligarchy. Whatever other Greeks may have thought of the particulars of the Spartan system, they admired the Spartans' unswerving respect for their laws as a guide to life in hostile surroundings, albeit of their own making.

The Rise of Tyrants

Opposition to oligarchic domination brought the first Greek tyrants to power in various Greek states, although Sparta never experienced tyranny in this period. The most famous early tyranny arose at Corinth around 657 B.C. in opposition to the rule of an oligarchy led by a family called the Bacchiads. Under Bacchiad domination in the eighth and early seventh centuries B.C., Corinth had blossomed into the most economically advanced city in Archaic Greece. The Corinthians had forged so far ahead in naval engineering, for instance, that other Greeks contracted with them to have ships built. Corinth's strong fleet helped the Bacchiads in founding overseas colonies at Corcyra in northwest Greece and Syracuse on Sicily, city-states which would themselves become major naval powers.

The Bacchiads became unpopular despite the city's prosperity because they ruled violently. Cypselus, a member of the social elite whose mother was a Bacchiad, readied himself to take over by becoming popular with the masses: "He became one of the most admired of Corinth's citizens because he was courageous, prudent, and helpful to the people, unlike the oligarchs in power, who were insolent and violent," according to a later historian (Nicholaus of Damascus, FGrH 90 F57.4–5). Cypselus engineered the overthrow of Bacchiad rule by rallying popular support and securing an oracle from Delphi favoring his rebellion. After seizing power, he ruthlessly suppressed rivals, but his popularity with the people remained so high that he could govern without the protection of a bodyguard. Corinth added to its economic strength during Cypselus's rule by exporting large quantities of fine pottery, especially to Italy and Sicily. Cypselus founded additional colonies along the sailing route to the western Mediterranean to promote Corinthian trade in that direction.

When Cypselus died in 625 B.C., his son Periander succeeded him. Periander aggressively continued Corinth's economic expansion by founding colonies on the coasts both northwest and northeast of Greek territory to increase trade with the interior regions there, which were rich in timber and precious metals. He also pursued commercial contacts with Egypt, an interest commemorated in the Egyptian name Psammetichus that he gave to one of his sons. The city's prosperity encouraged flourishing development in crafts, art, and architecture. The foundations of the great stone temple to Apollo begun in this period can still be seen today. Unlike his father, however, Periander lost the support of Corinth's people by ruling harshly. He kept his power until his death in 585 B.C., but the persisting hostility toward his rule soon led to the overthrow of his successor, Psammetichus. The opponents of tyranny at Corinth thereupon installed a government based on a board of eight magistrates and a council of eighty men.

Greek tyranny represented a distinctive type of rule for several reasons. Although tyrants were by definition rulers who usurped power by force rather than inheriting it like legitimate kings, they then established family dynasties to maintain their tyranny, with sons inheriting their fathers' position as the head of state. Also, the men who became tyrants were usually members of the social elite, or at least nearly so, who nevertheless rallied support from ordinary citizens for their coups. In places where propertyless men may have lacked citizenship or at least felt substantially disenfranchised in the political life of the city-state, tyrants perhaps won adherents by extending citizenship and other privileges to these groups. Tyrants, moreover, sometimes preserved the existing laws and political institutions of their city-states as part of their rule, thus promoting social stability.

As at Corinth, most tyrannies needed to cultivate support among the masses of their city-states to remain in power because those were the men making up the majority of their armies. The dynasty of tyrants on the island of Samos in the eastern Aegean Sea, for example, who came to power about 540 B.C., built enormous public works to benefit their city-state and provide employment. They began construction of a temple to Hera meant to be the largest in the Greek world, and they dramatically improved the water supply of their urban center by excavating a great tunnel connected to a distant spring. This marvel of engineering with a channel eight feet high ran for nearly a mile through a nine-hundred-foot-high mountain. The later tyrannies that emerged in city-states on Sicily similarly graced their cities with beautiful temples and public buildings.

By working in the interests of their peoples, some tyrannies, like that founded by Cypselus, maintained their popularity for decades. Other tyrants experienced bitter opposition from rivals jealous of the tyrant's power or themselves provoked civil war by ruling brutally and inequitably. The poet Alcaeus of the city-state of Mytilene on the island of Lesbos in the northeastern Aegean, himself an opponent of the tyrant of his homeland, described such strife around 600 B.C.: "Let's forget our anger; let's quit our heart-devouring strife and civil war, which some god has stirred up among us, ruining the people but bestowing the glory on Pittacus, our tyrant, for which he prays" (PLF, no. 70). In short, the title "tyrant" in Archaic Greece did not automatically label a ruler as brutal or unwelcome, as the use of the same word in English implies. Greeks evaluated tyrants as good or bad depending on their behavior as rulers.

The Political Development of Athens

It was a traditional Greek practice to explain significant historical changes such as the founding of communities or the codification of law as the work of an individual "inventor" from the distant past. Just like the Spartans, for whom the legendary Lycurgus was remembered as the founder of their city-state, the Athenians also believed their polis owed its start to a

single man. Athenian legends made Theseus responsible for founding the
polis of Athens by the synoecism of villages in Attica, the name given to the
peninsula at the southeastern corner of the mainland of Greece that formed
the territory of the Athenian polis. Since Attica had several fine ports along
its coast, the Athenians were much more oriented to seafaring and communication with other peoples than were the almost landlocked Spartans.
Theseus was described as a traveling adventurer, sailing, for example, to
the island of Crete to defeat the Minotaur, a cannibalistic monster, half-
human and half-bull. This exploit, like his other legendary adventures, became favorite subject matter for vase painters. Theseus's "labors," as they are
called in imitation of the deeds performed by the most famous Greek hero,
Heracles (Hercules to the Romans), were mainly successful fights against
monsters and criminals threatening civilized life and thus made him a hero
who labored to promote the social and moral institutions of the city-state.
Heracles, by contrast, the hero of Dorian Greeks, was renowned for overcoming monsters and miscreants as a demonstration of his supreme physical prowess. The legend of Theseus made him a particularly appropriate
choice as the founder of a city like Athens that prided itself on its claim to
have taught the most important aspects of civilized life, agriculture and the
initiation ceremonies of Demeter, to the rest of the Greek world. The choice
of Theseus as the legendary founder of the city-state thus expressed an Athenian feeling of superiority by virtue of its claimed "civilizing mission."

Unlike most other important sites inhabited in the Mycenaean period,
Athens had apparently not suffered any catastrophic destruction at the end
of the Bronze Age, although it seems unlikely that the settlement entirely escaped the troubles of that time. In any case, the population of Attica shrank
in the early Dark Age, just as had the populations of the rest of Greece. By
around 850 B.C., however, archaeological evidence such as the model granary from a woman's burial already mentioned implies that the Athenian
agricultural economy was reviving. When the population of Attica apparently expanded at a phenomenal rate during the century from about 800
to 700 B.C., the free peasants constituted the fastest-growing segment of
the population as economic conditions improved in the early Archaic Age.
These small agricultural producers apparently began to insist on having a
say in making Athenian policies because they felt justice demanded at least
a limited form of political equality. Some of these modest landowners became wealthy enough to afford hoplite armor, and these men, like similarly prosperous men elsewhere, probably made strong demands on the
elite, who had up to this time ruled Athens as what amounted to a relatively broad oligarchy. Rivalries among the oligarchs for status and material
wealth prevented them from presenting a united front, and they had to re-

spond to these pressures to insure the participation of the hoplites in the citizen militia, on which depended Athenian military strength. The poor were also enfranchised as citizens in early Athens, but we are in no better position in this case than in that of the rest of Greece to explain the details of this significant development.

Was Athens already on the road toward democracy at this early stage in its political development as a city-state? Opinions differ strongly on this question, but the evidence, admittedly scarce and obscure as it is, can be interpreted to mean that by the late seventh century B.C., Athens's male citizens—rich, hoplite-level, and poor alike—had established the first limited form of democratic government. Determining why, on this interpretation, they moved toward democracy instead of, for example, toward a narrow oligarchy like that of Sparta remains a difficult problem. Two factors perhaps encouraging the emergence of the Athenian polis as an incipient democracy were rapid population growth and a rough sense of egalitarianism among male citizens surviving from the frontier-like conditions of the early Dark Age, when most people had shared the same meager existence. These same factors, however, do not necessarily differentiate Athens from other city-states that did not evolve into democracies, because the same conditions generally pertained across the Greek world in the Archaic Age. Perhaps population growth was so rapid among Athenian peasants that they had greater power than at other places to demand a share in governing. Their power and political cohesion were evident, for example, in about 632 B.C., when they rallied "from the fields in a body" (Thucydides 1.126.7) to foil the attempted coup of an Athenian nobleman named Cylon. A former champion in the Olympics and married to a daughter of Theagenes, tyrant of Megara, Cylon and some of his friends had planned to install a tyranny.

The scanty evidence seems to indicate that by the seventh century all free-born adult male citizens of Athens had the right to attend open meetings, in a body called the assembly (*ecclesia*), which elected nine magistrates called archons ("rulers") each year. The archons headed the government and rendered verdicts in disputes and criminal accusations. As earlier, the elite still dominated Athenian political life and exploited their status to secure election for themselves as archons, perhaps by marshaling their bands of followers as supporters and by making alliances with others of their socio-economic level. The right of poorer men to serve as members of the assembly as yet had only limited significance because little business besides the election of archons was conducted in its gatherings, which in this period probably took place only rarely, when the current archons decided the time was right.

Political alliances among members of the elite often proved temporary,

however, and rivalries among men jealous of each other's status continued
to be the order of the day. In the aftermath of Cylon's attempted tyranny,
an Athenian named Draco was appointed in 621 B.C., perhaps after pressure by the hoplites, to establish a code of laws promoting stability and
equity. Unfortunately, Draco's laws somehow further destabilized the political situation; the Athenians later remembered them as having been as harsh
as the meaning of his name (drakon, the Greek word for "dragon, serpent").
A deterioration, which had been slowly building for a long time, in the
well-being of Athens's free peasants, further undermined social peace. Later
Athenians did not know what had caused this economic crisis, only that it
had pitted the rich against the peasants and the poor.

One cause may have been that the precariousness of agriculture in this
period sometimes led to the gradual accumulation of the available farmland
in the hands of fewer and fewer people. In subsistence agriculture, the level
at which many Athenian farmers operated, a lean year could mean starva-
tion. Moreover, farmers lacked any easy method to convert the surplus of
a good year into imperishable capital, such as coined money, which then
could be stored up to offset bad years in the future, because coinage was
not even invented until late in the seventh century B.C. in Lydia in Anatolia
and took a long time to become common in Greece. Failed farmers had to
borrow food and seed to survive. When they could borrow no more, they
had to leave their land to find a job to support their families, most likely by
laboring for successful farmers. Under these conditions, farmers who became more effective, or simply more fortunate, than others could acquire
the use and even the ownership of the land of failed farmers. Whatever the
reasons may have been, many poor Athenians had apparently lost control of
their land to wealthier proprietors by the late seventh century. The crisis became so acute that impoverished peasants were even being sold into slavery
to pay off debts.

The Reforms of Solon

Twenty-five years after Draco's legislation, conditions had become so
acute that a civil war threatened to break out. In desperation, the Athenians
in 594 B.C. gave Solon special authority to revise the laws to deal with the
crisis. As he explains in his autobiographical poetry, Solon tried to steer a
middle course between the demands of the rich to preserve their financial
advantages and the call of the poor for a redistribution of land to themselves from the holdings of the large landowners. His famous "shaking off
of obligations" somehow freed those farms whose ownership had become
formally encumbered without, however, actually redistributing any land.
He also forbade the selling of Athenians into slavery for debt and secured

the liberation of citizens who had become slaves in this way, commemorating his success in the verses he wrote about his reforms: "To Athens, their home established by the gods, I brought back many who had been sold into slavery, some justly, some not . . ." (West, no. 36).

Attempting to balance political power between rich and poor, Solon ranked male citizens into four classes according to their income: "five-hundred-measure men" (*pentakosiomedimnoi*, those with an annual income equivalent to that much agricultural produce), "horsemen" (*hippeis*, income of three hundred measures), "yoked men" (*zeugitai*, two hundred measures), and "laborers" (*thetes*, less than two hundred measures). The higher a man's class, the higher the governmental office for which he was eligible, with the laborer class barred from all posts. Solon did reaffirm the right of this class to participate in the assembly, however. Solon probably also created a council (*boule*) of four hundred men to prepare an agenda for the discussions in the assembly, although some scholars date this innovation after Solon's time. The elite could not dominate the council's deliberations because council members were chosen by lot, probably only from the top three income classes. Solon also may have initiated a schedule of regular meetings for the assembly. These reforms gave added impetus to the assembly's legislative role and thus indirectly laid a foundation for the political influence that the laborer class would gradually acquire over the next century and a half.

Despite the restriction on office holding by the lowest income class, Solon's classification scheme supported further development of conditions leading to democracy because it allowed for upward social mobility, and the absence of direct taxes on income made it easier for entrepreneurial citizens to better their lot. If a man managed to increase his income, he could move up the scale of eligibility for office. One man who did so had an inscription erected in the center of Athens along with a statue of a horse to commemorate his elevation from the fourth to the second income class: "Anthemion son of Diphilus set up this dedication to the gods when he exchanged his ranking in the laborer class for one in the horsemen class" (*Ath. Pol.* 7). From Solon's reforms, Athenian male citizens gained a political and social system far more open to individual initiative and change than that of Sparta.

Equally important to restoring stability in a time of acute crisis was Solon's ruling that any male citizen could bring charges on a wide variety of offenses against wrongdoers on behalf of any victim of a crime. Furthermore, he provided for the right of appeal to the assembly by persons who believed a magistrate had rendered unjust judgments against them. With these two measures, Solon made the administration of justice the concern of ordinary citizens and not just of the elite, who filled the official positions of government. He balanced these judicial reforms favoring the people, however, by granting broader powers to the "Council which meets on the Hill of the god of war, Ares," the Areopagus ("Ares' hill"). Archons became members of the Areopagus after their year in office. This body of ex-archons could, if the members chose, exercise great power because at this period it judged the most serious judicial cases, in particular accusations against archons themselves. Solon probably also expected the Areopagus to use its power to protect his reforms.

For its place and time, Athens's political system was remarkable, even at this early stage in its development toward greater democracy, because it granted all male citizens the possibility of participating meaningfully in the making of laws and the administration of justice. But not everyone found the system admirable. A visiting foreign king in the time of Solon is reputed to have remarked scornfully that he found Athenian government ludicrous. Observing the procedure in the Athenian assembly, he expressed his amazement that leading politicians could only recommend policy in their speeches, while the male citizens as a whole voted on what to do: "I find it astonishing that here wise men speak on public affairs, while fools decide them" (Plutarch, *Solon* 5). Some Athenians who agreed with the king that the wealthy should count as wise and the poor as foolish did their best to undermine Solon's reforms, and such oligarchic sympathizers continued to challenge Athenian democracy at intervals throughout its history.

From Tyranny to Democratic Reorganization

Despite Solon's best efforts at conciliation, strife flared up again at Athens following his reforms and lasted into the mid-sixth century B.C. The conflict sprang from rivalries for office and status among the members of the elite and the continuing discontent of the poorest Athenians. The outcome of this protracted unrest was Athens's first tyranny when a prominent Athenian named Pisistratus began a long and violent effort to make himself sole ruler with the help of wealthy friends and also the poor, whose interests he championed. On his third try he finally established himself securely as tyrant at Athens in 546 B.C. Pisistratus courted poor supporters by providing funds to help peasants acquire needed farm equipment and by offering employment for poorer men on public works projects, such as road improvements, a huge temple to Zeus, and fountains to increase the supply of drinking water in the city. The tax that he imposed on agricultural production, one of the rare instances of direct taxation in Athenian history, financed the loans to farmers and the construction projects. He also arranged for judicial officials to go on circuits through the outlying villages of Attica to hear cases, thus saving farmers the trouble of having to leave their fields to seek justice in the city courts. Like the earlier tyrants of Corinth, he promoted the economic, cultural, and architectural development of Athens. Athenian pottery, for example, now began to crowd out Corinthian in the export trade.

Hippias, the eldest son of Pisistratus, inherited the position of tyrant of Athens after his father's death in 527 B.C. He governed by making certain that his relatives and friends occupied magistracies, but for a time he also allowed rivals from the social elite to serve as archons, thereby defusing some of the tension created by their jealousy of his superior status. Eventually, however, the wealthy family of the Alcmaeonids arranged to have the Spartans send an army to expel Hippias. In the ensuing vacuum of power, the leading Alcmaeonid, a man named Cleisthenes, sought support among the masses by promising dramatic democratic reforms when his bitterest rival, Isagoras, another scion of an elite family, became archon in 508 B.C. When Isagoras tried to block Cleisthenes' reforms by calling in the Spartans again, the Athenian people united to force him and his foreign allies out. The conflict between Athens and Sparta ended quickly but sowed the seeds of mutual distrust between the two city-states.

His popular support gave Cleisthenes the authority to begin to install the democratic system for which Athens has become famous, and the importance of his reforms led later Athenians to think of him as a principal founder of the democracy of the Classical period. First, he made the pre-existing villages of the countryside and the neighborhoods of the city of Athens (both called "demes," demoi) the constituent units of Athenian political organization. Organized in their demes, the male citizens participated directly in the running of their government: they kept track in deme registers of which males were citizens and therefore eligible at eighteen to attend the assembly to vote on laws and public policies. Each deme was in turn assigned according to its location to one of thirty different intermediate groupings called "thirds" (trittyes), which were drawn up to represent three territorial areas of Attica (ten "thirds" each for coast, plain, and city, respectively). Finally, ten administrative divisions called "tribes" (phylai) were created by assigning one "third" from each of the three regional categories to each tribe.

This complex system, which replaced an earlier division into four tribes, thus created "tribes" whose members did not all necessarily live near one another. Cleisthenes' rearrangement of the political map of Athenian government meant that local notables no longer could easily control election results just by exercising influence on the poorer people in their immediate area. This effect may have been especially directed at the political power of his oligarchic enemies. In any case, the system of ten tribes, each made up of demes from all over Attica, provided an administrative basis for spreading service in Athenian government widely throughout the male citizen body, such as by choosing fifty representatives by lot from each tribe to serve for one year on a new council of five hundred (replacing Solon's council of four hundred). The number of representatives from each deme was proportional to its population. Most importantly, the ten men who served each year as "generals" (strategoi), the officials with the highest civil and military authority, were elected one from each tribe. The citizen militia was also organized by tribes. Cleisthenes' reorganization was complicated and most likely incorporated various goals. His motives for the changes are not easy to discern, but his undermining of existing political alliances among the elite had the undeniable effect of promoting the interests of greater democracy and political stability.

By about 500 B.C. Cleisthenes succeeded in devising a system of government based on direct participation by as many adult male citizens as possible. That he could put such a system in place successfully in a time of turmoil and have it endure, as it did, means that he must have been building on preexisting conditions favorable to this kind of democracy. Certainly, as a member of the social elite looking for popular support, Cleisthenes had reason to invent the kind of system he thought ordinary people wanted. That he based his system on the demes, the great majority of which were country villages, suggests that some conditions favoring democracy may have stemmed from the traditions of village life. Possibly, the notion of widespread participation in government gained support from the custom village residents often have of dealing with each other on relatively egalitarian terms. Each man is entitled to his say in running local affairs and must persuade others of the wisdom of his recommendations rather than resorting to compulsion. In the daily affairs of life in a small community, especially the organization and accomplishment of religious festivals and sacrifices, villagers of all statuses, from the poorest peasant to the richest landowners, had to deal with each other through negotiation and compromise more often than not. Furthermore, since many wealthy landowners in this period increasingly seem to have preferred to reside primarily in the city (even if they maintained a house in the country as well), they could no longer dominate discussion and affairs in the rural demes as they had when they lived outside the urban center. In any case, the idea that persuasion, rather than force or status, should constitute the mechanism for political decision making in the emerging Athenian democracy fit well with the spirit of the intellectual changes which were taking place during the late Archaic Age. That is, the idea that people had to present plausible reasons for their recommendations corresponded to one of the period's new ways of thought. This development has proved one of the most influential legacies of Greek civilization.

New Literature and New Thinking

Poetry represented the only form of Greek literature until the late Archaic Age. The earliest Greek poetry, that of Homer and Hesiod, had been confined to a single rhythm. A much greater rhythmic diversity characterized the new form of poetry, called lyric, that emerged during the Archaic Age. Lyric poems were far shorter than the narrative poetry of Homer or the didactic poetry of Hesiod, and they encompassed many forms and subjects, but they were always performed with musical accompaniment, especially the lyre (a kind of harp that gives its name to the poetry) and a reed instrument called the *aulos*. Choral poets like Alcman of Sparta wrote songs to be performed by groups on public occasions to honor the gods, to celebrate famous events in a city-state's history, for wedding processions, and to praise victors in athletic contests. Lyric poets writing songs for solo performance on social occasions stressed a personal level of expression on a variety of topics.

The most personal of those topics was the passion of love, and the most famous poet on this topic was Sappho. Born about 630 B.C. on the island of Lesbos, she was already renowned for her poems by the time she was thirty years old. She was forced into exile in far-away Sicily, perhaps because she and her family had opposed the tyrant of her home city-state of Mytilene. Her poems are passionate in describing the psychological effects of love but reticent about physical love, as in this artful lyric about her feelings for another woman:

> Equal to the gods appears that one,
> the man sitting close by you now,
> who hears the sound of your sweet voice
> from so close by
> and drinks in your charming laugh. That sight,
> I swear, sets my heart racing;
> the briefest glance at you renders me
> speechless!
> My tongue loses its moorings, a delicate
> flame burns all over under my skin,
> My eyes no longer see, they are blinded, my ears
> ring, pulsate,
> a cold sweat overcomes me, fear
> grips my heart. Paler
> than grass in a meadow, I feel myself
> nearly dead.   (PLF, no. 31)

Archilochus of Paros, whose lifetime probably fell in the early seventh century, became famous for his range of poems on themes as diverse as friends lost at sea, mockery of martial valor, and love gone astray. The bitter power of his poetic invective reportedly caused a father and his two daughters to commit suicide when Archilochus ridiculed them in anger after the father had put an end to Archilochus's affair with his daughter Neobule. Some modern literary critics think the poems about Neobule and her family are fictional, not autobiographical, and were meant to display Archilochus's dazzling talent for "blame poetry," the mirror image of lyric as the poetry of praise. Mimnermus of Colophon, another seventh-century lyric poet, rhapsodized about the glory of youth and lamented its brevity, "no longer than the time the sun shines on the plain" (West, no. 2).

Lyric poets also wrote poems focused on contemporary politics; Solon and Alcaeus were particularly known for poems on this topic. Sometimes lyric poets self-consciously adopted a critical attitude toward traditional values, such as strength in war. Sappho, for instance, once wrote, "Some would say the most beautiful thing on our dark earth is an army of cavalry, others of infantry, others of ships, but I say it's whatever a person loves" (PLF, no. 16). Lyric poetry's focus on the individual's feelings represented a new stage in Greek literary sensibilities, one that continues to inspire poets to this day.

Greece's earliest prose literature also belongs to the late Archaic Age. Thinkers usually referred to today as philosophers, but who could equally well be described as theoretical scientists studying the physical world, created prose in Greek to express their new ways of thought, although some of them also employed poetry as a medium to convey their ideas. These thinkers, who came from the city-states of Ionia, were developing radically new explanations of the world of human beings and its relation to the world of the gods. In this way began the study of philosophy in Greece. Ionia's geographical location next to the non-Greek civilizations of Anatolia, which were in contact with the older civilizations of Egypt and the Near East, meant that Ionian thinkers were in a position to acquire knowledge and intellectual inspiration from their neighbors in the eastern Mediterranean area. Since Greece in this period had no formal schools at any level, thinkers like those from Ionia had to make their ideas known by teaching pupils privately and giving public lectures, as well as writing in prose and poetry and reciting from their works to interested groups. People who studied with these thinkers or heard their presentations would then help to spread knowledge of the new ideas.

Knowledge from the ancient Near East influenced the Ionian thinkers, just as it had influenced Greek artists of the Archaic Age. Greek vase painters and specialists in decorating metal vessels imitated Near Eastern designs depicting animals and luxuriant plants; Greek sculptors produced narrative reliefs like those of Assyria and statues with the stiff, frontal poses familiar from Egyptian precedents; Egypt also gave inspiration to Greek architects to employ stone for columns, ornamental details, and, eventually, entire buildings. In a similar process of the transfer of knowledge from east to west, information about the regular movements of the stars and planets developed by astronomers in Babylonia proved especially important in helping Ionian thinkers reach their conclusions about the nature of the physical world. The first of the Ionian theorists, Thales (c. 625–545 B.C.) from the city-state of Miletus, was said to have predicted a solar eclipse in 585 B.C., an accomplishment implying he had been influenced by Babylonian learning. Modern astronomers doubt that Thales actually could have predicted an eclipse, but the story shows how influential eastern scientific and mathematical knowledge was to the thinkers of Ionia. Working from knowledge such as the observed fact that celestial bodies moved in a regular pattern, scientific thinkers like Thales and Anaximander (c. 610–540 B.C.), also from Miletus, drew the revolutionary conclusion that the physical world was regulated by a set of laws of nature rather than by the arbitrary intervention of divine beings. Pythagoras, who emigrated from Samos to south Italy about 530 B.C., taught that the entire world was explicable through numbers. His doctrines inspired systematic study of mathematics and the numerical aspects of musical harmony.

The Ionian thinkers insisted that the workings of the universe could be explained because the phenomena of nature were neither random nor arbitrary. The universe, the totality of things, they named *cosmos* because this word meant an orderly arrangement that is beautiful (hence our word "cosmetic"). The order characteristic of the cosmos, perceived as lovely because it was ordered, encompassed not only the motions of the heavenly bodies but also everything else: the weather, the growth of plants and animals, human health and psychology, and so on. Since the universe was ordered, it was intelligible; since it was intelligible, explanations of events could be discovered by thought and research. The thinkers who conceived this view believed it necessary to give reasons for their conclusions and to persuade others by arguments based on evidence. They believed, in other words, in logic (a word derived from the Greek term *logos*, meaning, among other things, a reasoned explanation). This way of thought based on reason represented a crucial first step toward science and philosophy as these disciplines endure today. The rule-based view of the causes of events and physical phenomena developed by these thinkers contrasted sharply with the traditional mythological view of causation. Naturally, many people had difficulty accepting such a startling change in their understanding of the world, and the older tradition explaining events as the work of gods lived on alongside the new ideas.

The ideas of the Ionian thinkers probably spread slowly because no means of mass communication existed, and few men could afford to spend the time to become followers of these thinkers and then return home to explain these new ways of thought to others. Magic remained an important preoccupation in the lives of the majority of ordinary people, who retained their notions that demons and spirits, as well as gods and goddesses, frequently and directly affected their fortunes and health as well as the events of nature. Despite their perhaps limited immediate effect on the ancient world at large, the Ionian thinkers initiated a tremendously important development in intellectual history: the separation of scientific thinking from myth and religion. Demonstrating the independence of mind that characterized this new direction in thinking, Xenophanes of Colophon (c. 580–480 B.C.) severely criticized traditional notions about the gods that made them seem like nothing more than immortal human beings. For example, he decried the portrayal of gods in the poetry of Homer and Hesiod as subject to human moral failures such as theft, adultery, and fraud. He also rejected the common view that gods resemble human beings in their appearance: "There is one god, greatest among gods and men, who bears no similarity to humans either in shape or in thought. . . . But humans believe that the gods are born like themselves, and that the gods wear clothes and have bodies like humans and speak in the same way. . . . But if cows and horses or lions had hands or could draw with their hands and manufacture the things humans can make, then horses would draw the forms of gods like horses, cows like cows, and they would make the gods' bodies resemble those which each kind of animal had itself" (D.-K. 21B14,15,23).

Some modern scholars call these changes in Greek thinking the birth of rationalism, but it would be unfair to label myths and religious ways of thought as irrational if that term is taken to mean "unthinking" or "silly." Ancient people realized that their lives were constantly subject to forces beyond their control and understanding, and it was not unreasonable to attribute supernatural origins to the powers of nature or the ravages of disease. The new scientific ways of thought insisted, however, that observable evidence had to be sought and theories of explanation had to be logical. Just being old or popular no longer automatically bestowed veracity on a story purporting to explain natural phenomena. In this way, the Ionian thinkers parted company with the traditional ways of thinking of the ancient Near East as found in its rich mythology and repeated in the myths of early Greece.

Developing the view that people must give reasons to explain what they believe to be true, rather than just make assertions that they expect others to believe without evidence, was the most important achievement of the early Ionian thinkers. This insistence on rationality, coupled with the belief that the world could be understood as something other than the plaything of divine whim, gave human beings hope that they could improve their lives through their own efforts. As Xenophanes put it, "The gods have not revealed all things from the beginning to mortals, but, by seeking, human beings discover, in time, what is better" (D.-K. 21B18). Xenophanes, like other Ionian thinkers, believed in the existence of gods, but he nevertheless assigned the opportunity and the responsibility for improving human life squarely to human beings themselves. Human beings themselves were to "discover what is better."

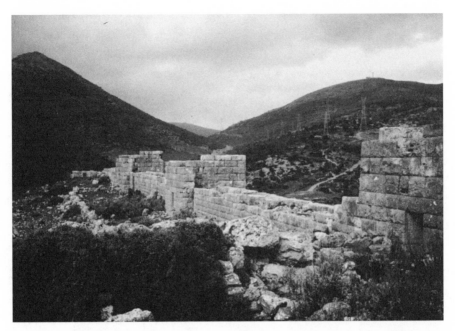

16. The circuit walls and towers of fourth-century Eleutherai, on the border of Athenian territory, exemplify the lengths to which Greeks had to go to defend themselves against each other. (Photo by author)

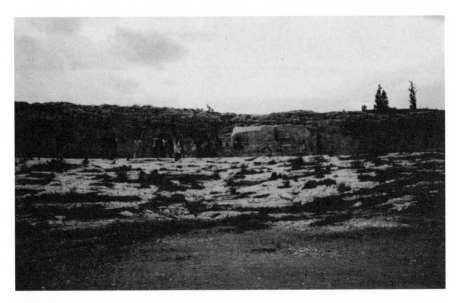

17. The assembly (*ecclesia*) of Athenian democracy, consisting of several thousand male citizens, usually met in the open air in this space on the Pnyx hill not far from the acropolis. (Photo by author)

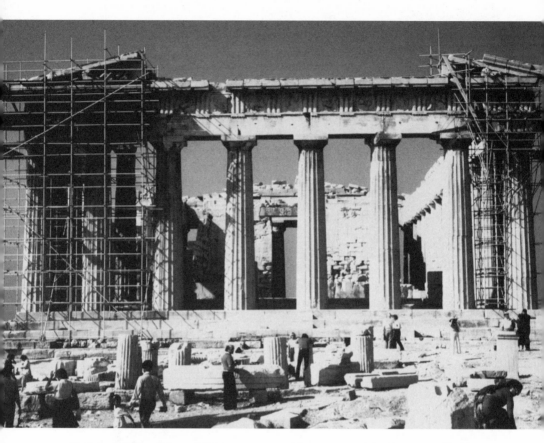

18. Conservators today are fighting to protect the remains of the Parthenon from the effects of the modern world, especially air pollution that is dissolving its marble. (Photo by author)

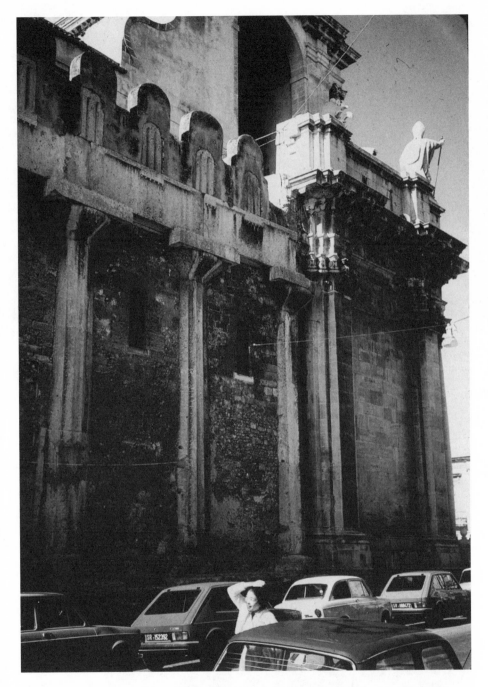

19. The interaction of the ancient and modern worlds is concrete in this cathedral in Syracuse on the island of Sicily, where the architecture of the church incorporates that of a fifth-century B.C. temple. (Photo by author)

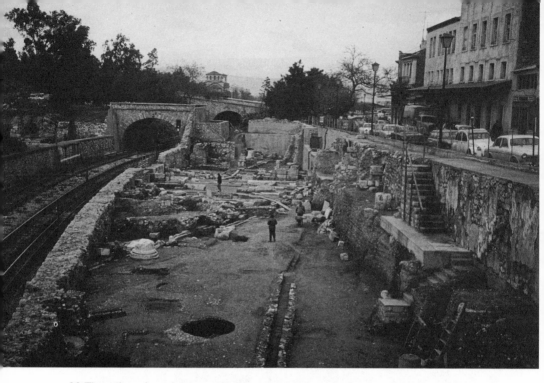

20. The railway from Athens to Piraeus was dug through the site of the ancient agora, an example of the archaeological difficulties created when human habitation on a site is continuous over the ages. (Photo by author)

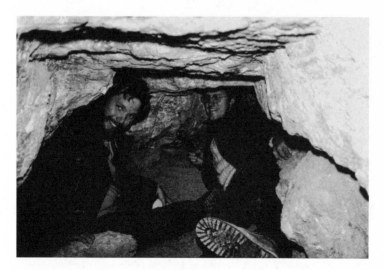

21. This narrow shaft of an Athenian silver mine near Laurion exemplifies the cramped and dangerous conditions in which slave miners were compelled to work. (Photo by author)

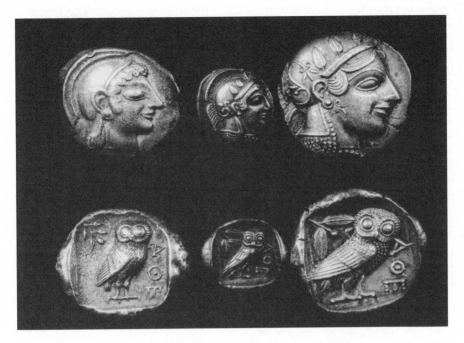

22. The output of the silver mines of Athens was minted into the city-state's internationally accepted currency, identified by Athena as its patron deity on the obverse of the coins and on the reverse by an owl (Athena's special bird), olive branch, and the initial letters of the city-state's name. (Courtesy of the American Numismatic Society)

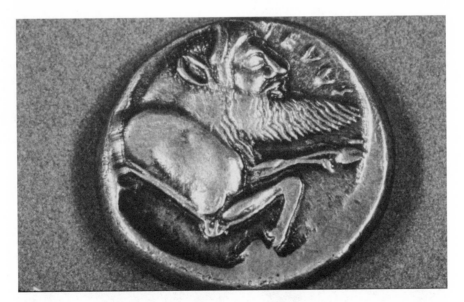

23. This silver coin of Gela on Sicily depicts a river god in the guise of a man/bull, illustrating the complex symbolism possible in Greek numismatic art. (Courtesy of Lawrence University and Miss Ottilia Buerger)

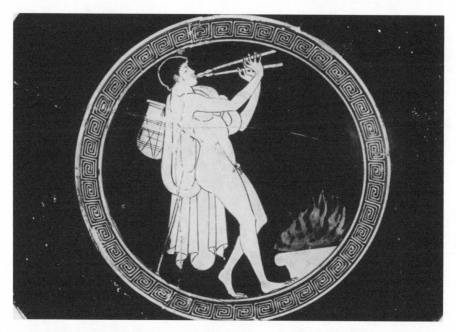

24. This vase painting of a youth playing an aulos (an oboe-like wind instrument) in front of an altar hints at the interaction of ritual elements, such as music, dance, and festival, that surrounded sacrifice, the central event of Greek religion. (Courtesy of the Yale University Art Gallery)

25. This third-century B.C. altar at Syracuse on Sicily was two hundred yards long to allow the sacrifice of cattle by the hundreds as a large-scale demonstration of civic piety and prosperity. (Photo by author)

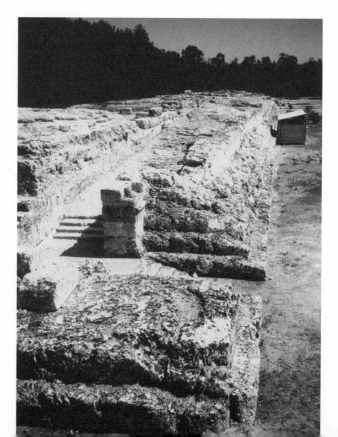

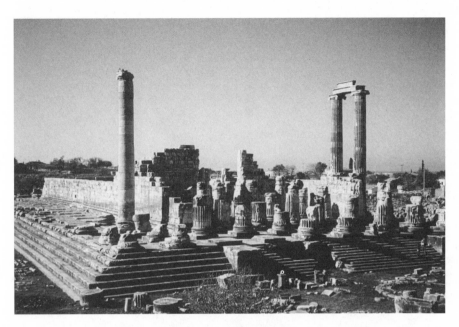

26. The massive size of the Hellenistic-era temple of Apollo at Didyma (on the coast of what is today western Turkey) demonstrates the continuing importance attached to spectacular affirmations of public piety in Greek religion. (Photo by author)

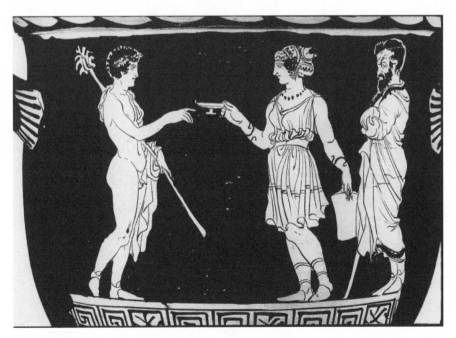

27. The variety of anthropomorphic representations of Dionysus, the god of wine and passionate emotion shown here (left) as beardless and youthful-looking, illustrates his status as the most ambiguous of Greek divinities. (Courtesy of the Yale University Art Gallery)

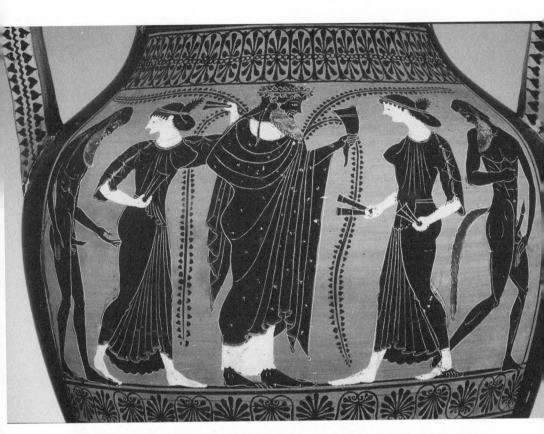

28. On this vase, by contrast with figure 27, Dionysus (center) is depicted as bearded, a sign of male maturity. (Courtesy of the Worcester Art Museum)

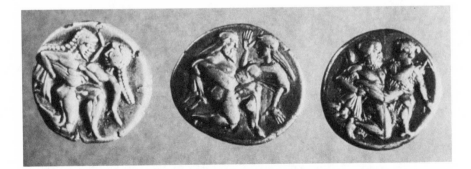

29. These coins of Thasos depict the rape of women by satyrs, mythological half-men/half-beasts associated with Dionysus; that such scenes could be placed on the official products of a Greek city-state emphasizes the complexity of the relation of gender, sexuality, reproduction, violence, and divine power in Greek religion. (Courtesy of the American Numismatic Society)

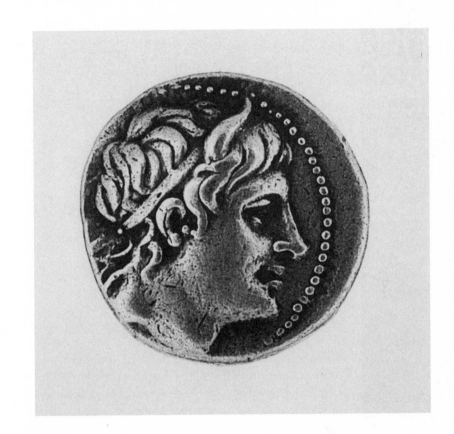

30. Hellenistic ruler cults instituted the worship of living human beings as gods. On this coin from the early third century B.C., the bull's horns sprouting from the head of the Macedonian king Demetrius signaled his divine status. (Photograph courtesy of Joel Villa)

From Persian Wars
to Athenian Empire

6

Background to War

Athenian blundering in international diplomacy set in motion the greatest military threat that the ancient Greeks ever faced. Fearing that the Spartans would again try to intervene at Athens in support of the city's oligarchic faction opposed to the democratic reforms of Cleisthenes, the Athenians in 507 B.C. had sent ambassadors to ask for a protective alliance with the king of Persia, Darius I. The Persian Empire by this time had become the richest, largest, and most militarily powerful state in the ancient world. The Athenian emissaries met with a representative of the king at Sardis, the Persian headquarters in western Anatolia. When the royal representative had heard their plea for an alliance to help protect them against the Spartans, he replied, "But who in the world are you and where do you live?" (Herodotus 5.73). From the Persian perspective, the Athenians were so insignificant that the king's representative had never heard of them. Yet within two generations Athens would be fully in control of what today we call the Athenian Empire. The transformation of Athens from insignificance to international power was startling and swift; it came about in a period of war that marks the beginning of the Classical Age, the modern designation of the period from about 500 B.C. to the death of Alexander the Great in 323 B.C.

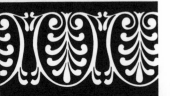

The dynamics of this incident between Athens and Persia expose the forces motivating the conflicts that would dominate the military and political history of mainland Greece throughout the fifth century B.C. First, the two major powers in mainland Greece—Sparta and Athens—remained suspicious of each other. The Spartans had sent King Cleomenes with an army to Athens in 508/7 B.C. to intervene on the side of Isagoras in his struggle for power with Cleisthenes, only to have their forces and their king humiliatingly expelled by the men of Athens. Sparta therefore from this date began to see Athens as a hostile state, a feeling naturally reciprocated at Athens after the abortive Spartan intervention, during which the Spartan troops had forced some seven hundred Athenian households into temporary exile. Second, the kingdom of Persia had expanded westward all the way to Anatolia and become the master of Greek city-states along its coast. The Greeks of the mainland therefore had reason to feel anxious about Persian intentions toward their territory. Neither the Persians nor the mainland Greeks yet knew much about each other, however, and their mutual ignorance opened the door to explosive misunderstandings.

Conflict between Unequals

The Athenian ambassadors dispatched to Sardis accepted the usual Persian terms for an alliance by offering tokens of earth and water to the king's representative, thereby indicating Athens's recognition of the superiority of the king, who acknowledged no one as his equal and therefore did not make alliances as if with an equal. The Athenian ambassadors, in their ignorance of Persian diplomatic procedure, had naively assumed that they could strike a kind of partnership with the Persian kingdom because Greeks made alliances on those sorts of terms. Even after they understood that the earth and water demanded by the king's representative, the local governor (a satrap in Persian terminology), amounted to an admission of inferiority on their part, the Athenian ambassadors were evidently reluctant to return to Athens empty-handed. They therefore complied with the symbolic demand. Once the mission had returned home, the men of the Athenian assembly, although outraged at their envoys' symbolic submission to a foreign power, never overtly repudiated the alliance and never sent another embassy to the satrap in Sardis to announce that Athens was unilaterally dissolving the pact. In the aftermath of this fumbled diplomacy the Athenians continued to think of themselves as independent and unencumbered by any obligation to the Persian king. The king, for his part, had no indication that the relationship had changed; as far as he knew, the Athenians remained voluntarily allied to him and still owed him the loyalty and deference all mere mortals should pay to him.

---

499 B.C.: Beginning of the Ionian revolt.

494 B.C.: Final crushing of the Ionian revolt by the Persians.

490 B.C.: Darius sends Persian force against Athenians; battle of Marathon.

483 B.C.: Discovery of large deposits of silver in Attica; Athenians begin to build large navy at instigation of Themistocles.

482 B.C.: Ostracism of Aristides (recalled in 480 B.C.).

480 B.C.: Xerxes leads massive Persian invasion of Greece; battles of Thermopylae and Salamis.

479 B.C.: Battles of Plataea in Boeotia and Mycale in Anatolia.

478 B.C.: Spartans send Pausanias to lead Greek alliance against Persians.

477 B.C.: Athens assumes leadership of the Greek alliance (Delian League).

475 B.C.: Cimon returns the bones of the hero Theseus to Athens.

465 B.C.: Devastating earthquake in Laconia leads to helot revolt in Messenia.

465–463 B.C.: Attempt of Thasos to revolt from the Delian League.

462 B.C.: Cimon leads Athenian troops to help Spartans, who reject them.

461 B.C.: Ephialtes' reforms to democratize Athenian government further.

450s B.C.: Hostilities between Athens and Sparta; institution of stipends for jurors and other magistrates at Athens.

454 B.C.: Enormous losses of Delian League forces against Persians in Egypt; transfer of league's treasury from island of Delos to Athens.

451 B.C.: Passage of Pericles' law on citizenship.

450 B.C.: End of overseas expeditions against Persians by Delian League forces.

447 B.C.: Athenian building program begins.

446–445 B.C.: Peace treaty meant to last thirty years agreed to by Athens and Sparta.

443 B.C.: Pericles' main political opponent ostracized.

441–439 B.C.: Samos attempts to revolt from Delian League.

430s B.C.: Increasing political tension at Athens as Sparta threatens war.

This serious misunderstanding was to set in motion a sequence of events that was to culminate in invasions of mainland Greece by the enormous army and navy of the king of Persia. The Persian kingdom outstripped mainland Greece in every category of material resources, from precious metals to soldiers. The wars between Persians and Greeks pitted the equivalent of an elephant against a small swarm of mosquitoes. In such a conflict a Greek victory seemed improbable, to say the least. Equally improbable, given the propensity toward disunity and even mutual hostility of the independent Greek city-states, was the coalition of Greek states—although not all of Greece—united to repel the common foe.

The kingdom of Persia had originally taken shape when Cyrus (ruled 560–530 B.C.) established himself as its first king by overthrowing the monarchy of the Medes. The Median kingdom, centered in what is today northern Iran, had emerged in the late eighth century, and its army had joined that of Babylonia in destroying the Assyrian kingdom in 612 B.C. Median power had then been extended as far as the border of Lydia in central Anatolia. The languages of the Medes and the Persians descended from Indo-European, and the language of today's Iran is a descendant of ancient Persian. By taking over Lydia in 546 B.C., Cyrus also acquired dominion over the Greek city-states on the western coast of Anatolia that the Lydian king Croesus had previously subdued. This expansion of Persian power set the stage for the great conflict that erupted in the early fifth century between Persia and the coalition of Greek city-states.

By the reign of Darius I (ruled 522–486 B.C.), the Persian kingdom, whose ancestral heart lay in southern Iran east of Mesopotamia, covered a vast territory stretching east-west from modern Afghanistan to Turkey, and north-south from inside the southern border of the former Soviet Union to Egypt and the Indian Ocean. Its heterogeneous population numbered in the millions. The empire took its administrative structure from Assyrian precedents, and its satraps ruled enormous territories with little, if any, direct interference from the king. Their duties were to keep order, enroll troops when needed, and send revenues to the royal treasury. From the many different subject peoples of the kingdom, the Persian kings exacted taxes in food, precious metals, and other valuable commodities and demanded levies of soldiers to serve in the royal army.

The revenues of its vast kingdom made the Persian monarchy wealthy beyond comparison. Everything about the king was meant to emphasize his grandeur and superiority to ordinary mortals. His purple robes were more splendid than anyone's; the red carpets spread for him to walk upon could not be trod on by anyone else; his servants held their hands before their mouths in his presence to muffle their breath so that he would not have to breathe the same air as they; in the sculpture adorning his palace, he was depicted as larger than any other human being. To display his concern for his loyal subjects, as well as the gargantuan scale of his resources, the king provided meals for some fifteen thousand nobles, courtiers, and other followers every day, although he himself ate hidden from the view of his guests. The Greeks, in awe of the Persian monarch's power and lavishness, referred to him as "The Great King."

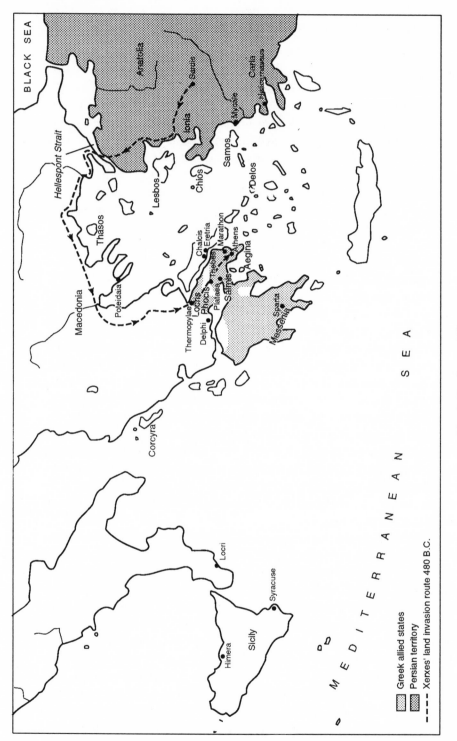

Map 5. The Persian Wars

Greek allied states

Persian territory

------- Xerxes' land invasion route 480 B.C.

The Persian kings did not, however, regard themselves as gods, but rather as the agents of the supreme god of Persian religion, Ahura Mazda. Persian religion, based on the teachings of the prophet Zoroaster, was dualistic, conceptualizing the world as the arena for a constant battle between good and evil. Unlike other peoples of the ancient Near East and the Greeks, the Persians shunned animal sacrifice. Fire, kindled on special altars, formed an important part of their religious rituals. The religion of ancient Persia survives in the modern world as Zoroastrianism, whose adherents have preserved the central role of fire in its practice. Despite their autocratic rule, the ancient Persian kings usually did not interfere with the religious practices or everyday customs of their subjects.

The Outbreak of Hostilities

The most famous series of wars in ancient Greek history — the so-called Persian Wars, which took place in the 490s and in 480–479 B.C. — broke out with a revolt of the Greek city-states of Ionia (a region on the western coast of Anatolia) against Persian rule. The Ionian Greeks had originally lost their independence not to the Persians but to the Lydian kingdom, which overpowered them during the reign of King Croesus (ruled c. 560–546). Buoyed by this success and his legendary riches, Croesus next tried to conquer territory in Anatolia that had previously been in the Median kingdom. Before initiating a campaign, he had requested advice from Apollo's oracle at Delphi about the advisability of attacking a region that the new Persian monarchy was now claiming. The oracle gave the famous response that if Croesus attacked the Persians, he would destroy a great kingdom. Encouraged, Croesus sent his army eastward in 546 B.C., but he was defeated and lost his territory, including Ionia, to Cyrus, the Persian king. When Cyrus later allowed Croesus to complain to the Delphic oracle that its advice had been disastrously wrong, the oracle testily replied that, if Croesus had been truly wise, he would have asked a second question: Whose kingdom was he going to destroy, his enemy's or his own?

By 499 B.C., local factional strife among the Ionian Greeks led to revolt against the tyrannies that the Persian kings had installed after taking over the area, in keeping with their policy of supporting local tyrants on whom they relied to maintain order in conquered Greek city-states. The Ionian rebels sent representatives to mainland Greece seeking support in their effort to throw off Persian control. The Spartan king, Cleomenes, ruled out any chance of help from his city-state after he saw the map that the Ionians had brought and learned that an attack on the Persian capital (in modern Iran) would entail a march of three months inland from the Ionian coast. He, like the other Spartans and most Greeks in general, had previously had no idea of the geography and dimensions of the Near East. The men of the Athenian assembly, in contrast to the Spartan leaders, voted to join the city-state of Eretria on the neighboring island of Euboea in sending military aid to the Ionian revolt. Their force proceeded as far as Sardis, Croesus's old capital and now a Persian headquarters. After burning Sardis to the ground, including a famous sanctuary, the Athenians and Eretrians returned home when a Persian counterattack caused the Ionian allies to lose their coordination. Subsequent campaigns by the Persian king's commanders crushed the Ionian rebels entirely by 494 B.C. King Darius then sent his general Mardonius to reorganize Ionia, where some democratic regimes were now permitted in place of the unpopular tyrannies.

King Darius was doubly furious when he learned that the Athenians had aided the Ionian revolt: not only had they dared attack his kingdom, but they had done so after having indicated their submission to him by offering the tokens of earth and water. Insignificant though the Greeks were in his eyes, he vowed to avenge their disloyalty as a matter of justice, if not of grand strategy. The Greeks later claimed that, to keep himself from forgetting his vow in the press of his many other concerns as the ruler of a huge kingdom, Darius ordered one of his slaves to say to him three times at every meal, "Sire, remember the Athenians" (Herodotus, History 5.105). In 490 B.C. Darius dispatched a flotilla of ships carrying troops to punish the misguided Greeks. This force burned Eretria and landed on the northeastern coast of Attica near a village called Marathon. The Persians brought with them the elderly Hippias, exiled son of Pisistratus, expecting to reinstall him as tyrant of Athens under their sway. Since the Persian troops outnumbered the citizen militia of Athenian hoplites, the Athenians asked the Spartans and other Greek city-states for military help. The Athenian courier dispatched to Sparta became famous because he ran the hundred and forty miles from Athens to Sparta in less than two days. But by the time the battle of Marathon took place, the only troops to arrive were a contingent from the small city-state of Plataea in Boeotia, the region just north of Athenian territory.

Everyone expected the Persians to win. The Greek soldiers, who had never seen Persians before, grew afraid just gazing at their (to Greek eyes) frighteningly outlandish outfits. Moreover, the Persian troops greatly outnumbered the Athenian and Plataean contingents. The Athenian commanders—the board of ten generals elected each year as the civil and military leaders of Athens—felt enormous pressure to act because they feared that the disparity in forces might induce the assembly to surrender rather than fight or that the oligarchic sympathizers in the city might try to strike a treacherous deal with the Persians. They therefore prepared for an attack on the wider line of the enemy by thinning out the center of their own line of soldiers from the citizen militia while putting more men on the wings. Carefully planning their tactics to minimize the time their soldiers would be exposed to the fire of Persian archers, the generals, led by Miltiades (c. 550–489 B.C.), sent their hoplites against the Persian line at a dead run. The Greek hoplites clanked across the Marathon plain in their metal armor under a hail of arrows. Once engaged in hand-to-hand combat with the Persians, the Greek infantrymen benefited from their superior armor and longer weapons. In a furious struggle the strengthened wings of the Greek army defeated the Persians opposite them and then turned inward to crush the Persian center from the flanks. They then drove the Persians back into a swamp where any invaders unable to escape to their ships could be picked off one by one.

The Athenian army hurried the more than twenty miles from Marathon to Athens to guard the city against a naval attack by the Persian fleet. Today's long foot races called marathons commemorate in their name and distance this famous trek in 490 B.C. When the Persians sailed home without taking Athens, the Athenians (at least those who favored democracy) rejoiced in disbelief. The Persians, whom they had feared as invincible, had retreated. For decades afterwards, the greatest honor an Athenian man could claim was to say he had been a "Marathon fighter."

The symbolic importance of the battle of Marathon far outweighed its military significance. The defeat of his punitive expedition enraged Darius because it insulted his prestige, not because it represented any threat to the security of his kingdom. The ordinary Athenian men who made up the city-state's army, on the other hand, had dramatically demonstrated their commitment to preserving their freedom by refusing to capitulate to an enemy whose reputation for power and wealth had made a disastrous Athenian defeat appear certain. The unexpected victory at Marathon gave an unparalleled boost to Athenian self-confidence, and the city-state's soldiers and leaders thereafter always boasted that they had stood fast before the feared barbarians even though the Spartans had not come in time to help them.

Full-scale Invasion

This newly won confidence helped steel the population of Athens to join in the resistance to the gigantic Persian invasion of Greece that arrived in 480 B.C. Darius had vowed the invasion as revenge for the defeat at Marathon, but it took so long to marshal forces from all over the far-flung Persian kingdom that he died before it could be launched. His son, Xerxes I (ruled 486–465), therefore led the massive invasion force of infantry and ships against the Greek mainland. So huge was Xerxes' army, the Greeks later claimed, that it required seven days and seven nights of continuous march-

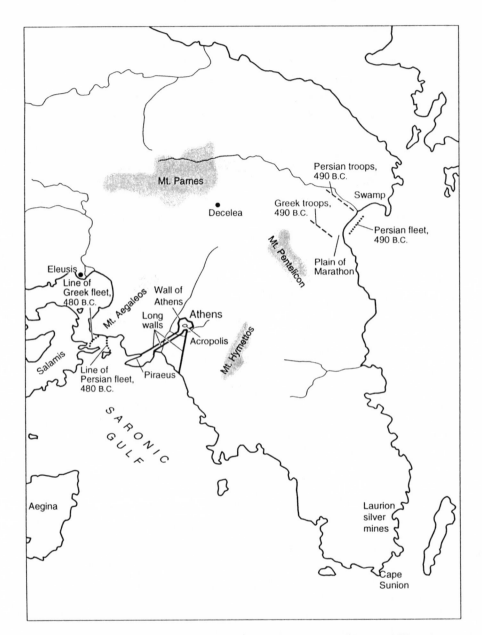

Plan 1. Attica Showing Battle of Marathon (490 B.C.) and Battle of Salamis (480 B.C.)

ing to cross the Hellespont, the narrow passage of sea between Anatolia and mainland Greece, on a temporary bridge lashed together from boats and pontoons. Xerxes expected the Greek states simply to surrender without a fight once they realized the size of his forces. The city-states in northern and central Greece did just that because their location placed them directly in the line of the invading Persian forces, while the small size of their populations left them without any hope of effective defense. The important Boeotian city-state of Thebes, about forty miles north of Athens, also supported the Persian invasion, probably hoping to gain an advantage over its Athenian neighbors in the aftermath of the expected Persian victory. Thebes and Athens had previously become hostile to one another about 519 B.C. when Plataea successfully sought Athenian protection from Theban dominance.

Thirty-one Greek states, however, most of them located in southern Greece, formed a military coalition to fight the Persian invasion, and they chose Sparta as leader because it fielded Greece's most formidable hoplite army. The coalition sought aid from Gelon, the tyrant of Syracuse, the most powerful Greek city-state on Sicily. The appeal failed, however, when Gelon demanded command of the Greek forces in return for his assistance, a price the Spartan and Athenian leaders were unwilling to meet. In this same period Gelon was engaged in a struggle with Carthage, a powerful Phoenician city on the coast of North Africa, over territory in Sicily, and in 480 his forces defeated a massive Carthaginian expedition in battle at Himera, on the island's northern coast. It is possible that the Carthaginian expedition to Sicily and the Persian invasion of mainland Greece were purposely coordinated to embroil the Greek world simultaneously in a two-front war in the west and the east.

The Spartans showed their courage when three hundred of their men led by Leonidas, along with allies, held off Xerxes' huge army for several days at the narrow pass called Thermopylae ("warm gates") on the eastern coast of central Greece. Xerxes was flabbergasted that this paltry force did not immediately retreat when confronted with his magnificent force. The Spartan troops characteristically refused to be intimidated. When one of Xerxes' scouts was sent ahead to observe the situation at the pass, he reported that the Spartans were standing casually in front of their fortification, leisurely combing their long hair. The Persians were astonished at this behavior, but it was in fact customary for Spartan soldiers to fix their hair as a mark of pride before proceeding into battle. Their defiant attitude was summed up by the reputed response of a Spartan hoplite to the remark that the Persian archers were so numerous that their arrows darkened the sky in battle. "That's good news," said the Spartan, "we will get to fight in the shade" (Herodotus, *History* 7.226). The pass was so narrow that the Persians could not employ their superior numbers to overwhelm the Greek defenders, who were more skilled at close-in fighting. Only when a local Greek, hoping for a reward from the Persian king, revealed to him a secret route around the pass was his army able to massacre its defenders by attacking them from the front and the rear simultaneously. The Persian army then continued its march southward into Greece.

The Athenians soon proved their mettle. Rather than surrender when Xerxes arrived in Attica with his army, they abandoned their city for him to sack. Women, children, and noncombatants packed up their belongings as best they could and evacuated to the northeast coast of the Peloponnese. The Athenian commander Themistocles (c. 528–462), purposely spreading misinformation in his characteristically shrewd manner, maneuvered the other, less aggressive Greek leaders into facing the larger Persian navy in a sea battle in the narrow channel between the island of Salamis and the west coast of Attica. Athens was able to supply the largest contingent to the Greek navy at Salamis because the assembly had been financing the construction of warships ever since a rich strike of silver had been made in Attica in 483 B.C. The proceeds from the silver mines went to the state, and, at the urging of Themistocles, the assembly had voted to use the financial windfall to build a navy for defense, rather than to disburse the money to individual citizens. As at Thermopylae, the Greeks in the battle of Salamis in 480 B.C. used their country's topography to their advantage. The narrowness of the channel prevented the Persians from using all their forces at once and minimized the advantage of their ships' greater maneuverability, while the heavier Greek ships could employ their underwater rams to sink the less sturdy Persian craft. When Xerxes observed that the most energetic of his naval commanders appeared to be the one woman among them, Artemisia, the ruler of Caria (today the southwest corner of Turkey), he reportedly remarked, "My men have become women, and my women, men" (Herodotus, History 8.88).

The Greek victory at Salamis in 480 B.C. induced Xerxes to return to Persia, but he left behind an enormous infantry force under his best general, Mardonius, and an offer for the Athenians: If they capitulated, they would remain unharmed and become the king's overlords over the other Greeks. The assembly refused, the population evacuated again, and Mardonius wrecked Athens for the second time in as many years. In 479 B.C., the Greek infantry headed by the Spartans under the command of a royal son named Pausanias (c. 520–470 B.C.) outfought the Persian infantry at the battle of Plataea in Boeotia, while a Greek fleet caught the Persian navy napping at Mycale in Ionia. The coalition of Greek city-states had thus done the astonishing: they had protected their homeland and their independence from the strongest power in the world.

The Greeks' superior armor and weapons and adroit use of topography to counterbalance their enemy's greater numbers help to explain their victories on the military level. What is truly remarkable about the Persian Wars, however, is the decision of the citizen militias of the thirty-one Greek city-states to fight in the first place. They could easily have surrendered and agreed to become Persian subjects to save themselves. Instead, these Greek warriors chose to strive together against apparently overwhelming odds. Their courage found support in the encouragement to fight offered by noncombatants in their communities, such as the women of Corinth, who as a group offered public prayers to the goddess Aphrodite for the Greek cause. Since the Greek forces included not only the wealthiest men and hoplites but also thousands of poorer men, who rowed the warships, the effort against the Persians cut across social and economic divisions. The Greek decision to fight the Persian Wars demonstrated courage inspired by a deep devotion to the ideal of political freedom, which had emerged in the preceding Archaic Age.

The Establishment of the Athenian Empire

The struggle against the Persian invasion had occasioned a rare interval of interstate cooperation in ancient Greek history. The two most powerful city-states, Athens and Sparta, had put aside their mutual suspicions stemming from their clash at the time of the reforms of Cleisthenes to share the leadership of the united Greek military forces. Their attempt to continue this cooperation after the repulse of the Persians, however, ended in failure, despite the lobbying of pro-Spartan Athenians who believed that the two city-states should be partners rather than rivals. Out of this failure arose the so-called Athenian Empire, a label invented to point out the harsh dominance Athens came to exercise over numerous other Greek states in an alliance that had originated as a voluntary coalition against Persia.

Following its victories in 479 B.C., the Greek coalition decided to continue as a naval alliance aimed at driving out the Persian outposts that still existed in far northern Greece and western Anatolia, especially Ionia. The Spartan Pausanias, the victor of the battle of Plataea, was chosen to lead the first expedition in 478. The Greek forces under his command soon became enraged by his arrogant and violent behavior toward both his allies and local Greek citizens in Anatolia, especially women. This kind of outrageous conduct was to prove common in the future for Spartan men in positions of power when away from home. Their regimented training in Sparta apparently left them ill prepared to operate humanely and effectively once they had escaped from the constraints imposed by their way of life at home, where they were always under the scrutiny of one another.

By 477 B.C., the Athenian leader Aristides (c. 525–465 B.C.) had successfully persuaded the other Greeks to request Athenian leadership of the alliance against the Persians. The leaders at Sparta were happy to cede their
position at the head of the alliance because, in the words of the Athenian
historian Thucydides (c. 460–400 B.C.), "they were afraid any other commanders they sent abroad would be corrupted, as Pausanias had been, and
they were glad to be relieved of the burden of fighting the Persians . . . .
Besides, at the time they still thought of the Athenians as friendly allies"
(History of the Peloponnesian War 1.95). Sparta's ongoing need to keep its army at
home most of the time to guard against helot revolts also made prolonged
overseas operations difficult to maintain.

The Greek alliance against Persia now took on a permanent organiza-
tional structure under Athenian leadership. Member states swore a solemn
oath never to desert the coalition. The members were predominantly located
in northern Greece, on the islands of the Aegean Sea, and along the western
coast of Anatolia—that is, in the areas most exposed to Persian attack. Most
of the independent city-states of the Peloponnese, on the other hand, remained in their long-standing alliance with the Spartans, which had been in
existence since well before the Persian Wars. Thus, Athens and Sparta each
now dominated a separate coalition of allies. Sparta and its allies, whose
coalition modern historians refer to as the Peloponnesian League, had an assembly to set policy, but no action could be taken unless the Spartan leaders
agreed to it. The alliance headed by Athens also had an assembly of representatives to make policy. Members of this alliance were in theory supposed
to make decisions in common, but in practice Athens was in charge.

The special arrangements made to finance the Athenian-led alliance's
naval operations promoted Athenian domination. Aristides set the different
levels of dues the various member states were to pay each year, based on
their size and prosperity. Larger member states were to supply entire warships complete with crews and their pay; smaller states could share the cost
of a ship or simply contribute cash, which would be pooled with others'
dues to pay for ships and crews. The warship of the time was a narrow
vessel built for speed called a trireme, a name derived from its having three
stacked banks of oarsmen on each side for propulsion in battle. One hundred and seventy rowers were needed to propel a trireme, which fought by
ramming enemy ships with a metal-clad ram attached to the bow. Triremes
also usually carried a complement of ten hoplite warriors and four archers
on their decks to engage the enemy crews in combat when the ships became
entangled. Officers and other crew brought the total of men on board to
two hundred. The alliance's funds were kept on the Aegean island of Delos,

in the temple of Apollo to whom the whole island was sacred, and consequently the alliance is today customarily referred to as the Delian League.

Over time, more and more of the members of the Delian League paid their dues in cash rather than by going to the trouble of furnishing warships. Most members of the alliance preferred this option because it was beyond their capacities to build ships as specialized as triremes and to train crews in the intricate teamwork required to work triple banks of oars. Athens, far larger than most of the allies, had the shipyards and skilled workers to build triremes in large numbers, as well as a large population of men eager to earn pay as rowers. Therefore, Athens built and manned most of the alliance's warships, using the dues of allies to supplement its own contribution. The Athenian men serving as rowers on these warships came from the poorest social class, that of the laborers (thetes), and their essential contribution to the navy earned them not only money but also additional political importance in Athenian democracy as naval strength increasingly became the city-state's principal source of military power. Athens continued to be able to muster larger numbers of hoplite infantry than many smaller city-states, but over time its fleet became its most powerful force.

Since most allies eventually lacked warships of their own, members of the Delian League had no effective recourse if they disagreed with decisions made for the league as a whole under Athenian leadership. By dispatching the superior Athenian fleet to compel discontented allies to adhere to league policy and to continue paying their annual dues, the men of the Athenian assembly came to exercise the dominant power. The modern reference to allied dues as "tribute" is meant to indicate the compulsory nature of these payments. As Thucydides observed, rebellious allies "lost their independence," making the Athenians as the league's leaders "no longer as popular as they used to be" (History of the Peloponnesian War 1.98–99).

The most egregious instance of Athenian compulsion of a reluctant ally was the case of the city-state of the island of Thasos in the northern Aegean Sea. Thasos in 465 B.C. unilaterally withdrew from the Delian League after a dispute with Athens over control of gold mines on the neighboring mainland. To compel the Thasians to keep their sworn agreement to stay in the league, the Athenians led allied forces against them in a protracted siege, which ended in 463 B.C. with the island's surrender. As punishment, the league forced Thasos to pull down its defensive walls, give up its navy, and pay enormous tribute and fines.

The Delian League did accomplish its principal strategic goal: within twenty years after the battle of Salamis, league forces had expelled almost all the Persian garrisons that had continued to hold out in some city-states along the northeastern Aegean coast and had driven the Persian fleet from the Aegean Sea, ending the direct Persian military threat to Greece for the next fifty years. Athens meanwhile grew stronger from its share of the spoils captured from Persian outposts and the tribute paid by its members. By the middle of the fifth century B.C., league members' annual tribute alone totaled the equivalent of perhaps $200 million in contemporary terms (assuming $80 as the average daily pay of an ordinary worker today). For a state the size of Athens (around thirty to forty thousand adult male citizens), this annual income meant general prosperity.

The male citizens meeting in the assembly decided how to spend the city-state's income. Rich and poor alike had a self-interested stake in keeping the fleet active and the allies paying for it. Well-heeled leaders such as Cimon (c. 510–450), the son of Miltiades, the victor of Marathon, enhanced their prestige by commanding successful league campaigns and spending their share of the spoils on benefactions to Athens. Cimon, for example, reportedly paid for the foundations of the massive defensive walls that were eventually to connect the city's urban core with its harbor several miles away. Such financial contributions to the common good were expected of wealthy and prominent men. Political parties did not exist in ancient Athens, and political leaders formed informal circles of friends and followers to support their ambitions. Disputes among these ambitious leaders often stemmed more from competition for election to the highest public offices of the city-state and influence in the assembly than from disagreements over pure matters of policy. Arguments tended to concern how Athens should exercise its growing power internationally, not whether it should refrain from interfering with the affairs of the other members of the Delian League in the pursuit of Athenian interests. The numerous Athenian men of lesser means who rowed the Delian League's ships came to depend on the income they earned on league expeditions. Since these men represented the numerically largest group in the male population eligible to vote in the assembly of Athens, where decisions were rendered by majority vote, they could make certain that assembly votes were in their interest. If the interests of the allies did not coincide with theirs, the allies were given no choice but to acquiesce to official Athenian opinion concerning league policy. In this way, alliance was transformed into empire, despite Athenian support of democratic governments in some allied city-states previously ruled by oligarchies. From the Athenian point of view, this transformation was justified because it kept the alliance strong enough to carry out the overall mission of the Delian League: protecting Greece from the Persians.

The Democratic Reform of the Athenian System of Justice

Poorer men of the thete class powered the Athenian fleet, and in the decades following the Persian Wars, both their military and their political importance grew. As these poorer citizens came to recognize that they provided the foundation of Athenian security and prosperity, they apparently felt the time had come to make the administration of justice at Athens just as democratic as the process of making policy and passing laws in the assembly, which was open to all male citizens over eighteen years old. Although at this time the assembly could serve as a court of appeals, most judicial verdicts were rendered by the nine annual magistrates of the city-state, the archons, and the Areopagus council of ex-archons. The nine archons had been chosen by lot rather than by election since 487 B.C., thus making access to those offices a matter of random chance and not liable to domination by wealthy men from the highest Solonian income class, who could afford expensive electoral campaigns. Filling public offices by lot was felt to be democratic because it gave an equal chance to all eligible contestants and was thought to be overseen by the gods. But even democratically selected magistrates were susceptible to corruption, as were the members of the Areopagus. A different judicial system was needed if those men who decided cases were to be insulated from pressure by socially prominent people and from bribery by those rich enough to buy a favorable verdict. That laws were enacted democratically meant little if they were not applied fairly and honestly.

The final impetus to a reform of the judicial system came from a crisis in foreign affairs. The crisis had its roots in a tremendous earthquake near Sparta in 465 B.C. It killed so many Spartans that the helots of Messenia, the Greeks in the western Peloponnese who had long ago been subjugated by the Spartans, instigated a massive revolt against their weakened masters. By 462 B.C. the revolt had become so serious that the Spartans appealed to Athens for military help, despite the chill that had fallen over their relations since the days of their cooperation against the Persians. The tension between the former allies had arisen because rebellious members of the Delian League had received at least moral support from the leaders at Sparta, who felt that Athens was growing powerful enough someday to threaten Spartan interests in the Peloponnese. Cimon, the hero of the Delian League's campaigns, marshaled all his prestige to persuade a reluctant Athenian assembly to send hoplites to help the Spartans in 462 B.C. against a serious revolt of the helots. Cimon, like many among the Athenian elite, had always been an admirer of the Spartans, and he was renowned for registering his opposition to proposals in the assembly by saying, "But that is not what the Spartans would do" (Plutarch, *Cimon* 16). His Spartan friends let him down, however, by soon changing their minds and sending him and his army home. Spartan leaders feared that the democratically inclined Athenian soldiers might decide to help the helots escape from Spartan domination.

This humiliating rejection of their help outraged the Athenian assembly and provoked hostile relations between the two states. The disgrace it brought to Cimon carried over to the elite in general, thereby establishing a political climate ripe for further democratic reforms. A man named Ephialtes promptly seized the moment in 461 B.C. and convinced the assembly to pass measures limiting the power of the Areopagus. The details are obscure, but it appears that up to this time the Areopagus council had held authority to judge accusations of misconduct brought against magistrates, a competence referred to as "guardianship of the laws." The Areopagus was constituted by ex-magistrates, who would presumably have been on generally good terms with current magistrates, the very ones whose conduct they were responsible for punishing if necessary. There existed, therefore, at least the appearance of a conflict of interest, and instances of illegal conduct by magistrates being whitewashed or excused by the Areopagus no doubt had occurred. The reforms apparently removed the guardianship of the laws from the Areopagus, although the council remained the court for premeditated murder and wounding, arson, and certain offenses against the religious cults of the city-state.

The most significant of the Ephialtic reforms was the establishment of a judicial system of courts manned by juries of male citizens over thirty years old, chosen by lot to serve for a year. Previously, judicial power had belonged primarily to the archons and the Areopagus council of ex-archons, but now that power was largely transferred to the jurors, a randomly chosen cross-section of the male citizen body, six thousand men in all, who were distributed into individual juries as needed to handle the case load. Under this new judicial system the magistrates were still entitled to render verdicts concerning minor offenses, the Areopagus had its few special judicial competencies, and the council and assembly could take action in certain cases involving the public interest, but the citizen-manned courts were otherwise given an extraordinary jurisdiction. Their juries in practice defined the most fundamental principles of Athenian public life because they interpreted the law by deciding on their own how it should be applied in each and every case. There were no judges to instruct the jurors and usually no prosecutors or defense lawyers to harangue them, although a citizen could be appointed to speak for the prosecution when a magistrate was on trial for misconduct in office or when the case involved the public interest. In most cases citizens brought the charges, and the only government official in court was a magistrate to keep fights from breaking out during the trial. All trials were concluded in a single day, and jurors made up their own minds after hearing speeches by the persons involved. They swore an oath to pay attention and judge fairly, but they were the sole judges of their own conduct as jurors and did not have to undergo a public scrutiny of their actions at the end of their term of service, as other officials in Athenian democracy regularly did. Improperly influencing the outcome of cases by bribing jurors was made difficult because juries were so large, numbering from several hundred to several thousand. Nevertheless, jury tampering apparently was a worry, because in the early fourth century the system was revised to assign jurors to cases by lot and not until the day of the trial.

Since few, if any, criminal cases could be decided by forensic evidence of the kind used in modern trials, such as blood tests and fingerprints, persuasive speech was the most important element in the legal proceedings. The accuser and the accused both had to speak for themselves in Athenian court, although they might pay someone else to compose the speech that they would deliver and frequently asked others to speak in support of their arguments and as witnesses to their good character. The characters and civic reputations of defendants and plaintiffs were therefore always relevant, and jurors expected to hear about a man's background and his conduct as citizen as part of the information necessary to discover where truth lay. A majority vote of the jurors ruled. No higher court existed to overrule their decisions, and there was no appeal from their verdicts. The power of the court system after Ephialtes epitomized the power of Athenian democracy in action. As a trial-happy juror boasts in Aristophanes' comic play about the Athenian judicial system, *The Wasps*, produced in 422 B.C., "our power in court is no less than royal!" (548–549).

The structure of the new court system reflected underlying principles of what scholars today call the "radical" democracy of Athens in the mid-fifth century B.C. This system involved widespread participation by a cross-section of male citizens, selection of the participants at random for most public offices, elaborate precautions to prevent corruption, equal protection under the law for individual citizens regardless of wealth, and the authority of the majority over any minority or individual when the vital interests of the state were at stake. This last principle appears most dramatically in the official procedure for exiling a man from Athens for ten years, called ostracism. Every year the assembly voted on whether to go through this procedure, which gets its name from the word ostraca, meaning pieces of broken pottery, which were inscribed with names of candidates for expulsion and used as ballots. If the vote on whether to hold an ostracism in a particular year was affirmative, all male citizens on a predetermined day could cast a ballot on which they had scratched the name of the man they thought should be exiled. If six thousand ballots were cast, whichever man was named on the greatest number was compelled to go live outside the borders of Attica for ten years. He suffered no other penalty, and his family and property could remain behind undisturbed. Ostracism was emphatically not a criminal penalty, and men returning from their period of exile enjoyed undiminished rights as citizens.

Ostracism existed because it helped protect the Athenian system from real or perceived threats. At one level, it provided a way of removing a citizen who seemed extremely dangerous to democracy because he was totally dominating the political scene, whether because he was simply too popular and thus a potential tyrant by popular demand or whether he was genuinely subversive. This point is made by a famous anecdote concerning the Aristides who set the original level of dues for the members of the Delian League. Aristides had the nickname "The Just" because he was reputed to be so fair-minded. On the day of the balloting for an ostracism, an illiterate man from the countryside handed Aristides a potsherd, asking him to scratch the name of the man's choice for ostracism on it. "Certainly," said Aristides. " Which name shall I write?" "Aristides," replied the countryman. "Very well," remarked Aristides as he proceeded to inscribe his own name. "But tell me, why do you want to ostracize Aristides? What has he done to you?" "Oh, nothing; I don't even know him," sputtered the man. "I'm just sick and tired of hearing everybody refer to him as 'The Just' " (Plutarch, *Aristides* 7).

In most cases, ostracism served to identify a prominent man who could be made to take the blame for a failed policy that the assembly had originally approved and that was causing extreme political turmoil. Cimon, for example, was ostracized after the disastrous attempt to cooperate with Sparta during the helot revolt of the late 460s. There is no evidence that ostracism was used frivolously, despite the story about Aristides, and probably no more than several dozen men were actually ostracized before the practice fell into disuse after about 416 B.C., when two prominent politicians colluded to have a nonentity ostracized instead of one of themselves. Ostracism is significant for understanding Athenian democracy because it symbolizes the principle that the interest of the group must prevail over that of the individual citizen when the freedom of the group and the freedom of the individual come into conflict in desperate and dangerous cases. Indeed, the first ostracisms had taken place in the 480s B.C., after the ex-tyrant Hippias had appeared with the Persians at Marathon in 490 and some feared he would again become tyrant over the community.

Although Aristides was indeed ostracized in 482 and recalled in 480 to fight the Persians, the anecdote about his encounter with the illiterate citizen sounds apocryphal. Nevertheless, it makes a valid point: the Athenians assumed that the right way to protect democracy was always to trust the majority vote of free-born, adult male citizens, without any restrictions on a man's ability to say what he thought was best for democracy. This conviction required making allowances for irresponsible types like the kind of man depicted in the story about Aristides. It rested on the belief that the cumulative political wisdom of the majority of voters would outweigh the eccentricity and irresponsibility of the few.

The Leadership of Pericles

The idea that democracy at Athens was best served by involving a cross-section of the male citizenry received further backing in the 450s B.C. when Pericles (c. 495–429 B.C.), whose mother was the niece of the democratic reformer Cleisthenes and whose father had been a prominent leader, successfully proposed that state revenues be used to pay a daily stipend to men who served on juries, in the council of five hundred established by Cleisthenes, and in other public offices filled by lot. Without this stipend, poorer men would have found it hard to leave their regular work to serve in these time-consuming positions. By contrast, the most influential public officials—the annual board of ten generals who had responsibility both for military and civil affairs, especially public finances—were elected and received no stipends. They were elected by the assembly rather than chosen by lot because their posts required expertise and experience. Nor were they paid, because mainly rich men like Pericles, who had access to the education required to handle this top job and had the free time to fill it, were expected to win election as generals. Generals were compensated by the prestige their office carried. The stipend that other officials and jurors received was not lavish, certainly no more than an ordinary laborer could earn in a day. Nevertheless, the provision of a living allowance enabled poorer Athenians to serve in government. Like Cleisthenes before him, Pericles was a man of privilege who became the most influential leader in the Athens of his era by devising innovations to strengthen the egalitarian tendencies of Athenian democracy.

Pericles and others of his economic status had inherited enough wealth to spend their time in politics without worrying about money, but remuneration for public service was essential for Athenian democracy if it were truly going to be open to the mass of working men. Pericles' proposal for state stipends for jurors made him overwhelmingly popular with ordinary citizens. Consequently, beginning in the 450s B.C., he was able to introduce dramatic changes in both Athenian foreign and domestic policy. On the latter front, for instance, Pericles sponsored a law in 451 stating that henceforth citizenship would be conferred only on children whose mother and father both were Athenians. Previously, the offspring of Athenian men who married non-Athenian women had been granted citizenship. As Pericles' own maternal grandfather had done, wealthy Athenian men in particular had tended to marry rich foreign women. The new law not only solidified the notion of Athenian identity as special and exclusive but also emphatically recognized the privileged status of Athenian women as possessors of citizenship, putting their citizenship on a par with that of men in the crucially important process of establishing the citizenship of new generations of Athenians. Not long after the passage of the citizenship law, a review of the citizenship rolls of Athens was conducted to expel any persons who had claimed citizenship fraudulently. The advantages of citizenship included, for men, the rights to participate in politics and juries, to influence decisions that directly affected their lives, to have equal protection under the law, and to own land and houses in Athenian territory. Citizen women had fewer direct rights because they were excluded from politics, had to have their male legal guardian speak for them in court, and were not legally entitled to make large financial transactions on their own. They did, however, enjoy the fundamental guarantees of citizenship: the ability to control property and to have the protection of the law for their persons and their property. Female and male citizens alike experienced the advantage of belonging to a city-state that was enjoying unparalleled material prosperity and an enhanced sense of communal identity.

The involvement of Pericles in foreign policy in the early 450s is less clear, and we cannot tell how he felt about the massive Athenian intervention in support of a rebel in Egypt trying to overthrow Persian rule there. This expedition, which began perhaps in 460, ended in utter disaster in 454 with the loss of perhaps two hundred ships and their crews, an overwhelming death toll given that each ship had approximately two hundred men on board. Some of these men would have been allies, not Athenians, but the loss of manpower to Athens must have been large in any case. After this catastrophe, the treasury of the Delian League was moved from Delos to Athens, ostensibly to insure its safety from possible Persian retaliation. Whatever the real motive behind this change, it signified the overwhelming dominance that Athens had achieved as leader of the league by this time.

The 450s were a period of intense military activity by Athens and its allies. At the same time that Athenian and Delian League allies were fighting in Egypt, they were also on campaign on the eastern Mediterranean seacoast against Persian interests. In this same decade Pericles supported an aggressive foreign policy against Spartan interests in Greece. Athenian forces were defeated by Peloponnesian forces at the battle of Tanagra in Boeotia in central Greece in 457, but Athenian troops subsequently gained control of that region and neighboring Phocis as well. Victories were won also over the powerful northern Peloponnesian state of Corinth and the island of Aegina. When Cimon, who had returned from ostracism, died in 450 while leading a naval force against the Persians on the island of Cyprus, the assembly finally decided to end military campaigns directed at Persian interests and sent no more fleets to the eastern Mediterranean.

Operations in Greece also failed to secure enduring victory over Sparta's allies in central Greece, and Boeotia and Phocis threw off Athenian control in 447. In the winter of 446–445 B.C. Pericles engineered a peace treaty with Sparta designed to freeze the balance of power in Greece for thirty years and thus preserve Athenian dominance in the Delian League. He was then able to turn his attention to his political rivals at Athens, who were jealous of his influence over the board of ten generals. Pericles' overwhelming political prominence was confirmed in 443 when he managed to have his chief rival, named Thucydides (not the historian), ostracized instead of himself. He was subsequently elected general fifteen years in a row. His ascendancy was challenged, however, after his rashly taking sides in a local political crisis on the island of Samos led to a war with that valuable Delian League ally from 441 to 439 B.C. The war with Samos was not the first break between Athens and its Delian League allies in the period since 450 when action against the Persians—the main goal of the league in its early years after 478—had ceased to be an active part of the league's mission. Strains developed between Athens and several allied city-states that wished to leave the league and end their tribute payments, which were no longer paying for war with Persia. Pericles' position apparently was that the league was indeed fulfilling its primary mission of keeping the allies safe from Persia; that no Persian fleet was to be seen venturing far from its eastern Mediterranean home base was proof that the allies had no cause for complaint. Inscriptions from the 440s in particular testify to the unhappiness of various Athenian allies and to Athenian determination to retain control over its fractious partners in alliance.

When the city-state of Chalcis on the island of Euboea rebelled from the Delian League in 446 B.C., for example, the Athenians soon put down the revolt and forced the Chalcidians to swear to a new set of arrangements. Copies of the arrangements inscribed on stone were then set up in Chalcis and Athens. The differences in the oaths exchanged by the two sides as recorded in this copy of the inscription found at Athens reveal the imperiousness of Athens's dominance of its Greek allies in this period: "The Athenian Council and all the jurors shall swear the oath as follows: 'I shall not deport Chalcidians from Chalcis or lay waste the city or deprive any individual of his rights or sentence him to a punishment of exile or put him in prison or execute him or seize property from anyone without giving him a chance to speak in court without (the agreement of) the People [i.e., the assembly] of

Athens. I shall not cause a vote to be held, without due notice to attend trial, against either the government or any private individual whatever. When an embassy [from Chalcis] arrives [in Athens], I shall see that it has an audience before the Council and People within ten days when I am in charge of the procedure, so far as I am able. These things I shall guarantee to the Chalcidians if they obey the People of Athens.' The Chalcidians shall swear the oath as follows: 'I shall not rebel against the People of Athens either by trickery or by plot of any kind either by word or by action. Nor shall I join someone else in rebellion and if anyone does start a rebellion, I shall denounce him to the Athenians. I shall pay the dues to the Athenians which I persuade them [to assess], and as I shall be the best and truest possible ally to them. And I shall send assistance to the People of Athens and defend them if anyone attacks the People of Athens, and I shall obey the People of Athens'" (IG, 3d ed., no. 40).

Pericles in the mid-430s faced an even greater challenge than restive and rebellious allies as relations with Sparta greatly worsened despite the provisions of the peace that had been struck in 446/5. An impasse developed when the Spartans finally threatened war unless the Athenians ceased their interference in the affairs of the Corinthian colonies of Corcyra and Potidaea, but Pericles prevailed upon the assembly to refuse all compromises. His critics claimed he was sticking to his hard line against Sparta and insisting on provoking a war in order to revive his fading popularity by whipping up a jingoistic furor in the assembly. Pericles retorted that no accommodation to Spartan demands was possible because Athenian freedom of action was at stake. By 431 B.C. the thirty-years' peace made in 445 B.C. had been shattered beyond repair. The Peloponnesian War (as modern historians call it) between Athens and its allies and Sparta and its allies thus began in 431; at that point no one could know that its violence would drag on for twenty-seven years.

Prosperous Athens

Athens reached the height of its power and prosperity in the decades just before the Peloponnesian War, the period accordingly referred to today as the Golden Age of ancient Athens. Private homes, whether in the city or in the countryside, retained their traditionally modest size even during this period of communal abundance. Farmhouses were usually clustered in villages, while homes in the urban center were wedged tightly against one another along narrow, winding streets. Even the residences of rich people followed the same basic design, which grouped bedrooms, storerooms, work rooms, and dining rooms around the one constant in a Greek house: an open-air courtyard in the center. The courtyard was not open to the street, however, thus insuring privacy, a prime goal of Greek domestic architecture. Wall paintings or works of art were as yet uncommon as decoration in private homes, with sparse furnishings and simple furniture the rule. Sanitary facilities usually consisted of a pit dug just outside the front door, which was emptied by collectors paid to dump manure outside the city at a distance set by law. Poorer people rented houses or small apartments.

Benefactions donated by the rich provided some public improvements, such as the landscaping with shade trees and running tracks that Cimon paid to have installed in open areas. On the edge of the central market square and gathering spot at the heart of the city, the agora, Cimon's brother-in-law paid for the construction of the renowned building known as the Painted Stoa. Stoas were narrow buildings open along one side, and their purpose was to provide shelter from sun or rain. The crowds of men who came to the agora daily for conversation about politics and local affairs would cluster inside the Painted Stoa, whose walls were decorated with paintings of great moments in Greek history commissioned from the most famous painters of the time, Polygnotus and Mikon. That one of the stoa's paintings portrayed the battle of Marathon in which Cimon's father, Miltiades, had won glory was only appropriate since the building had been donated to the city by the husband of Cimon's sister, probably with financial assistance from Cimon himself. The social values of Athenian democracy called for leaders like Cimon and his brother-in-law to provide such gifts for public use to show their good will toward the city-state and thereby earn increased social eminence as their reward. Wealthy citizens were also expected to fulfill costly liturgies, or public services, such as providing theatrical entertainment at city festivals or fitting out a fully equipped warship and then serving on it as a commander. This liturgical system for wealthy men compensated to a certain extent for the lack of any regular income or property taxes in peacetime after the reign of the tyrant Pisistratus. (A levy on property, the *eisphora*, could be voted for war costs.)

Athens received substantial public revenues from harbor fees, sales taxes, and the tribute of the allies. Buildings paid for by public funds from these sources constituted the most conspicuous architecture in the city of the Classical period of the fifth and fourth centuries. The scale of these public buildings was usually no greater than the size required to fulfill their function, such as the complex of buildings on the agora's western edge in which the council of five hundred held its meetings and the public archives were kept. Since the assembly convened in the open air on a hillside above the agora, it required no building at all except for a speaker's platform. In 447 B.C., however, at Pericles' instigation, a great project be-

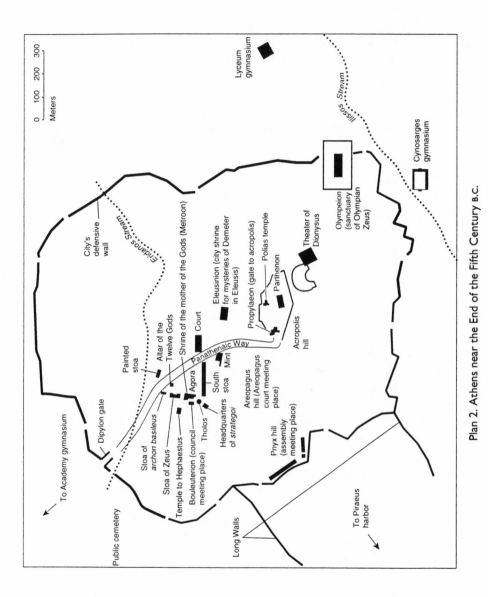

Plan 2. Athens near the End of the Fifth Century B.C.

gan atop the Acropolis, the mesa-like promontory at the center of the city, which towered over the agora. Most conspicuous of all were a mammoth gate building with columns straddling the broad entrance to the acropolis at its western end and a new Athena temple, the Parthenon, to house a towering image of the goddess. These buildings alone cost easily more than the equivalent of a billion dollars in modern terms, a phenomenal sum for an ancient Greek city-state. The program was so expensive that the political enemies of Pericles railed at him for squandering public funds. The finances for the program apparently came in part from the tribute paid by the members of the Delian League. Other funds came from the financial reserves of the goddess, whose sanctuaries, like those of the other gods throughout Greece, received both private donations and public support. The new buildings seemed spectacular not only because they were expensive but also because their large scale, decoration, and surrounding open spaces contrasted so vividly with the private architecture of Athens in the fifth century B.C.

Parthenon, the name of the new temple built for Athena on the Acropolis, meant "the house of the virgin goddess." As the patron goddess of Athens, Athena had long had another sanctuary on the acropolis honoring her in her role as Athena Polias ("guardian of the city"). The focus of this earlier shrine was an olive tree regarded as the sacred symbol of the goddess, who in this capacity provided for the agricultural and thus the essential prosperity of the Athenians. The temple in the Athena Polias sanctuary had largely been destroyed by the Persians in the invasion of 480 B.C. For thirty years, the Athenians purposely left the Acropolis in ruins as a memorial to the sacrifice of their homeland in that war. When at Pericles' urging the assembly decided to rebuild the temples on the Acropolis, it conspicuously turned first not to reconstruction of the olive-tree sanctuary but rather to building the Parthenon. This spectacular new temple was to honor Athena in her capacity as a warrior serving as the divine champion of Athenian military power. Inside the Parthenon was placed a gold-and-ivory statue over thirty feet high portraying the goddess in battle armor and holding in her outstretched hand a six-foot statue of the figure of Victory (Nike in Greek).

Like all Greek temples, the Parthenon was meant as a house for its divinity, not as a gathering place for worshippers. In its general design, the Parthenon was representative of the standard architecture of Greek temples: a rectangular box with doors on a raised platform, a plan that the Greeks probably derived from the stone temples of Egypt. The box was fenced in by columns all around. The columns were carved in the simple style called Doric, in contrast to the more elaborate Ionic or Corinthian styles that have often been imitated in modern buildings (for example, in the Corinthian-style façade of the Supreme Court Building in Washington, D.C.). Only

priests and priestesses could enter the temple, but public religious ceremonies took place around the altar outside its east end.

The Parthenon was extraordinary in its great size and expense, but it
was truly remarkable in the innovation of its refined architecture and elaborate sculptural decoration. Constructed from twenty thousand tons of Attic
marble, it stretched nearly 230 feet in length and 100 feet in width, with
eight columns across the ends instead of the six normally employed in Doric
style, and seventeen instead of thirteen along the sides. These dimensions
gave it a massive look conveying an impression of power. Since perfectly
rectilinear architecture appears curved to the human eye, subtle curves and
inclines were built into the Parthenon to produce an optical illusion of
completely straight lines: the columns were given a slight bulge in their
middles, the corner columns were installed at a slight incline and closer
together, and the platform was made slightly convex. These technical refine-
ments made the Parthenon appear ordered and regular in a way a building
built entirely on straight lines would not. By overcoming the distortions of
nature, the Parthenon's sophisticated architecture made a confident statement about human ability to construct order out of the entropic disorder
of the natural world.

✸The sculptural decoration of the Parthenon also proclaimed Athenians'
confidence about their city-state's relationship with the gods. The Parthenon
had sculptured panels along its exterior above the columns and tableaux of
sculptures in the triangular spaces (pediments) underneath the roof line at
either end of the building. These decorations were part of the Doric style,
but the Parthenon also presented a unique sculptural feature. A continuous
band of figures was carved in relief around the top of the walls inside the
porch formed by the columns along the edges of the building's platform.
This sort of continuous frieze was usually put only on Ionic-style buildings. Adding an Ionic frieze to a Doric temple was a startling departure
from architectural tradition intended to attract notice to its subject, even
though the frieze itself was difficult to see clearly from ground level. The
Parthenon's frieze probably depicted the Athenian religious ritual in which
a procession of citizens paraded to the Acropolis to present to Athena in her
olive-tree sanctuary a new robe woven by specially selected Athenian girls,
although it has also been suggested that the frieze refers to the myth of the
sacrifice of the daughers of Erechtheus to save the city in a time of crisis.
Depicting the procession in motion, like a filmstrip in stone, the frieze
showed men riding spirited horses, women walking along carrying sacred
implements, and the gods gathering at the head of the parade to observe
their human worshippers. As usual in the sculptural decoration on Greek
temples, the frieze sparkled with shiny metal attachments serving, for ex-

ample, as the horsemen's reins and brightly colored paint enlivening the figures and the background.

⁂ No other city-state had ever gone beyond the traditional function of temples — glorifying and paying honor to the community's special deities — by adorning a temple with representations of its citizens. The Parthenon frieze made a unique statement about the relationship between Athens and the gods by showing its citizens in the company of the gods, even if the assembled deities carved in the frieze were understood to be separated from and perhaps invisible to the humans in the procession. A temple adorned with pictures of citizens, albeit idealized citizens of perfect physique and beauty, amounted to a claim of special intimacy between the city-state and the gods and a statement of confidence that these honored deities favored the Athenians. Presumably, this claim reflected the Athenian interpretation of their success in helping to turn back the Persians and thus playing their role as the defenders of Greek civilized life, in achieving leadership of a powerful naval alliance, and in controlling, from their silver mines and the allies' tribute, an amount of revenue that made Athens richer than all its neighbors in mainland Greece. The Parthenon, like the rest of the Periclean building program, paid honor to the gods with whom the city-state was identified and expressed the Athenian view that the gods looked favorably on their empire. Their success, the Athenians would have said, proved that the gods were on their side.

Representing the Body

Like the design of the sculpture attached to the outside of the Parthenon, the enormous size and expense of the free-standing figure of Athena placed inside the temple expressed the innovative and confident spirit of Athens in the mid-fifth century B.C. The statue's creator, the Athenian Phidias, gained such fame that he became a close friend of Pericles and was invited by other Greek states to make great statues for their temples, such as the giant seated Zeus for the main temple at Olympia.

Other artists as well as sculptors were experimenting with new techniques and artistic approaches in this period, but free-standing sculpture provides the clearest demonstration of the innovation and variety in the representation of the human body that characterized Greek art in the fifth century. Such sculptures could either be public in the sense of having been paid for with state funds, as was the Parthenon, or private, but they did not serve as pieces of private art in the modern sense. Greeks who ordered statues privately from sculptors had not yet developed the habit of using them to decorate the interior of their homes. Instead, they set them up on public display for a variety of purposes. Privately commissioned statues of gods could be placed in a sanctuary as a proof of devotion. In the tradition of offering lovely crafted objects to divinities as commemorations of important personal experiences such as economic success or victories in athletic contests, people also donated sculptures of physically beautiful human beings to the sanctuaries of the gods as gifts of honor. Wealthy families would commission statues of their deceased members, especially if they had died young, to be placed above their graves as memorials of their virtue. In every case, private statues were meant to be seen by other people. In this sense, then, private sculpture in the Golden Age served a public function: it broadcast a message to an audience.

Archaic statues had been characterized by a stiff posture imitating the style of standing figures from Egypt. Egyptian sculptors had gone on producing this style unchanged for centuries. Greek artists, on the other hand, had begun to change their style by the time of the Persian Wars, and the fifth century B.C. saw new poses become ever more prevalent in free-standing sculpture, continuing an earlier evolution toward movement visible in the sculpture attached to temples. Human males were still being generally portrayed nude as athletes or warriors, while women were still clothed in fine robes. But their postures and their physiques were evolving toward ever more naturalistic renderings. While Archaic male statues had been made striding forward with their left legs, arms held rigidly at their sides, male statues might now have bent arms or the body's weight on either leg. Their musculature was anatomically correct rather than sketchy and almost impressionistic, as had been the style in the sixth century B.C. Female statues, too, now had more relaxed poses and clothing, which hung in such a way as to hint at the shape of the body underneath instead of disguising it. The faces of Classical sculptures, however, reflected an impassive calm rather than the smiles that had characterized Archaic figures.

Bronze was the preferred material of the sculptors who devised these daring new styles, although marble was also popular. Creating bronze statues, which were cast in molds made from clay models, required a particularly well-equipped workshop with furnaces, tools, and foundry workers skilled in metallurgy. Because sculptors and artists labored with their hands, the wealthy elite regarded them as workers of low social status, and only the most famous ones, like Phidias, could move in high society. Properly prepared bronze had the tensile strength to allow outstretched poses of arms and legs, which could not be done in marble without supports. (Hence the intrusive tree trunks and other such supporting members introduced in the marble copies made in Roman times of Greek statues in bronze. These Roman copies of the sort commonly seen in modern museums are often the only surviving examples of the originals.) The strength and malleability of bronze allowed innovative sculptors like the Athenian Myron and Polyclitus of Argos to push the development of the free-standing statue of the human form to its physical limits. Myron, for example, sculpted a discus thrower crouched at the top of his backswing, a pose far from the relaxed and serene symmetry of early Archaic statuary. The figure not only assumes an asymmetrical pose but also seems to burst with the tension of the athlete's effort. Polyclitus's renowned statue of a walking man carrying a spear is posed to give a different impression from every angle of viewing and to impart a powerful sensation of motion. The same is true of the famous statue by an unknown sculptor of a female (perhaps the goddess of love, Aphrodite) adjusting her diaphanous robe with one upraised arm. The message these statues conveyed to their ancient audience was one of energy, motion, and asymmetry in delicate balance. Archaic statues impressed a viewer with their appearance of stability; not even a hard shove looked likely to budge them. Statues of the Classical period, by contrast, showed greater range, a variety of poses and impressions. The spirited movement of some of these statues suggests the energy of the times but also the possibility of change and instability that underlies even a Golden Age.

7

Culture and Society in Classical Athens

Old and New in the Athenian Golden Age

Nowhere is the dominance of Athens in modern treatments of ancient Greek history more pronounced than in discussion of the Classical period of the fifth and fourth centuries B.C., and within that period nowhere is Athens more prominent than in the fifth century. The prosperity and cultural achievements of Athens in the mid-fifth century have led to this period in Athenian history being called a Golden Age. The state of the surviving evidence, which consistently comes more from Athens than from other city-states, and the focus of modern popular interest in ancient Greece, which has traditionally remained on the magnificent architectural remains of Athens, have combined to push Greek history of this period mightily in the direction of Athenian history. This limitation must be kept in mind so that one can avoid the trap of substituting "Greece" for "Athens" when talking about this period.

That being said, it is important to add that Athenian prominence in the story of Classical Greece is no accident and reflects the unprecedented changes that occurred in the culture and society of Athens in the fifth century B.C. At the same time, central aspects of Athenian life remained unchanged. The result was a mix of innovation and continuity that created tensions sometimes productive and sometimes corrosive. Tragic drama developed as

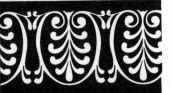

a publicly supported art form performed before mass audiences that explored serious ethical issues of concern to the community. Also emerging in the fifth century was a new and—to traditionalists—upsetting form of education for wealthy young men with ambitions in public life. For upperclass women, public life remained constrained by the limitations of modesty and their exclusion from the political affairs that were the lifeblood of many of their husbands. Women of the poorer classes, however, might have more contact with the public, male world because they had to work to help support their families. The interplay of continuity and change created tensions that were tolerable until the pressure of conflict with Sparta in the Peloponnesian War strained Athenian society to the breaking point. All these changes took place against the background of traditional Greek religion, which permeated public and private life.

Classical Greek Religion

As the design of the Parthenon revealed so dramatically, the Athenians in the mid-fifth century B.C. believed they enjoyed the favor of the gods and were willing to spend public money to erect monuments in honor of the deities protecting them. This belief corresponded to the basic tenet of Greek religion: humans both as individuals and as groups paid honors to the gods to thank them for blessings received and to receive blessings in return. Those honors consisted of public sanctuaries, sacrifices, gifts to the sanctuaries, and festivals of songs, dances, prayers, and processions. A seventh-century B.C. bronze statuette in the Boston Museum of Fine Arts, which a man named Mantiklos gave to a (now unknown) sanctuary of Apollo to honor the god, makes clear why individuals gave such gifts. On its legs Mantiklos inscribed his understanding of the transaction: "Mantiklos gave this from his share to the Far Darter of the Silver Bow [Apollo]; now you, Apollo, do something for me in return." This idea of reciprocity between gods and humans underlay the Greek understanding of the divine. Gods did not love human beings, except sometimes literally in mythological stories of gods taking earthly lovers and producing half-divine children. Rather, they supported humans who paid them honor and avoided offending them. Gods whom humans offended sent in response such calamities as famines, earthquake, epidemic disease, or defeat in war.

The greatest difficulty for human beings lay in anticipating what might offend a god. Fortunately, some of the gods' expectations were codified in a moral order with rules of behavior for human beings. For example, the Greeks believed that the gods demanded hospitality for strangers and proper burial for family members and that the gods punished human arrogance and murderous violence. When things went awry between humans and gods,

458 B.C.: Aeschylus's trilogy of tragedies, the *Oresteia (Agamemnon, Libation Bearers, Eumenides)*, produced at Athens.

c. 450 B.C.: The sophist Protagoras makes his first visit to Athens.

c. 447 B.C.: Sophocles' tragedy *Ajax* probably produced at Athens.

444 B.C.: Protagoras makes laws for colony of Athenians and others being sent to Thurii in southern Italy.

c. 441 B.C.: Sophocles' tragedy *Antigone* produced at Athens.

431 B.C.: Euripides' tragedy *Medea* produced at Athens.

430s B.C.: Increasing political tension at Athens as Sparta threatens war.

---

oracles, dreams, divination, and the prophecies of seers were all regarded as clues to what humans might have done to anger the gods. Offenses could be acts such as forgetting a sacrifice, violating the sanctity of a temple area, or breaking an oath or sworn agreement made to another person. The gods were regarded as especially concerned with certain transgressions (such as violating oaths), but as generally uninterested in common crimes, which humans had to police for themselves. Homicide, however, the gods were thought to punish by casting a state of pollution (*miasma*, as it was called) upon murderers and upon all those around them as well. Unless the members of the affected group took steps to purify themselves by punishing the murderer, they could all expect to suffer divine punishment such as bad harvests or disease. Since a corpse itself, whether a murder victim or not, exuded a miasma, the need for ritual purification through proper burial procedures was keenly felt.

The Greeks believed their gods lived easy lives, exposed to pain sometimes in their dealings with one another or sometimes sad at the misfortunes of favored humans but essentially carefree in their immortality. The twelve most important of the gods, headed by Zeus, were envisioned assembling for banquets atop Mount Olympus, the highest peak in mainland Greece. Like the prickly warriors of the stories of Homer, the gods were much concerned with slights to their honor. "I am well aware that the gods are envious of human success and prone to disrupt our affairs," is Solon's summary of their nature in one famous (and probably fictitious) anecdote in which he is portrayed as giving advice to another famous person, in this case Croesus before the Lydian king lost his kingdom to the Persians (Herodotus, *History* 1.32).

To interact with a god, worshippers prayed, sang hymns of praise, offered sacrifices, and presented offerings at the god's sanctuary. In the sanctuaries of the gods a person could honor and thank them for blessings and propitiate them when misfortune, taken as a sign of divine anger at human behavior, had struck the petitioner. Private individuals offered sacrifices at home with the household gathered around, and sometimes the family's slaves were allowed to join the gathering. The sacrifices of public cults were conducted by priests and priestesses, who were in most cases chosen from the citizen body as a whole and otherwise existed as ordinary citizens. The priests and priestesses of Greek cults were usually attached to a sanctuary or shrine and did not seek to influence political or social matters. Their special knowledge consisted in knowing how to perform the gods' rites according to tradition. They were not guardians of theological orthodoxy because Greek religion had no systematic theology or canonical dogma, nor did it have any institutions comparable to today's religious institutions that oversee doctrine.

The ritual of sacrifice provided the primary occasion of contact between the gods and their worshippers. The great majority of sacrifices took place as regularly scheduled events on the community's civic calendar. At Athens the first eight days of every month were marked by demonstrations of the citizens' piety toward the deities of the city-state's official cults. The third day of each month, for example, was celebrated as Athena's birthday and the sixth as that of Artemis, the goddess of wild animals, who was also the special patroness of the Athenian council of five hundred. Artemis's brother, Apollo, was honored on the following day. Athens boasted of having the largest number of religious festivals in all of Greece, with nearly half the days of the year featuring one, some large and some small. Not everyone attended all the festivals, and hired laborers' contracts would specify how many days off they received to attend religious ceremonies. Major occasions such as the Panathenaic festival, whose procession probably was portrayed on the Parthenon frieze, attracted large crowds of both women and men. The Panathenaic festival honored Athena not only with sacrifices and parades but also with contests in music, dancing, poetry, and athletics. Valuable prizes were awarded to the winners. Some festivals were for women only: one was the three-day festival for married women in honor of the goddess Demeter, the protectress of agriculture and life-giving fertility.

Different cults had differing rituals, but sacrifice served as their centering experience. Sacrifices ranged from the bloodless offering of fruits, vegetables, and small cakes to the slaughter of large animals. As noted in the section on prehistory, it seems possible that the tradition of animal sacrifice originally stemmed from the practice of prehistoric hunters, for whom such rites might have expressed their uneasiness about the paradox of having to kill other living beings so that they could eat and survive themselves. The Greeks of the Classical period sacrificed valuable domestic animals such as cattle, which their land supported in only small numbers, to express their reverence for the majesty of the gods, to ensure their own good fortune, to symbolize their control over the animal world, and to have a rare meal of meat. Looking back on fifth-century Athens, the orator Lysias explained the necessity for public sacrifice: "Our ancestors handed down to us the most powerful and prosperous community in Greece by performing the prescribed sacrifices. It is therefore proper for us to offer the same sacrifices as they, if only for the sake of the success which has resulted from those rites" (*Orations* 30.18). The sacrifice of a large animal provided an occasion for the community to reassemble to reaffirm its ties to the divine world and, by sharing the roasted meat of the sacrificed beast, for the worshippers to benefit personally from a good relationship with the gods.

The actual sacrificing of the animal proceeded along strict rules meant to ensure the purity of the occasion, and the elaborate procedures required for a blood sacrifice show how seriously and solemnly the Greeks regarded the sacrificial killing of animals. Sacrifices were performed at altars placed outside in front of temples. The victim had to be an unblemished domestic animal, specially decorated with garlands and induced to approach the altar as if of its own volition. The assembled crowd had to maintain a strict silence to avoid possibly impure remarks. The sacrificer sprinkled water on the victim's head so it would, in shaking its head in response to the sprinkle, appear to consent to its death. After washing his hands, the sacrificer scattered barley grains on the altar fire and the victim's head, and then cut a lock of the animal's hair to throw on the fire. Following a prayer, he swiftly cut the animal's throat while musicians played flute-like pipes and female worshippers screamed, presumably to express the group's ritual sorrow at the victim's death. The carcass was then butchered, with some portions thrown on the altar fire so their aromatic smoke could waft upward to the god of the cult. The rest of the meat was then distributed among the worshippers.

Greek religion encompassed many activities besides those of the cults of the twelve Olympian deities. Families marked important moments like birth, marriage, and death with prayers, sacrifices, and rituals. In the fifth century it became increasingly common for ordinary citizens, not just members of the elite, to make offerings at the tombs of their relatives. Nearly everyone consulted seers about the meanings of dreams and omens and sought out magicians for spells to improve their love lives or curses to harm their enemies. Particularly important both to the community and to individuals were what we call hero cults, rituals performed at the tomb of a man or woman, usually from the distant past, whose remains were thought to retain special power. Athenian soldiers in the battle of Marathon in 490 B.C., for example, had reported having seen the ghost of the hero Theseus leading the way against the Persians. When Cimon in 475 B.C. brought back to Athens bones agreed to be those of Theseus, who was said to have died on a distant island, the people of Athens celebrated the occasion as a major triumph for their community and had the remains installed in a special shrine at the center of the city. The power of a hero's remains was local, whether for revealing the future through oracles, for healing injuries and disease, or for providing assistance in war. The only hero to whom cults were established internationally, all over the Greek world, was the strongman Heracles (Hercules). His superhuman feats in overcoming monsters and generally doing the impossible gave him an appeal as a protector in many city-states.

International in a different sense was the cult of Demeter and her daughter Kore (or Persephone), whose headquarters were located at Eleusis, a settlement on the west coast of Attica. The central rite of this cult was called the Mysteries, a series of ceremonies of initiation into the secret knowledge of the cult. If they were free of pollution, all free speakers of Greek from anywhere in the world — women and men, adults and children — were eligible for initiation, as were some slaves who worked in the sanctuary. Initiation proceeded in several stages. The main stage took place during an annual festival lasting almost two weeks. So important were the Eleusinian Mysteries that the states of Greece honored an international agreement setting a period of fifty-five days for guaranteed safe transit through their territories for travelers to and from the festival. Prospective initiates participated in a complicated set of ceremonies that culminated in the revelation of Demeter's central secret after a day of fasting. The revelation was performed in an initiation hall constructed solely for this purpose. Under a roof fifty-five yards square supported on a forest of interior columns, the hall held three thousand people standing around its sides on tiered steps. The most eloquent proof of the sanctity attached to the Mysteries of Demeter and Kore is that throughout the thousand years during which the rites were celebrated, we know of no one who ever revealed the secret. To this day, all we know is that it involved something done, something said, and something shown. It is certain, however, that initiates expected to fare better in their lives on earth and were also promised a better fate after death. "Richly blessed is the mortal who has seen these rites; but whoever is not an initiate and has no share in them, that one never has an equal portion after death, down in the gloomy darkness," are the words describing the benefits of initiation in the sixth-century B.C. poem *The Hymn to Demeter* (lines 480–482).

The Eleusinian Mysteries were not the only mystery cult of the Greek world, nor were they unique in their concern with what lay beyond death for human beings. Most mystery cults emphasized protection for initiates in their daily lives, whether against ghosts, illness, poverty, shipwrecks, or the countless other daily dangers of life. Divine protection was provided, however, as a reward for appropriate conduct, not by any abstract belief in the gods. For the ancient Greeks, gods expected honors and rites, and Greek religion required action from its worshippers. Greeks had to say prayers and sing hymns honoring the gods, perform sacrifices, and undergo purifications. These rites represented an active response to the precarious conditions of human life in a world in which early death from disease, accident, or war was commonplace. Furthermore, the Greeks believed the same gods were responsible for sending both good and bad into the world. As Solon warned Croesus, "In all matters look to the end, and to how it turns out. For many people have enjoyed prosperous happiness as a divine gift, only afterwards to be uprooted utterly" (Herodotus, *History* 1.32). The Greek gods mirrored human frailty in that each could be both good and evil. As a result, the Greeks had no expectation that they would achieve paradise at some future time when evil forces would finally be vanquished forever. Their assessment of existence made no allowance for change in the relationship between the human and the divine. That relationship encompassed sorrow as well as joy, punishment in the here and now, with perhaps the uncertain hope for favored treatment both in this life and in an afterlife for initiates of the Eleusinian Mysteries and other similar cults.

Tragic Drama and Public Life

The problematic relationship between gods and humans formed the basis of Classical Athens's most enduring cultural innovation: the tragic dramas performed over three days at the major annual festival of the god Dionysus held in the late spring. These plays, still read and produced on stage today, were presented in ancient Athens as part of a drama contest, in keeping with the competitive spirit characteristic of many events held in the gods' honor. Athenian tragedy reached its peak as a dramatic form in the fifth century B.C., as did comedy, the other equally significant public drama of Athens (which will be discussed subsequently).

Every year, one of Athens's magistrates chose three playwrights to present four plays each at the festival of Dionysus. Three were tragedies and one a satyr play, so named from the actors portraying the half-human, half-animal (horse or goat) satyrs who were featured in this more light-hearted form of theater. The term *tragedy*—derived, for reasons now lost, from two Greek words meaning "goat" and "song"—referred to plays with plots involving fierce conflicts and characters representing powerful human and divine forces. Tragedies were composed in verse in elevated, solemn language and frequently based on stories about the violent consequences of the interaction between gods and people. The story commonly ended with a resolution to the trouble—after considerable suffering and bloodshed.

The performance of Athenian tragedies bore little resemblance to conventional modern theater productions. They took place during the daytime in an outdoor theater sacred to the god Dionysus, located on the slope of the southern hillside of Athens's Acropolis. This theater of Dionysus held around fourteen thousand spectators overlooking an open circular area in front of a slightly raised stage platform. Seating was temporary in the fifth century, and the first stone theater was not installed until the fourth century. To ensure fairness in the competition, all tragedies were required to have the same-size cast, all of whom were men: three actors to play the speaking roles of all male and female characters and fifteen chorus members. Although the chorus leader sometimes engaged in dialogue with the actors, the chorus primarily performed songs and dances in the circular area in front of the stage, called the orchestra. Since all the actors' lines were in verse with special rhythms, the musical aspect of the chorus's role was simply an elaboration of the overall poetic nature of Athenian tragedy.

Even though scenery on the stage was sparse, a good tragedy presented a vivid spectacle. The chorus wore elaborate decorative costumes and trained hard to put on intricate dance routines. The actors, who wore masks, used broad gestures and booming voices to reach the upper tier of seats. A powerful voice was crucial to a tragic actor because words represented the heart of a tragedy, in which dialogue and long speeches were far more common than physical action. Special effects were, however, part of the spectacle. For example, a crane allowed actors playing the roles of gods to fly suddenly onto the stage, like superheroes in a modern movie. The actors playing the lead roles, called the protagonists ("first competitors"), were also competing against each other for the designation of best actor. So important was it to have a first-rate lead actor to provide a successful tragedy that protagonists were assigned by lot to the competing playwrights of the year to give all three of them an equal chance to have the finest cast. Great protagonists, who had to have prodigious vocal skills, became enormously popular figures, although, unlike many playwrights, they were not usually members of the social elite.

The author of a slate of tragedies in the festival of Dionysus also served as director, producer, musical composer, choreographer, and sometimes even one of the actors. Only men of some wealth could afford the prodigious amounts of time such work demanded because the prizes in the tragedy competition were probably modest. As citizens, playwrights also fulfilled the normal military and political obligations of an Athenian man. The best-known Athenian tragedians—Aeschylus (525–456 B.C.), Sophocles

(c. 496–406 B.C.), and Euripides (c. 485–406 B.C.)—all served in the army, held public office at some point in their careers, or did both. Aeschylus fought at Marathon and Salamis; the epitaph on his tombstone, which says nothing of his great success as a playwright, reveals how highly he valued his contribution to his city-state as a citizen-soldier: "Under this stone lies Aeschylus the Athenian, son of Euphorion . . . the grove at Marathon and the Persians who landed there were witnesses to his courage" (Pausanias, *Description of Greece* 1.14.5).

Aeschylus's pride in his military service to his homeland points to a fundamental characteristic of Athenian tragedy: it was at its base a public art form, an expression of the polis that explored the ethical quandaries of human beings in conflict with the gods and with one another in a polis-like community. Even though the plots of most tragedies were based on stories that hearkened back to a time before the polis, such as tales of the Trojan War, the moral issues illuminated by the plays always pertained to the society and obligations of citizens in a polis. Sophocles, for example, presented probably in the early 440s a play entitled *Ajax*, the name of the second-best warrior (Achilles had been preeminent) in the Greek army fighting the Trojans. When his fellow Greeks voted to award the armor of the now-dead Achilles to the wily Odysseus instead of himself, Ajax went berserk on a rampage against his former friends. The goddess Athena thwarted Ajax because he had once rejected her help in battle. Disgraced by his failure to secure revenge, Ajax committed suicide despite the pleas of his wife, Tecmessa, not to abandon his family in the midst of his enemies. Odysseus then stepped in to convince the hostile Greek chiefs to bury Ajax because the future security of the army and the obligations of friendship demanded that they obey the divine injunction always to bury the dead, regardless of the person's conduct while living. Odysseus's arguments in favor of burying Ajax anachronistically treat the army as if it were a polis, and his use of persuasive speech to achieve accommodation of conflicting individual interests to the benefit of the community corresponds to the way in which disputes in the polis were supposed to be resolved.

In *Antigone* (probably produced in 441 B.C.), Sophocles presented a drama of harsh conflict between the family's moral obligation to bury its dead in obedience to divine command and the male-dominated city-state's need to preserve its order and defend its values. Antigone, the daughter of Oedipus, the now-deceased former king of Thebes, comes into conflict with her uncle, the new ruler, when he forbids the burial of one of Antigone's two brothers on the grounds that he was a traitor. This brother had attacked Thebes after the other brother had broken an agreement to share the kingship. Both brothers died in the ensuing battle, but Antigone's uncle had allowed the burial only of the brother who had remained in power. When Antigone defies her uncle by symbolically burying the allegedly traitorous brother, her uncle condemns her to die. He realizes his error only when sacrifices to the gods go wrong. His decision to punish Antigone ends in personal disaster when his son and then his wife kill themselves in despair. In this horrifying story of anger and death, Sophocles deliberately exposes the right and wrong on each side of the conflict. Although Antigone's uncle eventually acknowledges a leader's responsibility to listen to his people, the play offers no easy resolution of the competing interests of divinely sanctioned moral tradition expressed by a woman and the political rules of the state enforced by a man.

A striking aspect of Greek tragedies is that these plays written and performed by men frequently portray women as central, active figures. At one level, the frequent depiction of women in tragedy allowed men accustomed to spending most of their time with other men to peer into what they imagined the world of women must be like. But the heroines portrayed in fifth-century Athenian tragedies also served to explore the tensions inherent in the moral code of contemporary society by strongly reacting to men's violations of that code, especially as it pertained to the family. The heroines through their actions are made to display masculine qualities. Sophocles' Antigone, for example, confronts the male ruler of her city because he deprived her family of its traditional prerogative to bury its dead. Antigone is remarkable in fearlessly criticizing a powerful man in a public debate about right and wrong. Sophocles, in other words, shows a woman who can speak like an Athenian man.

So, too, does Aeschylus have Clytemnestra, the wife of Agamemnon, the leader of the Greek army in the Trojan War, act like a man in his tragedy entitled *Agamemnon* (produced in 458 B.C.). In the story, Clytemnestra takes a lover and rules her city in her husband's place when Agamemnon subverts his marriage, first by sacrificing their daughter to appease an angry goddess who is holding up the army and then by staying away from home for ten years to besiege Troy. When Agamemnon finally returns, he brings with him a captive Trojan princess whom he intends to install in his home as a concubine. In rage at this final insult to her status as wife and mother, Clytemnestra murders Agamemnon, ensuring tragic destruction but avenging her honor.

Of the three best-known tragedians, Euripides depicts the most sensational heroines. The Euripidean heroine Medea, the main character in the *Medea* produced in 431 B.C., reacts with a shattering violence when Jason, her husband, proposes to divorce her in order to marry a richer, more prominent woman. Jason's plans flout the social code governing marriage: a husband had no moral right to divorce a wife who had fulfilled her primary duty by bearing legitimate children, especially sons. To gain revenge, Medea uses magic to kill her and Jason's children and his prospective bride. Medea's murder of her own children subverts her proper role as wife and mother, yet she argues forcefully for a reevaluation of that role. She insists that women who bear children are due respect at least commensurate with that granted men who fight as hoplites: "People say that we women lead a safe life at home, while men have to go to war. What fools they are! I would much rather fight in the phalanx three times than give birth to a child only once" (248–251).

Despite their often gloomy outcomes, Sophocles' plays were overwhelmingly popular, and he earned the reputation as Athens's favorite author of tragedies. In a sixty-year career as a playwright, he competed in the dramatic festival about thirty times, winning at least twenty times and never finishing with less than second prize. Since winning plays were selected by a panel of ordinary male citizens who were apparently influenced by the audience's reaction, Sophocles' record clearly means his works appealed to the large number of citizens attending the drama competition of the festival of Dionysus. These audiences most likely included women as well as men, and the issues raised by the plays certainly gave prominence to gender relations both in the family and in the community. The spectators' precise understanding of Sophocles' messages and those of others' tragedies we cannot know, but they must have been aware that the central characters of the plays were figures who fell into disaster from positions of power and prestige. Their reversals of fortune come about not because they are absolute villains but because, as human beings, they are susceptible to a lethal mixture of error, ignorance, and hubris ("violent arrogance"). The Athenian Empire was at its height when audiences at Athens were seeing the plays of Sophocles. The presentation of the plays at the festival of Dionysus was preceded by a procession in the theater to display the revenues of Athens received from the tribute of the allies in the Delian League. All the Athenian men in the audience were actual or potential combat veterans in the citizen militia of the city-state and thus personally acquainted with the possibility of having to endure or inflict violence in the service of their community. Thoughtful spectators would have perhaps reflected on the possibility that Athens's current power and prestige, managed as it was by human beings, remained hostage to the same forces that the playwrights taught controlled the often bloody fates of the heroes and heroines of tragedy. Tragedies certainly had appeal because they were engrossing purely as entertainment, but they also had an educative function: to remind citizens, especially those who in the assembly made policy for the polis, that success and the force needed to maintain it engendered problems of a moral complexity too formidable to be fathomed casually or arrogantly.

Athenian Life for Women

Athenian women exercised power and earned status in both private and public life through their central roles in the family and religion, respectively. Their absence from politics, however, meant that their contributions to the city-state might be overlooked by men. One heroine in a tragedy by Euripides, Melanippe, vigorously expresses this judgment in a famous speech denouncing men who denigrate women: "Empty is the slanderous blame men place on women; it is no more than the twanging of a bowstring without an arrow; women are better than men, and I will prove it: women make agreements without having to have witnesses to guarantee their honesty. . . . Women manage the household and preserve its valuable property. Without a wife, no household is clean or happily prosperous. And in matters pertaining to the gods—this is our most important contribution—we have the greatest share. In the oracle at Delphi we propound the will of Apollo, and at the oracle of Zeus at Dodona we reveal the will of Zeus to any Greek who wishes to know it. Men cannot rightly perform the sacred rites for the Fates and the Anonymous Goddesses, but women make them flourish . . ." (*Melanippe the Captive*, fragment 13a; production date uncertain).

Greek drama sometimes emphasized the areas in which Athenian women contributed to the polis: publicly by acting as priestesses and privately by bearing and raising legitimate children, the future citizens of the city-state, and by serving as managers of the household's property. Women's property rights in Classical Athens reflected both the importance of the control of property by women and the Greek predisposition to promote the formation and preservation of households headed by property-owning men. Under Athenian democracy, women could control property, even land —the most valued possession in their society—through inheritance and dowry, although they faced more legal restrictions than men did when they wanted to sell their property or give it away as gifts. Like men, women were supposed to preserve their property to be handed down to their children. Daughters did not inherit a portion of their father's property if there were any living sons, but perhaps one household in five had only daughters, to whom the father's property fell. Women could also inherit from other male relatives who had no male offspring. A woman's regular share in her father's estate came to her in her dowry at marriage. A son whose father was still alive at the time of the son's marriage similarly might receive a share of his inheritance to allow him to set up a household. A bride's husband had legal control over the property in his wife's dowry, and their respective holdings frequently became commingled. In this sense husband and wife were co-owners of the household's common property, which had to be allotted between its separate owners only if the marriage were dissolved. The husband was legally responsible for preserving the dowry and using it for the support and comfort of his wife and any children she bore him, and a groom often had to put up valuable land of his own as collateral to guarantee the safety of his bride's dowry. Upon her death, the dowry became the inheritance of her children. The expectation that a woman would have a dowry tended to encourage marriage within groups of similar wealth and status. As with the rules governing women's rights to inheritances, customary dowry arrangements supported the society's goal of enabling males to establish and maintain households—because daughters' dowries were usually smaller in value than their brothers' inheritances—and therefore kept the bulk of a father's property attached to his sons.

The same goal shows up clearly in Athenian law concerning heiresses. If a father died leaving only a daughter to survive him, his property devolved upon her as his heiress, but she did not own it in the modern sense of being able to dispose of it as she pleased. Instead, Athenian law (in the simplest case) required her father's closest male relative—her official guardian after her father's death—to marry her himself, with the aim of producing a son. The inherited property then belonged to that son when he reached adulthood. As a disputant in a fourth-century court case about an heiress said, "We think that the closest kin should marry her and that the property should belong to the heiress until she has sons, who will take it over two years after coming of age" (Isaeus, *Orations*, fragment 25).

The law theoretically applied regardless of whether the heiress was already married (without any sons) or whether the male relative already had a wife. The heiress and the male relative were both supposed to divorce their present spouses and marry each other, although in practice this aspect of the rule could be circumvented by various legal maneuvers. The law on heiresses served to keep the property in their fathers' families. The practice also prevented rich men from getting richer by engineering deals with wealthy heiresses' guardians to marry and therefore merge estates, and, above all, it prevented property from piling up in the hands of unmarried women. At Sparta, Aristotle reported, precisely this agglomeration of wealth took place as women inherited land or received it in their dowries without—to Aristotle's way of thinking—adequate regulations promoting remarriage. He claimed that women in this way had come to own 40 percent of Spartan territory. The law at Athens was more successful at regulating women's control over property in the interests of promoting the formation of households headed by property-owning men.

Medea's comment in Euripides' play bearing her name that women were said to lead a safe life at home reflected the expectation in Athenian society that a woman from the propertied class would avoid frequent or close contact with men who were not members of her own family or its circle of friends. Women of this socio-economic level were therefore supposed to spend much of their time in their own homes or the homes of women friends. There women dressed, slept, and worked in interior rooms and in the central open courtyard characteristic of Greek houses. Male visitors from outside the family were banned from entering the rooms in a house allotted as women's space, which did not mean an area to which women were confined but the places where they conducted their activities in a flexible use of domestic space varying from house to house. There women would spin wool for clothing while chatting with female friends over for a visit, play with their children, direct the work of female slaves, and offer their opinions on various matters to male family members as they came and went through the courtyard. One room in a house was usually set aside as the men's dining room (andron), where the husband could entertain male friends, reclining on couches set against the wall in Greek fashion, without their coming into contact with the women of his family. Poor women had much less time for domestic activities because they, like their husbands, sons, and brothers, had to leave their homes—often only a crowded rental apartment—to find work. They often set up small stalls to sell bread, vegetables, simple clothing, or trinkets. Poor men sought jobs as laborers in workshops or foundries or on construction projects.

Expectations of female modesty dictated that a woman with servants who answered the door of her house herself would be reproached as careless of her reputation. So, too, a proper woman went out only for an appropriate reason. Fortunately, Athenian life offered many such occasions: religious festivals, funerals, childbirths at the houses of relatives and friends, and trips to workshops to buy shoes or other articles. Sometimes a woman's husband would escort her, but more often she was accompanied only by a servant or female friends and had more opportunity for independent action. Social protocol demanded that men not speak the names of respectable women in public conversations and speeches in court unless practical necessity demanded it.

Since they stayed inside or in the shade so much, women rich enough not to have to work maintained very pale complexions. This pallor was much admired as a sign of an enviable life of leisure and wealth, much as an even, all-over tan is valued today for the same reason. Women regularly used powdered white lead as make-up to give themselves a suitably pallid look. Presumably, many upper-class women valued their life of limited contact with men outside the household as a badge of their superior social status. In a gender-divided society such as that of the wealthy at Athens, the primary opportunities for personal relationships in a wealthy woman's life probably came in her contact with her children and the other women with whom she spent most of her time.

The social restrictions on women's freedom of movement served men's goal of avoiding uncertainty about the paternity of children by limiting opportunities for adultery among wives and protecting the virginity of daughters. Given the importance of citizenship as the defining political structure of the city-state and of a man's personal freedom, Athenians felt it crucially important to be certain a boy truly was his father's son and not the offspring of some other man, who could conceivably even be a foreigner or a slave. Furthermore, the preference for keeping property in the father's line meant that the boys who inherited a father's property needed to be his legitimate sons. In this patriarchal system, citizenship and property rights therefore led to restrictions on women's freedom of movement in society. Women who did bear legitimate children, however, immediately earned a higher status and greater freedom in the family, as explained, for example, by an Athenian man in this excerpt from his remarks before a court in a case in which he had killed an adulterer whom he had caught with his wife: "After my marriage, I initially refrained from bothering my wife very much, but neither did I allow her too much independence. I kept an eye on her . . . . But after she had a baby, I started to trust her more and put her in charge of all my things, believing we now had the closest of relationships" (Lysias, Orations 1.6). Bearing male children brought special honor to a woman because sons meant security for parents. Adult sons could appear in court in support of their parents in lawsuits and protect them in the streets of the city, which for most of its history had no regular police force. By law, sons were required to support their parents in old age, a necessity in a society with no state-sponsored system for the support of the elderly, such as Social Security in the United States. So intense was the pressure to produce sons that stories were common of barren women who smuggled in babies born to slaves to pass them off as their own. Such tales, whose truth is hard to gauge, were credible only because husbands customarily stayed away at childbirth.

Men, unlike women, had sexual opportunities outside marriage that carried no penalties. "Certainly you don't think men beget children out of sexual desire?" wrote the upper-class author Xenophon. "The streets and the brothels are swarming with ways to take care of that" (*Memorabilia* 2.2.4). Besides having sex with female slaves, who could not refuse their masters, men could choose among various classes of prostitutes, depending on how much money they had to spend. A man could not keep a prostitute in the same house as his wife without causing trouble, but otherwise he incurred no disgrace by paying for sex. The most expensive female prostitutes the Greeks called "companions" (*hetairai*). Usually from another city-state than the one in which they worked, companions supplemented their physical attractiveness with the ability to sing and play musical instruments at men's dinner parties (to which wives were not invited). Many companions lived precarious lives subject to exploitation or even violence at the hands of their male customers. The most accomplished companions, however, could attract lovers from the highest levels of society and become sufficiently rich to live in luxury on their own. This independent existence strongly distinguished them from other women, as did the freedom to control their own sexuality. Equally distinctive was their cultivated ability to converse with men in public. Like the geisha of Japan, companions entertained men especially with their witty, bantering conversation. Their characteristic skill at clever taunts and verbal snubs endowed companions with a power of speech denied to proper women. Only very rich citizen women of advanced years, such as Elpinike, the sister of Cimon, occasionally enjoyed a similar freedom of expression. She, for example, once publicly rebuked Pericles for having boasted about the Athenian conquest of Samos after its rebellion. When other Athenian women were praising Pericles for his success, Elpinike sarcastically remarked, "This really is wonderful, Pericles, . . . that you have caused the loss of many good citizens, not in battle against Phoenicians or Persians, like my brother Cimon, but in suppressing an allied city of fellow Greeks" (Plutarch, *Pericles* 28).

A man speaking in a lawsuit succinctly described the theoretical purposes assigned the different categories of women by Athenian men: "We have 'companions' for the sake of pleasure, ordinary prostitutes for daily attention to our physical needs, and wives to bear legitimate children and to be faithful guards inside our households" ([Demosthenes,] *Orations* 59.122). In practice, of course, the roles filled by women did not necessarily correspond to this idealized scheme; a husband could expect his wife to perform all of them. The social marginality of companions—they were usually not citizens, they could not legally marry, they had unsavory reputations—empowered them in speech and in sexuality because by definition they were expected to break the norms of respectability. Other women, by contrast, earned respect and social status by obeying these norms.

Training for Public Life

Athenians learned the norms of respectable behavior for both women and men not in school but in the family and in the countless episodes of everyday life. Formal education in the modern sense hardly existed because schools subsidized by the state did not exist. Only well-to-do families could afford to pay the fees charged by private teachers, to whom they sent their sons to learn to read, to write, perhaps to learn to sing or play a musical instrument, and to train for athletics and military service. Physical fitness was considered so important for men, who could be called on for military service from the age of eighteen until sixty, that the city-state provided open-air exercise facilities for daily workouts. These gymnasia were also favorite places for political conversations and the exchange of news. The daughters of well-to-do families often learned to read, write, and do simple arithmetic, presumably from being instructed at home, because a woman with these skills would be better prepared to manage the household finances and supplies for the husband of property she was expected to marry and aid with daily estate management.

Poorer girls and boys learned a trade and perhaps some rudiments of literacy by helping their parents in their daily work, or, if they were fortunate, by being apprenticed to skilled crafts producers. The level of literacy in Athenian society outside the ranks of the prosperous was quite low by modern standards, with only a small minority of the poor able to do much more than perhaps sign their names. The inability to read presented few insurmountable difficulties for most people, who could find someone to read aloud to them any written texts they needed to understand. The predominance of oral rather than written communication meant that people were accustomed to absorbing information by ear (those who could read usually read out loud), and Greeks were very fond of songs, speeches, narrated stories, and lively conversation.

Young men from prosperous families traditionally acquired the advanced skills required for successful participation in the public life of Athenian democracy by observing their fathers, uncles, and other older men as they participated in the assembly, served as councilors or magistrates, and made speeches in court cases. The most important skill to acquire was the ability to speak persuasively in public. In many cases, an older man would choose an adolescent boy as his special favorite to educate. The boy would learn about public life by spending his time in the company of the older man and his adult friends. During the day, the boy would observe his mentor talking politics in the agora or giving speeches in the assembly or courts, help him perform his duties in public office, and work out with him in a gymnasium. Their evenings would be spent at a symposium, a drinking party for men and companions, which could encompass a range of behavior from serious political and philosophical discussion to riotous partying.

Such a mentor-protégé relationship commonly implied homosexual love as an expression of the bond between the boy and the older male, who would normally be married. Greeks by this period found it natural for an older man to be sexually aroused by the physical beauty of a boy (as also of a lovely girl). The love between the older "lover" and the younger "beloved" (to use the Greek terminology) implied more than just desire, however. The eroticism of the relationship had to be played out as a kind of contest for status, with the younger man wishing to appear desirable but sufficiently in control to reject or modify his older pursuer's demands and the older man wishing to demonstrate his power and ability to overcome resistance by winning a physical relationship with the young object of his pursuit. Although male homosexuality outside a mentor-protégé relationship and female homosexuality in general incurred disgrace, the special homosexuality between older mentors and younger protégés was generally accepted as appropriate behavior, so long as the older man did not exploit his younger companion purely for physical gratification or neglect his education in public affairs. The fourth-century philosopher Plato portrayed a plain-thinking fifth-century Athenian man summing up what was apparently a common opinion about appropriate homosexual love: "I believe that the greatest good for a youth is to have a worthy lover from early on and, for a lover, to have a worthy beloved. The values that men need who want to live lives of excellence lifelong are better instilled by love than by their relatives or offices or wealth or anything else. . . . I mean the values that produce feelings of shame for disgraceful actions and ambition for excellence. Without these values neither a city-state nor a private person can accomplish great and excellent things. . . . Even a small army of such men, fighting side by side, could defeat, so to speak, the entire world because a lover could more easily endure everyone else rather than his beloved seeing him desert his post or throw down his weapons. He would die many times over before allowing that to happen" (*Symposium* 178c–179a).

In the second half of the fifth century B.C., a new brand of self-proclaimed teachers appeared, offering more organized instruction to young men seeking to develop the skills in public speaking and argumentation needed to excel in democratic politics. These instructors were called sophists ("wise men"), a label that acquired a pejorative sense (preserved in the English word "sophistry") because they were so clever at public speaking and philosophic debates. Sophists were detested and even feared by many traditionally minded men, whose political opinions and influence they threatened. The earliest sophists arose in parts of the Greek world other than Athens, but from about 450 B.C. on they began to travel to Athens, which was then at the height of its material prosperity, to search for pupils who could pay the hefty prices the sophists charged for their instruction. Wealthy young men flocked to the dazzling demonstrations that these itinerant teachers put on to showcase their ability to speak persuasively, an ability that they claimed to be able to impart to students. The sophists were offering just what every ambitious young man wanted to learn because the greatest single skill that a man in democratic Athens could possess was to be able to persuade his fellow citizens in the debates of the assembly and the council or in lawsuits before large juries. For those unwilling or unable to master the new rhetorical skills of sophistry, the sophists (for stiff fees) would compose speeches to be delivered by the purchaser as his own composition. The overwhelming importance of persuasive speech in an oral culture like that of ancient Greece made the sophists frightening figures to many, for the new teachers offered an escalation of the power of speech that seemed potentially destabilizing to political and social traditions.

The most famous sophist was Protagoras, a contemporary of Pericles from Abdera in northern Greece. Protagoras emigrated to Athens around 450 B.C., when he was about forty, and spent most of his career there. His oratorical ability and his upright character so impressed the men of Athens that they chose him to devise a code of laws for a new colony to be founded in Thurii in southern Italy in 444 B.C. Some of Protagoras's ideas eventually aroused considerable controversy. One was his agnostic position concerning the gods: "Whether the gods exist I cannot discover, nor what their form is like, for there are many impediments to knowledge, [such as] the obscurity of the subject and the brevity of human life" (D.-K. 80B4).

Equally controversial was Protagoras's denial of an absolute standard of truth, his assertion that every issue has two, irreconcilable sides. For example, if one person feeling a breeze thinks it warm, while a different person judges the same wind to be cool, they cannot decide which judgment is correct because the wind simply is warm to one and cool to the other. Protagoras summed up his subjectivism (the belief that there is no absolute reality behind and independent of appearances) in the much-quoted opening of his work entitled Truth (most of which is now lost): "Man is the measure of all things, of the things that are that they are, and of the things that are not that they are not" (D.-K. 80B1). "Man" in this passage (anthropos in Greek, hence our word "anthropology") seems to refer to the individual human being, whether male or female, whom Protagoras makes the sole judge of his or her own impressions.

The Impact of New Ideas

The teachings of sophists such as Protagoras made many Athenians nervous, especially because leading figures like Pericles flocked to hear them. Two related views taught by sophists aroused special controversy: the idea that human institutions and values were only matters of convention, custom, or law (*nomos*) and not products of nature (*physis*), and the idea that, since truth was relative, speakers should be able to argue either side of a question with equal persuasiveness. The first idea implied that traditional human institutions were arbitrary rather than grounded in immutable nature and the second rendered rhetoric an amoral skill. The combination of the two ideas seemed exceptionally dangerous to a society so devoted to the spoken word because it threatened the shared public values of the polis with unpredictable changes. Protagoras himself insisted that his doctrines were not hostile to democracy, especially because he argued that every person had an innate capability for "excellence" and that human survival depended on the rule of law based on a sense of justice. Members of the community, he argued, should be persuaded to obey the laws not because they were based on absolute truth, which did not exist, but because it was expedient for people to live by them. A thief, for instance, who might claim that in his opinion a law against stealing was not appropriate, would have to be persuaded that the law forbidding theft was to his advantage because it protected his own property and permitted the community to function in which he, like all human beings, had to live in order to survive.

Training of the sort offered by Protagoras struck some Athenian men as ridiculous hair splitting. One of Pericles' sons, for example, who had become estranged from his father, made fun of him for disputing with Protagoras about the accidental death of a spectator killed by a javelin thrown by an athlete in a competition. The politician and the sophist had whiled away an entire day debating whether the javelin itself, the athlete, or the judges of the contest were responsible for the tragedy. Such criticism missed the point of Protagoras's teachings. He never meant to help wealthy young men undermine the social stability of the traditional city-state. Some later sophists, however, had fewer scruples about the uses to which their instruction in arguing both sides of a case might be put. An anonymous handbook compiled in the late fifth century B.C., for example, provided examples of how rhetoric could be used to stand common-sense arguments on their heads: "Greeks interested in philosophy propose double arguments about the good and the bad. Some of them claim that the good is one thing and the bad something else, but others claim that the good and the bad are the same thing. This second group also says that the identical thing might be good for some people but bad for others, or at a certain time good and at

another time bad for the same individual. I myself agree with those holding the latter opinion, which I shall investigate by taking human life as my
example and its concern for food, drink, and sexual pleasures: these things
are bad for a man if he is ill but good if he is healthy and has need of them.
Furthermore, overindulgence in these things is bad for the person who gets
too much of them but good for those who profit by selling these things
to these overindulgers. Here is another point: illness is a bad thing for the
patient but good for the doctors. And death is bad for those who die but
good for the undertakers and sellers of grave monuments . . . . Shipwrecks
are bad for the shipowners but good for the shipbuilders. When tools become blunt and worn down it is bad for their owners but good for the tool-
maker. And if a piece of pottery gets broken, this is bad for everyone else
but good for the pottery maker. When shoes wear out and fall apart it is bad
for others but good for the shoemaker . . . . In the stadion race for runners,
victory is good for the winner but bad for the losers" (Dissoi Logoi 1.1–6).

Skill in arguing both sides of a case and a relativistic approach to such
fundamental issues as the moral basis of the rule of law in society were not
the only aspects of these new intellectual developments that disturbed many
Athenian men. Philosophers such as Anaxagoras of Clazomenae in Ionia and
Leucippus of Miletus propounded unsettling new theories about the nature
of the cosmos in response to the provocative physics of the Ionian thinkers
of the sixth century B.C. Anaxagoras's general theory postulating an abstract
force that he called "mind" as the organizing principle of the universe probably impressed most people as too obscure to worry about, but the details
of his thought seemed to offend those who held to the assumptions of traditional religion. For example, he argued that the sun was in truth nothing
more than a lump of flaming rock, not a divine entity. Leucippus, whose
doctrines were made famous by his pupil Democritus of Abdera, invented
an atomic theory of matter to explain how change was possible and indeed
constant. Everything, he argued, consisted of tiny, invisible particles in eternal motion. Their random collisions caused them to combine and recom-
bine in an infinite variety of forms. This physical explanation of the source
of change, like Anaxagoras's analysis of the nature of the sun, seemed to
deny the validity of the entire superstructure of traditional religion, which
explained events as the outcome of divine forces.

Many people feared that the teachings of the sophists and philosophers
could offend the gods and therefore erode the divine favor that they believed
Athens to enjoy. Just like a murderer, a teacher spouting doctrines offensive
to the gods could bring pollution and therefore divine punishment on the
whole community. So deeply felt was this anxiety that Pericles' friendship
with Protagoras, Anaxagoras, and other controversial intellectuals gave his

rivals a weapon to use against him when political tensions came to a head in the 430s B.C. as a result of the threat of war with Sparta. Pericles' opponents criticized him as sympathetic to dangerous new ideas as well as autocratic in his leadership.

Sophists were not the only thinkers to emerge with new ideas in the mid-fifth century. In historical writing, for example, Hecataeus of Miletus, born in the later sixth century, had earlier opened the way to a broader and more critical vision of the past. He wrote both an extensive guide book to illustrate his map of the world as he knew it and a treatise criticizing mythological traditions. The Greek historians writing immediately after him concentrated on the histories of their local areas and wrote in a spare, chronicle-like style that made history into little more than a list of events and geographical facts. Herodotus of Halicarnassus (c. 485–425 B.C.), however, built on the foundations laid by Hecataeus and wrote a groundbreaking work called *The Histories*, which was pioneering in its wide geographical scope, critical approach to historical evidence, and lively narrative. To describe and explain the clash between East and West that exploded into wars between Persians and Greeks in the early fifth century, Herodotus searched for the origins of the conflict both by delving deep into the past and by examining the cultural traditions of all the peoples involved. With his interest in ethnography, he recognized the importance and the delight of studying the cultures of others as a component of historical investigation.

The emergence of new ideas in Greek medicine in this period is associated with the name of Hippocrates of Cos, a younger contemporary of Herodotus. Details are sketchy about the life and thought of this most famous of all Greek doctors, but he certainly made great strides in putting medical diagnosis and treatment on a scientific basis. Earlier medical practices had depended on magic and ritual. Hippocrates apparently viewed the human body as an organism whose parts must be understood as part of the whole. Greek doctors characteristically searched for a system of first principles to serve as a foundation for their treatments, but no consensus emerged. Even in antiquity medical writers disagreed about the theoretical foundation of Hippocrates' medicine. Some attributed to him the view, popular in later times, that four fluids, called humors, make up the human body: blood, phlegm, black bile, and yellow bile. This intellectual system corresponded to the division of the inanimate world into the four elements of earth, air, fire, and water.

Most important, Hippocrates taught that physicians should base their knowledge on careful observation of patients and their response to remedies. Empirically grounded clinical experience, he insisted, was the best guide to treatments that would not do the sick more harm than good. Hippocratic medical doctrine apparently made little or no mention of a divine role in sickness and its cures, although various cults in Greek religion, most famously that of the god Asclepius, offered healing to petitioners. Hippocrates' contribution to medicine is remembered today in the oath bearing his name that doctors customarily swear at the beginning of their professional careers.

The impact on ordinary people of the new developments in history and medicine is hard to assess, but their misgivings about the new trends in education, oratory, and philosophy with which Pericles was associated definitely heightened the political tension in Athens in the 430s B.C. These intellectual developments had a wide-ranging effect because the political, intellectual, and religious dimensions of life in ancient Athens were so intricately connected. A person could feel like talking about the city-state's foreign and domestic policies on one occasion, about novel theories of the nature of the universe on another, and on every occasion about whether the gods were angry or pleased with the community. By the late 430s B.C., the Athenians had new reasons to worry about each of these topics.

The Peloponnesian War and
Its Aftermath at Athens

8

Pel War

A Generation of Conflict

Athens and Sparta had cooperated in the fight against Xerxes' great invasion of Greece, but the relations between the two most powerful states of mainland Greece had deteriorated to such a point by the middle of the fifth century that open hostilities erupted. The peace struck in 446/5 was supposed to endure for thirty years, but events of the 430s led once again to a high level of tension. The resulting Peloponnesian War lasted twenty-seven years, from 431 to 404, and engulfed most of the Greek world at one time or another. This bitter conflict, extraordinary in Greek history for its protracted length, wreaked havoc on the social and political harmony of Athens, sapped its economic strength, decimated its population, and turned upside down the everyday life of most of its citizens. The sharp divisions in Athenian public opinion that the war exposed were expressed most eloquently and bitingly by the comic poet Aristophanes in the comedies that he produced during the war years. The trial and execution of the Athenian philosopher Socrates in 399 B.C. revealed that the bitterness dividing Athenians survived the end of the war.

The Peloponnesian War shows the consequences of the repeated reluctance of the Athenian assembly to negotiate peace terms with the enemy instead of simply dictating them. The other side of the coin is the remarkable

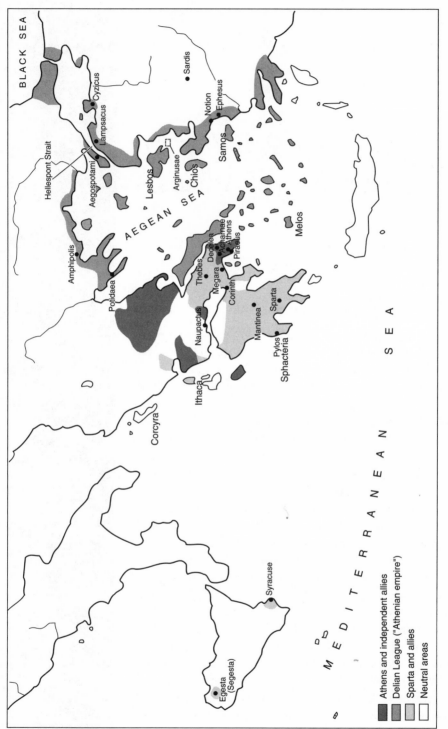

BLACK SEA

Sardis

Cyzicus
Lampsacus
Hellespont Strait
Aegospotami

Notion
Ephesus

Arginusae
Lesbos
Chios
Samos

AEGEAN SEA

Amphipolis

Melos

Potidaea

Thebes
Decelea
Acharnae
Athens
Megara
Piraeus
Corinth
Naupactus
Mantinea
Sparta

Ithaca
Pylos
Sphacteria

Corcyra

MEDITERRANEAN SEA

Syracuse

Egesta
(Segesta)

■ Athens and independent allies

▨ Delian League ("Athenian empire")

▨ Sparta and allies

☐ Neutral areas

Map 6. The Peloponnesian War

433 B.C.: Athens and Corinth clash over former Corinthian ally.

432 B.C.: Athens imposes economic sanctions on Megara.

431 B.C.: War begins with first Spartan invasion of Attica and Athenian naval raids on Peloponnese.

430 B.C.: Epidemic strikes Athens.

429 B.C.: Pericles dies in epidemic.

425 B.C.: Athenians commanded by Cleon capture Spartan hoplites at Pylos; Aristophanes' comedy *The Acharnians* produced at Athens.

424 B.C.: Aristophanes' comedy *The Knights* produced at Athens.

422 B.C.: Cleon and Brasidas killed in battle of Amphipolis.

421 B.C.: Peace of Nicias reestablishes prewar alliances.

418 B.C.: Athenians recommence hostilities at urging of Athenian Alcibiades; defeat at Mantinea.

416 B.C.: Athens attacks the island of Melos.

415 B.C.: Athenian expedition launched against Syracuse on the island of Sicily; Alcibiades defects to Sparta.

414 B.C.: Aristophanes' comedy *The Birds* produced at Athens.

413 B.C.: Destruction of Athenian forces in Sicily; establishment of Spartan base at Decelea in Attica.

411 B.C.: Athenian democracy temporarily abolished; Aristophanes' comedy *The Lysistrata* produced at Athens.

404 B.C.: Athens surrenders to Spartan army commanded by the Spartan general Lysander.

404–403 B.C.: Reign of terror of the Thirty Tyrants at Athens.

403 B.C.: Overthrow of the Thirty Tyrants and restoration of Athenian democracy.

399 B.C.: Trial and execution of Socrates at Athens.

by **393 B.C.:** Rebuilding of Long Walls of Athens completed.

---

resilience shown by Athens in recovering from defeats and losses of manpower. The magnitude of the conflict and the unprecedented, if controversial, evidence about it provided by Thucydides justify the attention traditionally devoted to it.

The Causes of the Peloponnesian War

Most of our knowledge of the causes and the events of this decisive war depends on the history written by the Athenian Thucydides (c. 460–400 B.C.). Thucydides served as an Athenian commander in northern Greece in the early years of the war until in 424 the assembly exiled him for twenty years as punishment for losing a valuable northern outpost, Amphipolis, to the enemy. During his exile, Thucydides was able to interview witnesses from both sides of the conflict. Unlike Herodotus, Thucydides concentrated on contemporary history and presented his account of the events of the war in an annalistic framework—that is, according to the years of the war, with only occasional divergences from chronological order. Like Herodotus, he included versions of direct speeches in addition to the description of events. The speeches in Thucydides, usually longer and more complex than those in Herodotus, deal with major events and issues of the war in difficult and dramatic language. Their contents often address the motives of the participants in the war and offer broad interpretations of human nature and behavior. Scholars disagree about the extent to which Thucydides has put words and ideas into the mouths of his speakers, but it seems indisputable that the speeches deal with the moral and political issues that Thucydides saw as central for understanding the Peloponnesian War as well as human conflict in general. His perceptive chronicle and interpretation made his book a pioneering work of history as the narrative of great contemporary events and power politics.

The Peloponnesian War, like most wars, had a complex origin. Thucydides reveals that the immediate causes centered on disputes between Athens and Sparta in the 430s concerning whether they had a free hand in dealing with each other's allies. Violent disputes broke out concerning Athenian aid to Corcyra, an island naval power in conflict with Corinth (a principal Spartan ally), concerning Athenian economic sanctions against the city-state of Megara, a Spartan ally located immediately west of Athenian territory, and concerning the Athenian blockade of Potidaea, a strategically positioned city-state in northern Greece formerly allied to Athens but now in revolt and seeking help from Corinth. The deeper causes involved the antagonists' ambitions for hegemony, fears of each other's power, and concern for freedom from interference by a strong rival.

The outbreak of the war finally came when the Spartans issued ultimatums to Athens that the Athenian assembly rejected at the urging of Pericles. The Spartans threatened open warfare unless Athens lifted its economic sanctions against Megara and stopped its military blockade of Potidaea. The Athenians had forbidden the Megarians from trading in all the harbors of the Athenian empire, a severe blow for Megara, which derived much income from seaborne trade. The Athenians had imposed the sanctions in retaliation for alleged Megarian encroachment on sacred land along the border between Megara and Athens. Potidaea retained ties to Corinth, the city that had originally founded it, and Corinth, an ally of Sparta, had protested the Athenian blockade of its erstwhile colony. The Corinthians were by this time already angry at the Athenians for having supported the city-state of Corcyra in its earlier quarrel with Corinth and securing an alliance with Corcyra and its formidable navy. The Spartans issued their ultimatums in order to placate the Megarians and, more important, the Corinthians with their powerful naval force. Corinth had threatened to withdraw from the Peloponnesian League and join the Athenian alliance if the Spartans delayed any longer in backing them in their dispute with the Athenians over Potidaea. In this way, the actions of lesser powers nudged the two great powers, Athens and Sparta, over the brink to war in 431 B.C. Hostilities were assured when Athens rejected a final Spartan ultimatum which required only that the Athenians rescind the Megarian Decree, as the economic sanctions are called today. To this demand, Pericles is said to have replied frostily that the Athenian assembly had passed a law forbidding anyone to take down the inscribed panel on which the text of the sanctions against Megara had been publicly displayed. "All right, then," exploded the head of the Spartan delegation, "you don't have to take the panel down. Just turn its face to the wall. Surely you have no law forbidding that!" (Plutarch, Pericles 30). This anecdote about the Megarian Decree eloquently expresses the rancor that had come to characterize Spartan-Athenian relations in the late 430s.

The disputes over Athenian sanctions against Megara, as well as over its use of force against Potidaea and alliance with Corcyra, reflected the larger issues of power motivating the hostility between Athens and Sparta. The Spartan leaders feared that the Athenians would use their superiority in long-distance offensive weaponry—the naval forces of the Delian League—to destroy Spartan control over the Peloponnesian League. The majority in the Athenian assembly, for their part, resented Spartan interference in their freedom of action. For example, Thucydides portrays Pericles as making the following arguments in a speech to his fellow male citizens: "If we do go to war, harbor no thought that you went to war over a trivial affair. For you this trifling matter is the assurance and the proof of your determination. If you yield to their demands, they will immediately confront you with some larger demand, since they will think that you only gave way on the first point out of fear. But if you stand firm, you will show them that they have to deal with you as equals. . . . When our equals, without agreeing to arbitration of the matter under dispute, make claims on us as neighbors and state those claims as commands, it would be no better than slavery to give in to them, no matter how large or how small the claim may be" (History of the Peloponnesian War, 1.141).

It is true that the Athenians had offered to submit to arbitration of the Spartan complaints, the procedure officially mandated under the sworn terms of the peace treaty of 445 B.C. The Spartans nevertheless refused arbitration because they could not risk the defection of Corinth from their alliance if the decision went against them. The Spartans needed Corinth's sizable fleet to combat Athens's formidable naval power. The Spartan refusal to honor an obligation imposed by an oath amounted to sacrilege. Although the Spartans continued to argue that the Athenians were at fault by refusing all concessions, they nevertheless felt uneasy about the possibility that the gods might punish them for refusing their sworn obligation. The Athenians, on the other hand, exuded confidence that the gods would favor them in the war because they had respected their obligation.

Periclean Strategy

Athens's fleet and fortifications made its urban center impregnable to direct attack. Already by the 450s the Athenians had encircled the city center with a massive stone wall and fortified a broad corridor with a wall on both sides leading all the way to the main harbor at Piraeus some four miles to the west. Cimon in the late 460s had spent great sums to lay the foundations for the first two Long Walls, as they were called, and Pericles had seen to their completion in the early 450s, using public funds. A third wall was added about 445. The technology of military siege machines in the fifth century was unequal to the task of breaching fortifications of the thickness of the Long Walls. Consequently, no matter what damage was done to the agricultural production of Attica in the course of the war by Spartan invasions of the territory outside the walls around the city center, the Athenians could feed themselves by importing food by ship through their fortified port. They could pay for the food with the huge financial reserves they had accumulated from the dues of the Delian League and the income from their silver mines. The Athenians could also retreat safely behind their walls in the case of attacks by the superior Spartan infantry. From this impregnable position, they could launch surprise attacks against Spartan territory by sending their ships from the fortified harbor to land troops behind enemy lines. Like aircraft in modern warfare before the invention of radar warning systems, Athenian warships could swoop down unexpectedly on their enemies before they could prepare to defend themselves. The two-pronged strategy, which Pericles devised for Athens, was therefore simple: avoid set battles with the Spartan infantry even if it ravaged Athenian territory, but attack Spartan territory from the sea. In the end, he predicted, the superior resources of Athens in money and men would enable it to win a war of attrition.

The difficulty in carrying out Pericles' strategy was that it required the many Athenians who resided outside the urban center to abandon their homes and fields to the depredations of the Spartan army during its regular invasions of Attica each year. As Thucydides reports, people hated coming in from the countryside where "most Athenians were born and bred; they grumbled at having to move their entire households [into Athens] . . . , abandoning their normal way of life and leaving behind what they regarded as their true city" (2.16). When in 431 B.C. the Spartans began the war by invading Attica for the first time and proceeded to destroy property in the countryside, hoping to force the Athenians into an infantry battle, the country dwellers of Attica became enraged as, standing in safety on Athens's walls, they watched the smoke rise from their burning homes and fields. The men of Acharnae, the most populous deme of Attica and visible just to the north from the city walls, were particularly furious, and Pericles barely managed to stop the citizen militia from rushing out to take on the Spartan hoplites. Somehow he managed to prevent the assembly from meeting to ratify a new strategy; precisely how Pericles blocked normal democratic procedures at this critical juncture, Thucydides does not reveal. The Spartan army returned home from this first attack on Athenian territory after about a month in Attica because it lacked the structure for resupply over a longer period and could not risk being away from Sparta too long for fear of helot revolt. For these reasons, the annual invasions of Attica that the Spartans sent in the early years of the war never lasted longer than forty days. Even in this short time, however, the Spartan army could inflict losses on the Athenian countryside that were felt very keenly by the Athenians holed up in their walled city.

Unforeseen Disaster

The innate unpredictability of war soon undermined Pericles' strategy for Athenian victory, for an epidemic began to ravage Athens's population in 430 B.C. and raged for several years with disastrous consequences. The disease struck while the Athenians from the countryside were jammed together in unsanitary conditions behind the city walls. The failure to provide adequate housing and sanitation for this mass of the population was a devastating oversight by Pericles and his fellow leaders. The symptoms of the disease, described in detail by Thucydides, were gruesome: vomiting, convulsions, painful sores, uncontrollable diarrhea, and fever and thirst so extreme that sufferers threw themselves into cisterns vainly hoping to find relief in the cold water. The rate of mortality was so high that it crippled Athenian ability to man the naval expeditions that Pericles' wartime strategy demanded. Pericles himself died of the disease in 429 B.C. He apparently had not anticipated the damage to Athens which the loss of his firm leadership could mean. The epidemic also seriously hampered the war effort by destroying the Athenians' confidence in their relationship with the gods. "As far as the gods were concerned, it seemed not to matter whether one worshipped them or not because the good and the bad were dying indiscriminately," Thucydides wrote (2.53).

The epidemic thus hurt the Athenians materially by devastating their population, politically by removing their foremost leader, Pericles, and psychologically by damaging their self-confidence and corroding social and religious norms. Nevertheless, they fought on resiliently. Despite the loss of manpower inflicted by the epidemic, the Athenian military forces proved effective in several locations. Potidaea, the ally whose rebellion had exacerbated the hostility between Athens and Corinth, was compelled to surrender in 430. The Athenian navy won two major victories in 429 off Naupactus in the western Gulf of Corinth under the general Phormio. A serious revolt in 428–427 of allies on the island of Lesbos, led by the city-state of Mytilene, was forcefully put down. One of the most famous passages in Thucydides is the set of vivid speeches on the fate of the Mytilenians presented by Cleon and Diodotus. The opposing speeches respectively argue for capital punishment based on justice and clemency based on expediency. Their arguments represent stirring and provocative positions that bear on larger political and ethical questions than the immediate issue of what to do about the rebels of Mytilene. Equally impressive and disturbing is Thucydides' report of the civil war that broke out on the island of Corcyra in 427 when the opposing factions, one supporting Athens and one Sparta, tried to gain advantage by appealing to these major powers in the Peloponnesian War. His blunt analysis reveals how civil war can bring out and inflame the worst features of human nature:

> [The citizens supporting democracy in the civil war in the city-state of Corcyra] captured and executed all their enemies whom they could find. . . . They then proceeded to the sanctuary of Hera and persuaded about fifty of the suppliants [from the opposing faction] who had sought sacred refuge there to agree to appear in court. The democrats thereupon condemned every last one of the erstwhile suppliants to death. When the other suppliants who had refused to go to trial comprehended what was going on, most of them killed each other right there in the sanctuary. Some hanged themselves from trees, while others found a variety of ways to commit suicide. [For a week] the members of the democratic faction went on slaughtering any fellow citizens whom they thought of as their enemies. They accused their victims of plotting to overthrow the democracy, but in truth they killed many people simply out of personal hatred or because they owed money to the victims. Death came in every way and fashion. And, as customarily occurs in such situations, the killers went to every extreme and beyond. There were fathers who

murdered their sons; men were dragged out of the temples to be put to death or simply butchered on the very altars of the gods; some people were actually walled up in the temple of Dionysus and left there to die [of starvation].

In numerous Greek cities these factional struggles produced many catastrophes—as happens and always will happen while human nature remains what it is. . . . During periods of peace and prosperity, cities and individuals alike adhere to more demanding standards of behavior, because they are not forced into a situation where they have to do what they do not want to do. But war is a violent teacher; in stealing from people the ability to fulfill their ordinary needs without undue difficulty, it reduces most people's temperaments to the level of their present circumstances.

So factional conflicts erupted in city after city, and in cities where the struggles took place at a later date than in other cities, the knowledge of what had already happened in other places led to even more inventiveness in attacking rivals and to unprecedented atrocities of revenge. In accordance with the changes in conduct, words, too, exchanged their customary meanings to adapt to people's purposes. What had previously been described as a reckless act of aggression was now seen as the courage demanded of a loyal co-conspirator in a faction; to give any thought to the future and not take immediate action was simply another way of calling someone a coward; any suggestion of moderation was just an attempt to cover up one's cowardice; ability to understand different sides of an issue meant that one was wholly unsuited to take action. Fanatical enthusiasm was the defining characteristic of a real man. . . . Ties of family were weaker obligations than belonging to a faction, since faction members were more prepared to go to any extreme for any reason whatsoever. (3.81–82)

The manpower losses of the great epidemic prevented Athens from launching as many naval expeditions as would have been needed to make Periclean strategy effective, and the annual campaigns of the war in the early 420s brought losses to both sides without any significant chance of one side overcoming the other. In 425 B.C., however, Athens stumbled upon a golden chance to secure an advantageous peace when the Athenian general Cleon won an unprecedented victory by capturing some 120 Spartan Equals and about 170 allied Peloponnesian troops after a protracted struggle on the tiny island of Sphacteria in the gulf fronting Pylos in the western Peloponnese. No Spartan soldiers had ever before surrendered under any circumstances. They had always taken as their martial creed the sentiment expressed by the legendary advice of a Spartan mother handing her son his shield as he went off to war: "Come home either with this or on it" (Plutarch, *Moralia* 241F), meaning that he should return either as a victor or as a corpse. By this date, however, the population of Spartan Equals had been so reduced that the loss of even such a small group was perceived as intolerable. The Spartan leaders therefore offered the Athenians favorable peace terms in return for the captives. Cleon's unexpected success at Pylos had vaulted him into a position of political leadership, and he advocated a hard line toward Sparta. Thucydides, who apparently had no love for Cleon, called him "the most violent of the citizens" (3.36). At Cleon's urging, the Athenian assembly refused to make peace with Sparta: he convinced his fellow citizens that they could win even more, and they took the gamble.

The lack of wisdom in the Athenian decision became clear with the next unexpected development of the war: a sudden reversal in the traditional Spartan policy against waging extended military expeditions far from home. In 424 the Spartan general Brasidas led an army on a daring campaign against Athenian strongholds in far northern Greece hundreds of miles from Sparta. His most important victory came with the conquest of Amphipolis, an important Athenian colony near the coast that the Athenians regarded as essential to their strategic position. Brasidas's success there robbed Athens of access to gold and silver mines and a major source of timber for warships. Even though he was not directly involved in the battle at Amphipolis, Thucydides lost his command and was forced into exile because he was the commander in charge of the region when the city was lost and was thus held responsible for the catastrophe.

A Fighting Peace

Cleon, the most prominent and influential leader at Athens after the Athenian victory at Pylos in 425, was dispatched to northern Greece in 422 to try to stop Brasidas. As it happened, both he and Brasidas were killed before Amphipolis in 422 B.C. in a battle won by the Spartan army. Their deaths deprived each side of its most energetic military commander and opened the way to negotiations. Peace came in 421 B.C., when both sides agreed to resurrect the balance of forces as it had been in 431. The agreement made in that year is known as the Peace of Nicias, after the Athenian general who was instrumental in convincing the Athenian assembly to agree to a peace treaty. The Spartan agreement to the peace revealed a fracture in the coalition of Greek states allied with Sparta against Athens and its allies because the Corinthians and the Boeotians refused to join the Spartans in signing the treaty.

The Peace of Nicias failed to quiet those on both sides of the conflict who were pushing for a decisive victory. A brash, rich, and young Athenian named Alcibiades (c. 450–404 B.C.) was especially active against the uneasy peace. He was a member of one of Athens's richest and most distinguished families, and he had been raised in the household of Pericles after his father had died in battle against allies of Sparta in 447, when his son was only about three years old. By now in his early thirties—a very young age at which to have achieved political influence, by Athenian standards— Alcibiades rallied some support in the Athenian assembly for action against Spartan interests in the Peloponnese. Despite the ostensible conditions of peace between Sparta and Athens, he managed to cobble together a new alliance among Athens, Argos, and some other Peloponnesian city-states that were hostile to Sparta. He evidently believed that Athenian power and security, as well as his own career, would be best served by a continuing effort to weaken Sparta. Since the geographical location of Argos in the northeastern Peloponnese placed it astride the principal north-south route in and out of Spartan territory, the Spartans had reason to fear the alliance created by Alcibiades. If the alliance held, Argos and its allies could virtually pen the Spartan army inside its own borders. Nevertheless, support for the coalition seems to have been shaky in Athens, perhaps because the memory of the ten years of war just concluded was still vivid. The Spartans, recognizing the threat to themselves, met and defeated the forces of the coalition in battle at Mantinea in the northeastern Peloponnese in 418. The Peace of Nicias was now a dead letter in practice, whatever its continuing validity in theory.

In 416 an Athenian force besieged the tiny city-state on the island of Melos situated in the Mediterranean southeast of the Peloponnese, a community sympathetic to Sparta that had taken no active part in the war, although it seems to have made a monetary contribution to the Spartan war effort. In any case, Athens had long considered Melos an enemy because Nicias had led an unsuccessful attack on the island in 426. Now once again Athens demanded that Melos support its alliance voluntarily or face destruction, but the Melians refused to submit despite the overwhelming superiority of Athenian force. What the Athenians hoped to gain by this campaign is not clear because Melos had neither much property worth plundering nor a strategically crucial location. When Melos eventually had to surrender to the besieging army of Athenian and allied forces, its men were killed and its women and children sold into slavery. An Athenian community was then established on the island. Thucydides portrays Athenian motives in the affair of Melos as concerned exclusively with the amoral politics of the use of force, while the Melians he shows as relying on a concept of justice that they insisted should govern relations between states. He represents the leaders of the opposing sides as participating in a private meeting to discuss their views of what issues are at stake. This passage in his history (5.84–114), called the Melian Dialogue, offers a chillingly realistic insight into the clash between ethics and power in international politics that is timeless in its insight and its bluntness.

The Sicilian Expedition

In 415 B.C. Alcibiades convinced the Athenian assembly to launch a massive naval campaign against the city-state of Syracuse, a Spartan ally on the great island of Sicily. With this expedition the Athenians and their allies would pursue the great riches awaiting conquerors there and prevent any Sicilian cities from aiding the Spartans. Formally speaking, in launching the Sicilian expedition, Athens was responding to a request for support from the Sicilian city of Egesta (also known as Segesta), with which an alliance had been struck more than thirty years earlier. The Egestans encouraged Athens to prepare a naval expedition to Sicily by misrepresenting the extent of the resources that they had to devote to the military campaign against their enemies on the island. The prosperous city of Syracuse near the southeastern corner of the island represented both the richest prize and the largest threat to Athenian ambitions.

In the debate preceding the vote on the expedition, Alcibiades and his supporters argued that the numerous warships in the fleet of Syracuse represented an especially serious potential threat to the security of the Athenian alliance because they could sail from Sicily to join the Spartan alliance in attacks on Athens and its allies. Nicias led the opposition to the proposed expedition, but his arguments for caution failed to counteract the enthusiasm for action that Alcibiades generated with his speeches. The latter's aggressive dreams of martial glory appealed especially to young men who had not yet experienced the realities of war for themselves. The assembly resoundingly backed his vision by voting to send to Sicily the greatest force ever to sail from Greece.

The arrogant flamboyance of Alcibiades' private life and his blatant political ambitions had made him many enemies in Athens, and this hostility came to the fore at the very moment of the expedition's dispatch when Alcibiades was suddenly accused of having participated in sacrilegious events on the eve of the sailing. One incident involved the herms of Athens. Herms, stone posts with sculpted sets of erect male organs and a bust of the god Hermes, were placed throughout the city as guardians of doorways, boundaries, and places of transition. A herm stood at nearly every street intersection, for example, because crossings were, symbolically at least, zones of special danger. Unknown vandals outraged the public by knocking off the statues' phalluses just before the fleet was to sail. When Alcibiades was accused of having been part of the vandalism, his enemies immediately upped the ante by reporting that he had earlier staged a mockery of the Eleusinian Mysteries. This was an extremely serious charge of sacrilege and caused an additional uproar. Alcibiades pushed for an immediate trial while his popularity was at a peak and the soldiers who supported him were still in Athens, but his enemies cunningly got the trial postponed on the excuse that the expedition must not be delayed. Alcibiades therefore set off with the rest of the fleet, but it was not long before a messenger was dispatched telling him to return alone to Athens for trial. Alcibiades' reaction to this order was unforeseen: he defected to Sparta.

The defection of Alcibiades left the Athenian expedition against Sicily without a strong and decisive leader. The Athenian fleet was so large that it won initial victories against Syracuse and its allies even without brilliant leadership, but eventually the indecisiveness of Nicias undermined the attackers' successes. The Athenian assembly responded to the setbacks by authorizing large reinforcements led by the general Demosthenes, but these new forces proved incapable of defeating Syracuse, which enjoyed effective military leadership to complement its material strength. Alcibiades had a decisive influence on the quality of Syracusan military leadership because Sparta adopted his suggestion to send an experienced Spartan commander to Syracuse to combat the invading expedition. The Athenian forces were eventually trapped in the harbor of Syracuse and completely crushed in a climactic naval battle in 413. When the survivors of the attacking force tried to flee overland to safety, they were either slaughtered or captured almost to a man, including Nicias. The Sicilian expedition ended in ignominious defeat for Athens and the crippling of its navy, its main source of military power.

Ten More Years of War

Alcibiades' defection turned out to cause Athens still more trouble after the Sicilian catastrophe. While at Sparta, he had advised the Spartan commanders to establish a permanent base of operations in the Attic countryside, and in 413 they at last acted on his advice. Taking advantage of Athenian weakness in the aftermath of the enormous losses in men and equipment sustained in Sicily, the Spartans installed a garrison at Decelea in northeastern Attica, in sight of the walls of Athens itself. Spartan forces could now raid the Athenian countryside year around, whereas earlier in the war the annual invasions dispatched from Sparta could never linger longer than forty days in Athenian territory. The presence of the garrison made agricultural work in the fields of Attica dangerous and forced Athens to rely even more heavily than in the past on food imported by sea. The damage to Athenian fortunes increased when twenty thousand slaves owned by the state who worked in Athens's silver mines sought refuge in the Spartan camp. The loss of these slave miners put a stop to the flow of revenue from the veins of silver ore. So immense was the distress caused by the crisis that an extraordinary change was made in Athenian government: a board of ten officials was appointed to manage the affairs of the city, virtually supplanting the council of five hundred.

The disastrous consequences of the Athenian defeat in Sicily in 413 were further compounded when Persia once again took a direct hand in Greek affairs. Athenian weakness seemed to make this an opportune time to reassert Persian dominance in western Anatolia by stripping away the allies of Athens there. The satraps governing the Persian provinces in the region therefore began to supply money to help outfit a fleet for the Spartans and their allies. Led by the powerful city-state of the island of Chios in the eastern Aegean, some restless allies of Athens in Ionia took advantage of the depleted state of their erstwhile leader to revolt from the Delian League. They were urged on by Alcibiades, whom the Spartans had sent to Ionia in 412 to foment rebellion among the members of the Athenian alliance there. A particularly dangerous result of these latter developments was the threat to the shipping lanes by which Athens imported grain from Egypt to the southeast and the fertile shores of the Black Sea to the northeast.

Athens demonstrated a strong communal will in the face of the great hardships that had begun in 413, however, by beginning to rebuild its fleet and train new crews to man it. The emergency reserve funds that had been stored on the Acropolis since the beginning of the war were tapped to finance the rebuilding. By 412–411 Athenian naval forces had revived sufficiently that they managed to prevent a Corinthian fleet from sailing to aid Chios, to lay siege to that rebellious island ally, and to win some other battles along the Anatolian coast.

Despite these successes, the turmoil in Athenian politics and revenues resulting from the Sicilian defeat opened the way for some influential Athenian men, who had long harbored contempt for the broad-based democracy of their city-state, to stage what amounted to an oligarchic coup d'état. They insisted that a small group of elite leaders could manage Athenian policy better than the democratic assembly. Alcibiades furthered their cause by letting it be known that he would make an alliance with the Persian satraps in western Anatolia and secure funds from them for Athens on condition that the democracy was overturned and an oligarchy installed. He apparently hoped that this would make it possible for him to return to Athens. He had reason to want to return because his negotiations with the satraps had by now aroused the suspicions of the Spartan leaders, who rightly suspected that he was intriguing in his own interests rather than theirs. He had also made Agis, one of Sparta's two kings, into a powerful enemy by seducing his wife.

Alcibiades' promises helped the oligarchic sympathizers in Athens to play on the assembly's hopes by holding out the lure of Persian gold. In 411 they succeeded in having the assembly members turn over all power to a group of four hundred men, hoping that this smaller body would provide better guidance for foreign policy in the war and improve Athens's finances. These four hundred were then supposed to choose five thousand men to act as the city's ultimate governing body, but the four hundred in fact kept all power in their own hands. Their oligarchic regime soon began to fall apart, however, because the oligarchs destroyed their unity by struggling with each other for dominance. The end came for them when the crews of the Athenian war fleet, which was stationed in the harbor of the friendly island city-state of Samos in the eastern Aegean, threatened to sail home to restore democracy by force unless the oligarchs stepped aside. In response, a mixed democracy and oligarchy called the Constitution of the Five Thousand was created, which Thucydides praised as "the best form of government that the Athenians had known, at least in my time" (*History of the Peloponnesian War* 8.97). This new government voted to recall Alcibiades and others in exile in the hope that they could improve Athenian military leadership.

With Alcibiades as one of the commanders, the revived Athenian fleet won a great victory over the Spartans in 410 at Cyzicus on the southern shore of the Black Sea. The Athenians intercepted the plaintive and typically brief dispatch sent by the defeated Spartans to their leaders at home: "Ships lost. Commander dead. Men starving. Do not know what to do" (Xenophon, *Hellenica* 1.1.23). The prodemocratic fleet demanded the restoration of full democracy at Athens, and in this year Athenian government returned to the form and membership that it had possessed before the oligarchic coup of 411. It also returned to the uncompromising bellicosity that had characterized the decisions of the Athenian assembly in the mid-420s. Just as after the defeat at Pylos in 425, the Spartans offered peace after their defeat at Cyzicus in 410. Athens refused and the Athenian fleet went on to reestablish the safety of the grain routes to Athens and to compel some of the allies who had revolted to return to the alliance.

The aggressive Spartan commander Lysander ultimately doomed Athenian hopes in the war by using Persian money to rebuild the Spartan fleet and by ensuring that it was well led. When in 406 he inflicted a defeat on an Athenian fleet at Notion, near Ephesus on the Anatolian coast, Alcibiades, who had not been present but was held to have been responsible for the safety of the Athenian forces, was forced into exile for the last time. The Athenian fleet nevertheless won a victory later in 406 off the islands of

Arginusae, south of the island of Lesbos, but a storm prevented the rescue of the crews of wrecked ships. The Athenian commanders were condemned to death for alleged negligence in a mass trial at Athens that contradicted the normal guarantee of individual trials. Once again the assembly rejected a Spartan offer of peace on the basis of the status quo. Lysander thereupon secured more Persian funds, strengthened the Spartan naval forces still further, and decisively eliminated the Athenian fleet in 405 in a battle at Aegospotami, near Lampsacus on the coast of Anatolia. He subsequently blockaded Athens and finally compelled Athens to surrender in 404 B.C. After twenty-seven years of near-continuous war, the Athenians were at the mercy of their enemies.

The Spartan leaders resisted the demand of their allies the Corinthians, the bitterest enemy of the Athenians, that Athens be totally destroyed. They feared that Corinth, with its large fleet and strategic location on the isthmus potentially blocking access to and from the Peloponnese, might grow too strong if Athens were no longer in existence to serve as a counterweight. Instead of ruining Athens, Sparta installed as the conquered city's rulers a regime of antidemocratic Athenian collaborators, who became known as the Thirty Tyrants. These men came from the wealthy elite, which had always harbored a faction despising democracy and admiring oligarchy. Brutally suppressing their opposition in Athens and stealing shamelessly from people whose only crime was to possess desirable property, these oligarchs embarked on an eight-month-long period of terror in 404–403 B.C. The metic and famous speechwriter-to-be Lysias, for example, whose father had earlier moved his family from their native Syracuse at the invitation of Pericles, reported that the henchmen of the Thirty seized his brother for execution as a way of stealing the family's valuables. The plunderers even ripped the gold earrings from the ears of his brother's wife in their pursuit of loot. So violent had been the rule of the Thirty Tyrants that the Spartans did not interfere when a prodemocracy resistance movement came to power in Athens after a series of street battles in 403 B.C. To put an end to the internal strife that threatened to tear Athens apart, the newly restored democracy proclaimed a general amnesty, the first known in Western history, under which all further charges and official recriminations concerning the terror were forbidden. Athens's government was once again a functioning democracy; its financial and military strength, however, was shattered, and its society harbored the memory of a bitter divisiveness that no amnesty could completely dispel.

Hardship and Comedy in Wartime Athens

Not only did the Peloponnesian War drain the state treasury of Athens, splinter its political harmony, and devastate its military power, but the long years of the war also exacted a heavy toll on the domestic life of Athenians. Many people both urban and rural found their livelihoods threatened by the economic dislocations of the war. Women without wealth whose spouses or male relatives were killed in the war experienced particularly difficult times because dire necessity forced them to seek work outside the home to support themselves and their children.

Perhaps the most ruinous personal losses and disruptions caused by wartime conditions at Athens were imposed on the many people who usually lived outside the walls of the urban center. These country dwellers periodically had to take refuge inside the city walls while the Spartan invaders wrecked their homes and damaged their fields. If they did not also own a house in the city or have friends who could take them in, these refugees had to camp in public areas in Athens in uncomfortable and unsanitary conditions, inevitably causing friction between them and the city dwellers.

The war meant drastic changes in their way of making a living for many working men and women of Athens, both those whose incomes depended on agriculture and those who operated their own small businesses. Wealthy families that had money and valuable goods stored up could weather the crisis by using their savings, but most people had no financial cushion to fall back on. When their harvests were destroyed by the enemy, farmers used to toiling in their own fields had to scrounge for work as day laborers in the city, but such jobs became increasingly scarce as the pool of men looking for them grew. Men who rowed the ships of the Athenian fleet could earn wages for the time the ships were at sea, but they had to spend long periods away from their families and faced death in every battle and storm. Men and women who worked as crafts producers and small merchants or business owners in the city still had their livelihoods, but their income levels suffered because consumers had less money to spend.

The pressure of war on Athenian society became especially evident in the severe damage done to the prosperity and indeed the very nature of the lives of many previously moderately well-off women whose husbands and brothers died during the conflict. Such women had traditionally done weaving at home for their own families and supervised the work of household slaves, but the men had earned the family's income by farming or practicing a trade. With no one to provide for them and their children, these women were forced to take the only jobs open to them in such low-paying occupations as wet nurse, weaver, or even vineyard laborer, in the event there were not enough men to meet the need. These circumstances brought more women into public view, but they did not lead to a woman's movement in the modern sense, or to any inclusion of women in Athenian political life.

The financial health of the city-state of Athens suffered during the Peloponnesian War from the many interruptions to agriculture and from the catastrophic loss of income from the state's silver mines that occurred after the Spartan army took up a permanent presence at Decelea in 413 B.C. Work could thereafter no longer continue at the mines, which were not far from the Spartan base, especially after the desertion of thousands of slave mine workers to the Spartan fort. Some public building projects in the city itself were kept going, like the Erectheum temple to Athena on the Acropolis, to demonstrate the Athenian will to carry on and also as a device for infusing some money into the crippled economy. But the demands of the war depleted the funds available for many nonmilitary activities. The great annual dramatic festivals, for example, had to be cut back. The financial situation had become so desperate by the end of the war that Athenians were required to exchange their silver coins for an emergency currency of bronze thinly plated with silver. The regular silver coins, along with gold coins that were minted from golden objects borrowed from Athens's temples, were then used to pay war expenses.

The stresses of everyday life were reflected in Athenian comedies produced during the Peloponnesian War. Comic plays were the other main form of dramatic art in ancient Athens besides tragedies. Like tragedies, comedies were composed in verse and had been presented annually since early in the fifth century B.C. They formed a separate competition in the Athenian civic festivals in honor of Dionysus in the same outdoor theater used for tragedies. The ancient evidence does not make it clear whether women could attend the performance of comedies, but if they could see tragedies, it seems likely that they could attend comedies as well. The all-male casts of comic productions consisted of a chorus of twenty-four members in addition to regular actors. Unlike tragedy, comedy was not restricted to having no more than three actors with speaking parts on stage at the same time. The beauty of the soaring poetry of the choral songs of comedy was matched by the ingeniously imaginative fantasy of its plots, which almost always ended with a festive resolution of the problems with which they had begun. The story of The Birds by Aristophanes, for example, produced in 414 B.C., has two men trying to escape the wrangles and disappointments of everyday life at Athens by running away to seek a new life in a world called Cloudcuckooland that is inhabited by talking birds, portrayed by the chorus in colorful bird costumes.

The immediate purpose of a comic playwright naturally was to create beautiful poetry and raise laughs at the same time in the hope of winning the award for the festival's best comedy. The plots of fifth-century Athenian comedies primarily dealt with current issues and personalities, while much of their humor had to do with sex and bodily functions and much of their ribaldry was delivered in a stream of imaginative profanity. Insulting attacks on prominent men such as Pericles or Cleon, the victor of Pylos, were a staple of the comic stage. Pericles apparently instituted a ban on such attacks in response to fierce treatment in comedies after the revolt of Samos in 441–439 B.C., but the measure was soon rescinded. Cleon was so outraged by the way he was portrayed on the comic stage by Aristophanes (c. 455–385 B.C.), the only comic playwright of the fifth century from whose works entire plays have survived, that he sued the playwright. When Cleon lost the case, Aristophanes responded by pitilessly parodying him in The Knights of 424 B.C. as a reprobate foreign slave. Other well-known men who were not portrayed as characters in the play could nevertheless come in for insults in the dialogue as sexually effeminate and cowards. On the other hand, women characters who are made figures of fun and ridicule in comedy seem to have been fictional.

Slashing satire directed against the mass of ordinary citizens seems to have been unacceptable in Athenian comedy, but fifth-century comic productions often criticized governmental policies that had been approved by the assembly by blaming political leaders for them. The strongly critical nature of comedy was never more evident than during the war. Several of the popular comedies of Aristophanes had plots in which characters arranged peace with Sparta, even though the comedies were produced while the war was still being fiercely contested. In The Acharnians of 425 B.C., for example, the protagonist arranges a separate peace treaty with the Spartans for himself and his family while humiliating a character who portrays one of Athens's prominent military commanders of the time. The play won first prize in competition for comedies that year.

The most remarkable of Aristophanes' comedies are those in which the main characters, the heroes of the story as it were, are women, who use their wits and their solidarity with one another to compel the men of Athens to overthrow basic policies of the city-state. Most famous of Aristophanes' comedies depicting powerfully effectual women is the Lysistrata of 411 B.C., named after the female lead. It portrays the women of Athens compelling their husbands to end the Peloponnesian War. The women first seize the Acropolis, where Athens's financial reserves are kept, and prevent the men from squandering them further on the war. They then beat back an attack on their position by the old men who have remained in Athens while the younger men are out on campaign. When their husbands return from battle, the women refuse to have sex with them. Teaming with the women of Sparta on this sex strike, which is portrayed in a series of risqué episodes, they finally coerce the men of Athens and Sparta to agree to a peace treaty.

The Lysistrata presents women acting bravely and aggressively against men who seem bent both on destroying their family life by staying away from home for long stretches while on military campaign and on ruining the city-state by prolonging a pointless war. In other words, the play's powerful women take on masculine roles to preserve the traditional way of life of the community. Lysistrata herself emphasizes this point in the very speech in which she insists that women have the intelligence and judgment to make political decisions. She came by her knowledge, she says, in the traditional way: "I am a woman, and, yes, I have brains. And I'm not badly off for judgment. Nor has my education been bad, coming as it has from my listening often to the conversations of my father and the elders among the men" (1124–1127). Lysistrata thus explains that she was schooled in the traditional way, by learning from older men. Her old-fashioned training and good sense allowed her to see what needed to be done to protect the community. Like the heroines of tragedy, Lysistrata is a reactionary: she wants to put things back the way they were. To do that, however, she has to act like a revolutionary, a response that Athenians in the audience would see as ludicrous. Ending the war would be so easy that women could do it, Aristophanes is telling Athenian men, and Athenians should concern themselves with preserving the old ways, lest they be lost.

Postwar Athenian Society

The losses of population, the ravages of the plague, and the financial constraints brought on by the war caused special difficulties for Athens. Not even the amnesty that accompanied the restoration of Athenian democracy in 403 B.C. could quell all the social and political animosities that the war and the rule of the Thirty Tyrants had exacerbated, and the most prominent casualty of this divisive bitterness was the famous philosopher Socrates, whose trial for impiety in 399 B.C. resulted in a sentence of death. The traditional institution of the Athenian household—the family members and their personal slaves—nevertheless survived the war as the fundamental unit of the city-state's society and economy, and over time Athens recovered much of its strength as an international power.

Many Athenian households lost fathers, sons, or brothers in the Peloponnesian War, but resourceful families found ways to compensate for the economic strain that such personal tragedies could create. An Athenian named Aristarchus, for example, is reported by the writer Xenophon (c. 428–354 B.C.) to have experienced financial difficulty because the turmoil of the war had severely diminished his income and also caused his sisters, nieces, and female cousins to come live with him. He found himself unable to support this swollen household of fourteen, not counting the slaves. Aristarchus's friend Socrates thereupon reminded him that his female relatives knew quite well how to make men's and women's cloaks, shirts, capes, and smocks, "the work considered the best and most fitting for women" (*Memorabilia* 2.7.10), although they had always just made clothing for the family and never had to try to sell it for profit. But others did make a living by selling such clothing or by baking and selling bread, Socrates pointed out, and Aristarchus could have the women in his house do the same. The plan was a success, but the women complained that Aristarchus was now the only member of the household who ate without working. Socrates advised his friend to reply that the women should think of him as sheep did a guard dog: he earned his share of the food by keeping away the wolves from the sheep.

Many Athenian manufactured goods were produced in households like that of Aristarchus or in small shops, although a few larger enterprises did exist. Among these were metal foundries, pottery workshops, and the shield-making business employing 120 slaves owned by the family of Lysias (c. 459–380 B.C.); businesses larger than this were unknown at this period. Lysias, a metic from Syracuse in Sicily whose father had been recruited by Pericles decades earlier to come live in Athens, had to use his education and turn to writing speeches for others to make a living after the Thirty Tyrants seized his property in 404 B.C. Metics could not own land in Athenian territory without special permission, but they enjoyed legal rights in Athenian courts that other foreigners lacked. In return, metics paid taxes and served in the army when called upon. Lysias lived near the harbor of Athens, Piraeus, where many metics were to be found because they played a central role in the international trade in such goods as grain, wine, pottery, and silver from Athens's mines that passed through Piraeus. The safety of Athenian trade was restored to prewar conditions when the Long Walls that connected the city with the port, demolished after the war as punishment, were rebuilt by 393 B.C. Another sign of the recovering economic health of Athens was that the city by the late 390s had resumed the minting of its famous silver coins to replace the emergency bronze coinage produced during the last years of the war.

The importation of grain through Piraeus was crucial for fourth-century Athens. Even before the war, Athenian farms had been unable to produce enough of this dietary staple to feed the population. The damage done to farm buildings and equipment during the Spartan invasions of the Peloponnesian War made the situation worse. The Spartan establishment of a year-round base at Decelea near Athens from 413 to 404 B.C. had given these enemy forces an opportunity to do much more severe damage in Athenian territory than the usually short campaigns of Greek warfare allowed. The invaders had probably even had time to cut down many Athenian olive trees, the source of valuable olive oil. The trees took a generation to replace because they grew so slowly. Athenian property owners after the war worked hard to restore their land and businesses to production not only to rebuild their incomes but also to provide for future generations, because Athenian men and women felt strongly that their property, whether in land, money, or belongings, represented resources to be preserved for their descendants. For this reason, Athenian law allowed prosecution of men who squandered their inheritance. The same spirit lay behind the requirement that parents must provide a livelihood for their children, by leaving them income-bearing property or training them in a skill.

Most working people probably earned little more than enough to clothe and feed their families. Athenians usually had only two meals a day, a light lunch in midmorning and a heavier meal in the evening. Bread baked from barley or, for richer people, wheat, constituted the main part of the diet. A family could buy its bread from small bakery stands, often run by women, or make it at home, with the wife directing and helping the household slaves to grind the grain, shape the dough, and bake it in a pottery oven heated by charcoal. Those few households wealthy enough to afford meat from time to time often grilled it over coals on a pottery brazier shaped much like modern picnic grills. For most people, vegetables, olives, fruit, and cheese represented the main variety in their diet, and meat was available only as part of animal sacrifices paid for by the state. The wine that everyone drank, usually much diluted with water, came mainly from local vineyards. Water from public fountains had to be carried into the house with jugs, a task that the women of the household had to perform themselves or see that the household slaves did. The war had hurt the Athenian state economically by giving a chance for escape to many of the slaves who worked in the silver mines in the Attic countryside, but few privately owned domestic slaves tried to run away, perhaps because they realized that they would simply be resold by the Spartans if they managed to escape their Athenian masters. All but the poorest Athenian families, therefore, continued to have at least a slave or two to do chores around the house and look after the children. If a mother did not have a slave to serve as a wet nurse to suckle her infants, she would hire a poor free woman for the job, if her family could afford the expense.

The Life of Socrates

The most infamous episode in Athenian history in the aftermath of the Peloponnesian War consisted of the trial, conviction, and execution of Socrates (469–399 B.C.), the most famous philosopher of the late fifth century. Socrates' life had been devoted to combating the idea that justice should be equated with power to work one's will. Coming as it did during a time of social and political turmoil, his death indicated the fragility of Athenian justice in practice. His passionate concern to discover valid guidelines for leading a just life and to prove that justice is better than injustice under all circumstances gave a new direction to Greek philosophy: an emphasis on ethics. Although other thinkers before him, especially the poets and dramatists, had dealt with moral issues, Socrates was the first philosopher to make ethics and morality his central concern.

Compared to the most successful sophists, Socrates lived in poverty and publicly disdained material possessions, but he nevertheless managed to serve as a hoplite in the army and support a wife and several children. He may have inherited some money, and he also received gifts from wealthy admirers. Nevertheless, he paid so little attention to his physical appearance and clothes that many Athenians regarded him as eccentric. Sporting, in his words, a stomach "somewhat too large to be convenient" (Xenophon, *Symposium* 2.18), Socrates wore the same nondescript cloak summer and winter and scorned shoes no matter how cold the weather. His physical stamina was legendary, both from his tirelessness when he served as a soldier in Athens's army and from his ability to outdrink anyone at a symposium.

Whether participating at a symposium, strolling in the agora, or watching young men exercise in a gymnasium, Socrates spent almost all his time in conversation and contemplation. In the first of these characteristics he resembled his fellow Athenians, who placed great value on the importance and pleasure of speaking with each other at length. He wrote nothing; our knowledge of his ideas comes from others' writings, especially those of his pupil Plato. Plato's dialogues, so called because they present Socrates and others in extended conversation about philosophy, portray Socrates as a relentless questioner of his fellow citizens, foreign friends, and various sophists. Socrates' questions had the unsettling aim of making his interlocutors examine the basic assumptions of their way of life. Employing what has come to be called the Socratic method, Socrates never directly instructed his conversational partners; instead, he led them to draw conclusions in response to his probing questions and refutations of their cherished but unexamined assumptions.

Socrates typically began one of his conversations by asking the interlocutor for a definition of an abstract quality such as happiness or a virtue such as courage. For instance, in the dialogue entitled *Laches*, after the Athenian general who appears as one of the dialogue's interlocutors, Socrates asks Laches and another distinguished military commander what makes a citizen a brave soldier. Socrates then proceeds by further questioning to show that the definitions of courage and instances of courageous behavior stated by the interlocutors actually conflict with their other beliefs about the behavior that constituted courage.

This indirect method of searching for the truth often left Socrates' conversational partners in a state of puzzlement and unhappiness because they were forced to admit that they were ignorant of what they began by assuming they knew perfectly well and that the principles by which they lived were unable to withstand close intellectual scrutiny. Socrates insisted that he, too, was ignorant of the best definition of virtue but that his wisdom consisted of knowing that he did not know. He was trying to improve rather than undermine his interlocutors' personal values and their beliefs in morality, even though, as one of them put it, a conversation with Socrates made a man feel numb just as if he had been stung by a stingray. Socrates wanted to discover through reasoning the universal standards that justified morality. He especially attacked the sophists' view of conventional morality as the "fetters that bind nature" (Plato, *Protagoras* 337d), asserting that it equated human happiness with power and "getting more."

Socrates passionately believed that just behavior was better for human beings than injustice and that morality was justified because it created happiness and well-being. Essentially, he seems to have argued that just behavior, or virtue, was identical to knowledge and that true knowledge of justice would inevitably lead people to choose good over evil and therefore to have truly happy lives, regardless of their material success. Since Socrates believed that knowledge itself was sufficient for happiness, he asserted that no one knowingly behaved unjustly and that behaving justly was always in the individual's interest. It might appear, he maintained, that individuals could promote their interests by cheating or using force on those weaker than themselves, but this appearance was deceptive. It was in fact ignorance to believe that the best life was the life of unlimited power to pursue whatever one desired. Instead, the most desirable human life was concerned with virtue and guided by rational reflection. Moral knowledge was all one needed for the good life, as Socrates defined it.

The Prosecution of Socrates

Although Socrates, unlike the sophists, offered no courses and took no fees, his effect on many people was as upsetting as the relativistic doctrines of the sophists had been. Indeed, Socrates' refutation of his fellow conversationalists' most treasured beliefs made some of his interlocutors decidedly uncomfortable. Unhappiest of all were the fathers whose sons, after listening to Socrates reduce someone to utter bewilderment, came home to try the same technique on their parents. Men who experienced this reversal of the traditional hierarchy of education between parent and child—the son was supposed to be educated by the father—had cause to feel that Socrates' effect, even if it was not his intention, was to undermine the stability of society by questioning Athenian traditions and inspiring young men to do the same with the passionate enthusiasm of their youth.

We cannot say with certainty what Athenian women thought of Socrates or he of them. His views on human capabilities and behavior could be applied to women as well as to men, and he perhaps believed that women and men had the same basic capacity for justice. Nevertheless, the realities of Athenian society meant that Socrates circulated primarily among men and addressed his ideas to them and their situations. He is, however, reported to have had numerous conversations with Aspasia, the courtesan who lived with Pericles for many years, and Plato has Socrates attribute his ideas on love to a woman, the otherwise unknown priestess Diotima of Mantinea. Whether these contacts were real or fictional devices remains uncertain.

The feeling that Socrates could be a danger to conventional society gave Aristophanes the inspiration for his comedy *The Clouds* of 423 B.C., so named from the role played by the chorus. In the play Socrates is presented as a cynical sophist, who, for a fee, offers instruction in the Protagorean technique of making the weaker argument the stronger. When the protagonist's son is transformed by Socrates' instruction into a rhetorician able to argue that a son has the right to beat his parents, the protagonist ends the comedy by burning down Socrates' "Thinking Shop."

Athenians with qualms about Socrates found confirmation of their fears in the careers of the outrageous Alcibiades and, especially, Critias, one of the Thirty Tyrants. Socrates' critics blamed him for Alcibiades' contempt for social conventions because Alcibiades had been one of Socrates' most devoted followers, while Critias, another prominent follower, had played a leading role in the murder and plunder perpetrated by the Thirty Tyrants in 404–403 B.C. In blaming Socrates for the crimes of Critias, Socrates' detractors chose to overlook his defiance of the Thirty Tyrants when they had tried to involve him in their violent schemes and his rejection of the immorality that Critias had displayed.

The hostility some Athenians felt toward Socrates after the violence of the Thirty Tyrants encouraged the distinguished Athenian Anytus, a supporter of democracy who had suffered personally under the tyrants, to join with two other men of lesser prominence in prosecuting Socrates in 399 B.C. Since the amnesty prevented their bringing any charges directly related to the period of tyranny in 404–403, they accused Socrates of impiety. As Athenian law did not specify precisely what offenses constituted impiety, the accusers had to convince the jurors chosen for the case that what Socrates had done and how he had behaved and what he believed constituted a crime. Impiety ranked as an extremely serious crime because the gods were believed to punish the entire city-state if it harbored impious individuals.

As usual in Athenian trials, no judge presided to rule on what evidence was admissible or how the law should be applied. Speaking for themselves as the prosecutors, as also required by Athenian law, the accusers argued their case against Socrates before a jury of 501 men that had been assembled by lot from that year's pool of eligible jurors, drawn from the male citizens over thirty years old.

The prosecution of Socrates had both a religious and a moral component. Religiously, the prosecutors accused Socrates of not believing in the gods of the city-state and of introducing new divinities. Morally, they charged, he had led the young men of Athens away from Athenian conventions and ideals. After the conclusion of the prosecutors' remarks, Socrates spoke in his own defense, as required by Athenian legal procedure. Plato presents Socrates as taking this occasion not to rebut all the charges or try to curry favor or beg for sympathy, as jurors expected in serious cases, but to reiterate his unyielding dedication to goading his fellow citizens into examining their preconceptions. This irritating process of constant questioning, he maintained, would help them learn to live virtuous lives. Furthermore, they should care not about their material possessions but about making their true selves—their souls—as good as possible. If he were to be acquitted, he baldly stated, he vowed to remain their stinging gadfly no matter what the consequences to himself.

After the jury narrowly voted to convict, standard Athenian legal procedure required the jurors to decide between alternative penalties proposed by the prosecutors and the defendant. Anytus and his associates proposed death. In such instances the defendant was then expected to offer exile as the alternative, which the jury would usually accept. Socrates, however, replied to the prosecutors' proposal of the death penalty with the brash claim that he deserved a reward rather than a punishment, until his friends at the trial in horror prevailed upon him to propose a fine as his penalty. The jury chose death, by a wider margin than for the conviction. Socrates accepted his sentence with equanimity because, as he put it in a famous paradox, "no evil can befall a good man either in life or in death" (Plato, *Apology* 41d). In other words, nothing can take away the knowledge that constitutes virtue, and only the loss of that wisdom can count as a true evil.

After his sentencing, Socrates had to wait in prison for some time before his execution because the city-state had a sacred delegation on the Cycladic island of Delos to honor Apollo and did not allow executions to be carried out while such official religious activity was in progress. While he waited, Socrates was visited regularly by a wealthy follower named Crito, who tried to convince Socrates to escape from his cell and flee Attica to his friends in other regions. Crito was apparently confident that he and his associates could secure Socrates' freedom through bribery. Socrates refused to go, explaining his reasons by imagining that the laws of Athens were brought to life and held a dialogue with him as the interlocutor in which they set out a notion of a voluntary, implicit social contract between citizens and the state:

> Consider, Socrates [the Laws would most likely say], whether we are correct in saying that you are now trying to do something to us that is wrong [that is, to escape from prison and execution]. Although we brought you into this world and reared you and educated you and gave you and all your fellow citizens a share in all the good things that we could, nevertheless by the very fact of granting our permission we openly proclaim this principle: that any Athenian, once he becomes an adult and understands the political organization of the city and us its Laws, is allowed, if he is dissatisfied with us, to move away to wherever he likes and take his family property with him. If any citizen who is unhappy with us and with the city decides to go to one of our colonies or to emigrate to any other country, not one of us Laws hinders or stops him from going to wherever he pleases, without any penalty of loss of property. On the other hand, if any one of you stays here once he grasps how we administer justice and the rest of the official organization of our city, we claim that the fact of his remaining here means that he has agreed to follow any order that we may give him; and we further believe that anyone in this situation who disobeys us is guilty of wrongdoing on three separate counts: first because we are his parents, and second because we are his guardians, and third because, after promising us obedience, he neither obeys us nor persuades us to change our decision if we are in any way in the wrong; and although we issue all our orders as proposals, not as fierce commands, and we give him the choice either to persuade us or to carry out our order, he in fact does neither. (Crito 51cd)

Spurning his friends' pleas to escape with arguments such as these, Socrates was executed in the normal Athenian way, by being given a poisonous drink concocted from powdered hemlock. The intellectual controversy that Socrates provoked in his life continued after his death, as philosophers and sophists churned out work after work in the genre called "Socratic conversations," arguing both for and against the positions on a wide variety of issues that they ascribed to Socrates. Xenophon, in a memoir on Socrates perhaps written decades after the philosopher's execution, summed up the feelings of his admirers: "All those who knew what sort of person Socrates was and who aim at excellence [arete] in their lives continue even now to long for him most of all because he was the most helpful of all in learning about excellence" (Memorabilia 4.8.11).

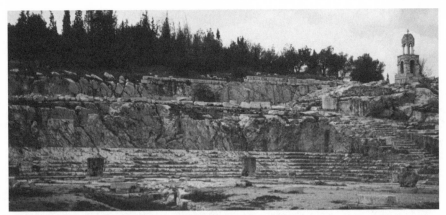

31. The large size of the initiation hall (telesterion) in the sanctuary of Demeter and Kore (Persephone) at Eleusis near Athens shows the popularity of this international Greek mystery cult. (Photo by author)

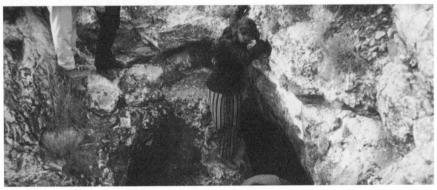

32. Greek religion found sacred space in a variety of locations; this cave near modern Vari in Athenian territory housed a shrine of the god Pan. (Photo by author)

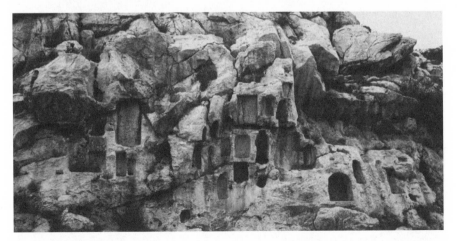

33. These niches cut in a cliff alongside a main road outside Athens housed dedications to Aphrodite, the goddess of erotic passion. (Photo by author)

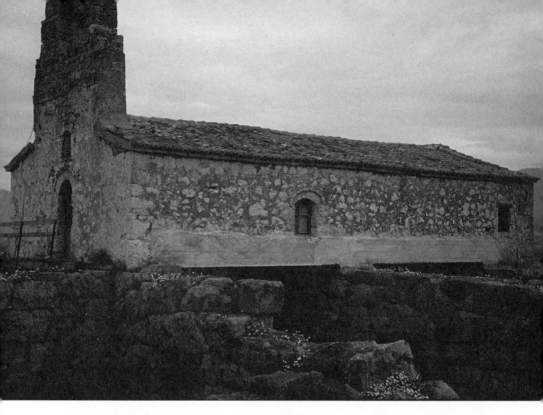

34. Under this church in northwest Greece lay a subterranean labyrinth housing an oracle of the dead (*nekromanteion*), where petitioners sought information that the everyday world could not supply. (Photo by author)

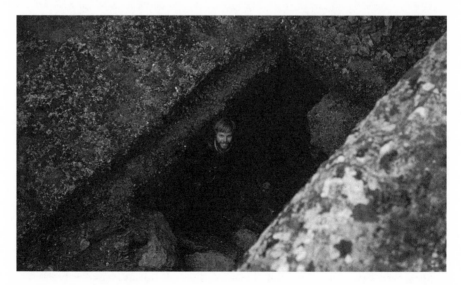

35. Petitioners had to descend into the earth, where the deceased resided, to consult the oracle of the dead. (Photo by author)

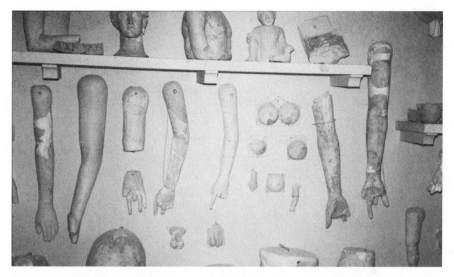

36. Worshipers of the god Asclepius sought healing in his sanctuaries, often dedicating models of body parts such as these to commemorate their experience. (Photo by author)

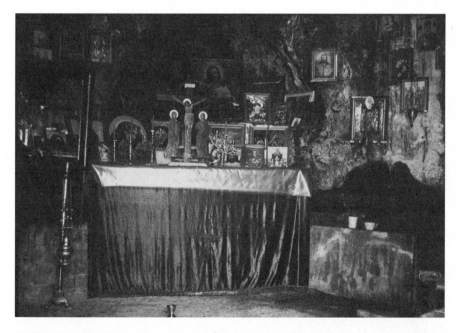

37. This Christian shrine is located in a cave at the site of an ancient sanctuary of the healing divinity Asclepius; modern worshipers seeking divine healing leave small plaques showing parts of the body. (Photo by author)

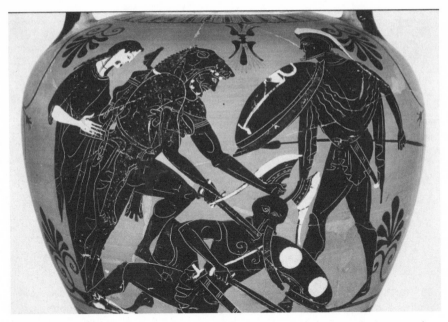

38. This vase painting of Heracles dispatching Kyknos ("Swan"), a brigand who preyed on travelers to the oracle of Apollo at Delphi, shows the most popular heroic figure of Greek mythology using his great power to benefit the Greek world. (Courtesy of the Worcester Art Museum)

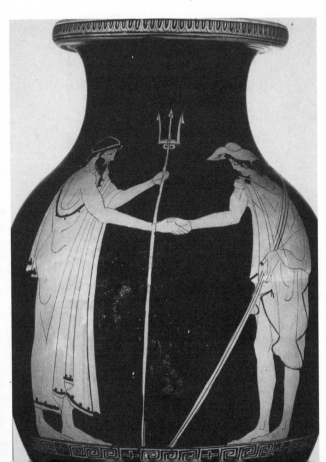

39. Theseus (right), shown here shaking hands with the god Poseidon, was the Athenian rival to Heracles as a famous hero. (Courtesy of the Yale University Art Gallery)

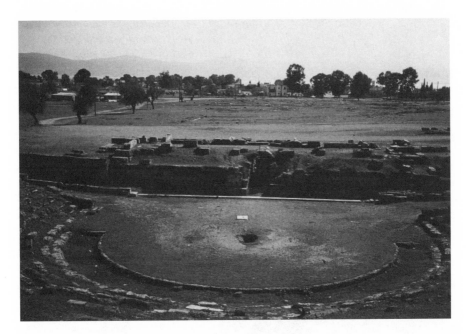

40. The civic theater at Eretria on the island of Euboea had a tunnel from backstage to the playing area that allowed actors to pop up from the ground as ghosts in dramas. (Photo by author)

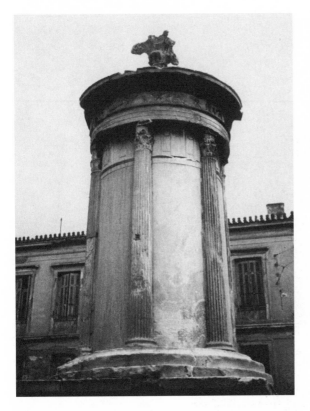

41. Wealthy citizens who sponsored winning plays in the public dramatic festivals at Athens were allowed to put up monuments such as this one to commemorate their victory and civic-minded generosity. (Photo by author)

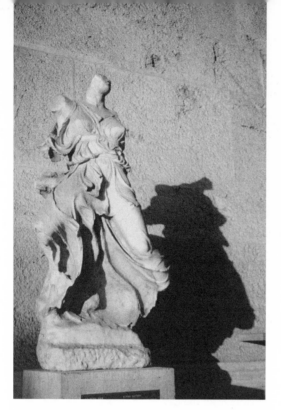

42. This statue of Victory (Nike), which originally stood atop the stoa of Zeus in the Athenian agora, illustrates the exuberant style of Greek sculpture of the Classical period. (Photo by author)

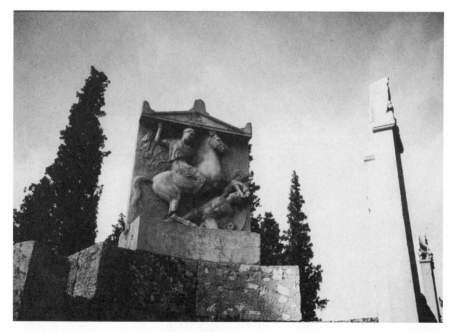

43. These Classical-period sculptures served as Athenian grave monuments, in a typically public function of Greek art. (Photo by author)

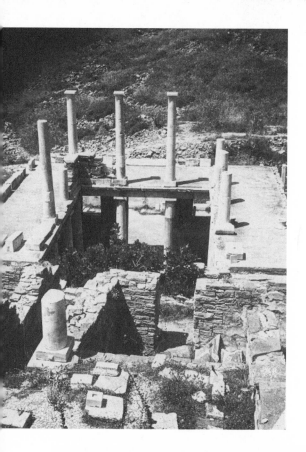

44. This terraced multistory house on Delos shows the scale of a luxurious residence in the Hellenistic period. (Photo by author)

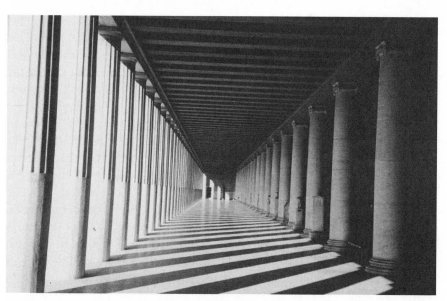

45. The stoa in the Athenian agora paid for in the Hellenistic period by King Attalus of Pergamum, now restored as a museum and archaeological workspace, was a magnificent example of the public architecture of Greek city-states designed to shelter people from the elements when they gathered in the city center for conversation, business, and politics. (Photo by author)

9

From the Peloponnesian War to Alexander the Great

Conflict and Achievement
in Fourth-Century Greece

The end of the Peloponnesian War did not bring an end to conflict among prominent Greek city-states contending for power over each other. In the fifty years following the war, Sparta, Thebes, and Athens struggled militarily to win a preeminent position without, in the end, achieving anything more than weakening each other and creating a vacuum of power on the international level. That void was filled by the unexpected rise to military and political power of the kingdom of Macedonia during the reign of Philip II (ruled 359–336 B.C.). Philip's reorganization of the Macedonian army saved the kingdom from invasion by northern enemies and gave him the power to extend his influence eastward and southward into Greek territory. His victory over an alliance of Greek city-states at Chaeronea in 338 B.C. led to his forming the League of Corinth, whose forces of Greeks and Macedonians he planned to lead on a belated war of revenge against Persia.

When Philip was murdered in 336, it was left to his son, Alexander the Great (ruled 336–323 B.C.), to astonish the world by conquering the Persian empire. Alexander's conquests, which reached from Greece to the western border of India, brought the Greek and Near Eastern worlds into more direct contact than ever before. Alexander died unexpectedly in 323, before he had a mature heir to succeed him as king of Macedonia and without having put into place a permanent political rearrangement of Greece that would reflect the new conditions of the late fourth century. Thus, his brilliant success as a conqueror left unresolved the problem of how to structure international power in a Greek world in which the citizen militias of the city-states could not withstand the mercenary armies of the ambitious commanders left over from Alexander's army.

Squabbling City-States in the Fourth Century

Athens in the fourth century never regained the great economic and military strength that it had wielded in the fifth century B.C., perhaps because its silver mines were no longer producing at the same level. Nevertheless, it did recover substantially after the reestablishment of democracy in 403 B.C. and soon became a major force in international politics once again. Moreover, Sparta's widespread attempts to extend its power in the years immediately after the Peloponnesian War gave Athens and the other Greek states ample provocation for diplomatic and military action. The first half of the fourth century saw frequently shifting alliances among the Greek city-states. Whichever ones happened to be weaker at a particular moment would temporarily join together against whichever city-state happened to be strongest, only to lose their unity once the common enemy had been humbled.

In 401 B.C., the Persian satrap Cyrus, son of a previous king, had hired a mercenary army to try to unseat the current Persian king, Artaxerxes II, who had ascended the throne in 404. Xenophon, an Athenian adventurer and author accompanying the rebel satrap on his campaign, wrote in his *Anabasis* a stirring account of the fate of the Greek soldiers in Cyrus's forces. After their expedition's disastrous defeat at Cunaxa near Babylon, the terrified Greek mercenaries had to make an arduous trek home through hundreds of miles of hostile territory. Sparta had supported Cyrus's rebellion, thereby arousing the hostility of Artaxerxes. In this same period, the Spartan general Lysander and the Spartan king Agesilaus pursued an aggressive policy of trying to extend Spartan power in Anatolia and northern Greece; other Spartan commanders meddled in Sicily. Thebes, Athens, Corinth, and Argos thereupon formed an anti-Spartan coalition because they saw this expansionist Spartan activity as threatening their own interests at home and abroad.

In a reversal of the alliances of the end of the Peloponnesian War, the Persian king initially allied with Athens and the other Greek city-states against Sparta in the so-called Corinthian War, which lasted from 395 to 386 B.C. But this alliance failed, too, because the king and his Greek allies were seeking their own advantage rather than a genuine and peaceful ac-

---

390s–370s B.C.: Spartans campaign first in Anatolia and then in Greece.

386 B.C.: King's Peace between Sparta and Persia.

377 B.C.: Athens reestablishes a naval alliance.

371 B.C.: Spartans defeated at battle of Leuctra in Boeotia.

370 B.C.: Jason, tyrant of Pherae in Thessaly, assassinated.

362 B.C.: Spartans defeated by Thebans, whose army is fatally weakened, in the battle of Mantinea in the Peloponnese.

359 B.C.: Philip II becomes king of Macedonia.

357–355 B.C.: Athenian-led naval alliance dissolves in internal war.

338 B.C.: Philip II defeats Greek alliance at Chaeronea in Boeotia and founds League of Corinth.

336 B.C.: Philip murdered; his son Alexander ("the Great") takes over as king.

334 B.C.: Alexander begins attack against the Persian Empire; wins victory at the Granicus River in northwest Anatolia.

333 B.C.: Alexander wins victory at Issus in southeastern Anatolia.

332 B.C.: Tyre (on coast of Lebanon) falls to Alexander's siege.

331 B.C.: Alexander takes Egypt and founds Alexandria; victory over Persian king at Gaugamela.

329 B.C.: Alexander reaches Bactria (modern Afghanistan).

327 B.C.: Alexander marries the Bactrian princess Roxane.

326 B.C.: Alexander's army mutinies at the Hyphasis River in India.

324 B.C.: Alexander returns to Persia after march through the Gedrosian Desert (in modern southern Iran).

323 B.C.: Alexander dies in Babylon (in modern Iraq).

322 B.C.: Death of Aristotle.

---

commodation on the international scene. The war ended with Sparta once again cutting a deal with Persia. In a blatant renunciation of its long-standing claim to be the defender of Greek freedom, Sparta acknowledged the Persian king's right to control the Greek city-states of Anatolia in return for permission to secure Spartan interests in Greece without Persian interference. The King's Peace of 386 B.C., as the agreement is called, effectively returned the Greeks of Anatolia to the dependent status of a century earlier, before the Greek victory in the Persian Wars of 490–479 had freed them from Persian domination.

Spartan forces attacked city-states all over Greece in the years after the treacherous peace of 386. Athens, meanwhile, had restored its invulnerability to invasion by rebuilding the Long Walls connecting the city and the harbor. The Athenian general Iphicrates also devised effective new tactics for light-armed troops called peltasts by improving their weapons, thus giving the army another tactical strength. The reconstruction of Athens's navy built up its offensive strength to a substantial level, and by 377 the city had again become the leader of a naval alliance of Greek states, but this time the members of the league had their rights specified in writing to prevent high-handed Athenian behavior and posted in public inscriptions for all to see. Spartan hopes for lasting power in these decades of turmoil after the Peloponnesian War were finally dashed in 371, when a resurgent Thebes defeated the Spartan army at Leuctra in Boeotia and then invaded the Spartan homeland in the Peloponnese. At this point the Thebans seemed likely to challenge Jason, tyrant of Pherae in Thessaly and an ambitious commander, for the position of the dominant military power in Greece.

The alliances of the various leading city-states on the Greek mainland shifted often in the repeated conflicts that took place in Greece during the opening decades of the fourth century. The threat from Thessaly disappeared suddenly with Jason's assassination in 370 B.C., and the former enemies Sparta and Athens momentarily allied against the Thebans in the famous battle of Mantinea in the Peloponnese in 362. Thebes won the battle but lost the war when its great leader Epaminondas fell at Mantinea and no credible replacement for him could be found. The Theban quest for dominance in Greece was now over. Xenophon adroitly summed up the situation after 362 with these closing remarks from the history that he wrote of the Greeks in his time: "Everyone had supposed that the winners of this battle would be Greece's rulers and its losers their subjects . . . but there was only more confusion and disturbance in Greece after it than before" (*Hellenica* 7.5.26–27). The truth of his analysis was confirmed when the naval alliance led by Athens dissolved in the mid-350s in a war among the leader and the allies.

All the efforts of the various major Greek states to extend their hegemony over mainland Greece in the first half of the fourth century therefore ended in failure. By the mid 350s B.C., no Greek city-state had the power to rule more than itself on a consistent basis. The struggle for supremacy in Greece that had begun eighty years earlier with the outbreak of the Peloponnesian War had finally ended in a stalemate of exhaustion that opened the way for a new power—the kingdom of Macedonia to the north, a rough land with a warrior tradition.

The Career of Plato

The most famous Greek from these decades of turmoil in the fourth century B.C. was not a politician or a general but Socrates' most brilliant follower, the philosopher Plato of Athens (c. 428–348 B.C.). His works are without doubt the most important legacy of this period to later times. Although his status as a member of the social elite propelled him into politics as a young man, he withdrew from Athenian public life after 399 B.C. The condemnation of Socrates had apparently convinced Plato that citizens in a democracy were incapable of rising above narrow self-interest to knowledge of any universal truth. In his works dealing with the organization of society, Plato bitterly rejected democracy as a justifiable system of government, calling it the "worst form of rule under law" (*Statesman* 303a). He said that Pericles' establishment of pay for service in public office, the linchpin of broad citizen participation in democracy, had made the Athenians "lazy, cowardly, gabby, and greedy" (*Gorgias* 515e). An honorable man committed to virtue, he concluded, could take no part in Athenian public life without incurring hatred and danger (*Apology* 32e).

Against the background of this fierce critique of his own city-state, Plato worked to describe an ideal for political and social organization headed by leaders imbued with philosophical wisdom. His utopian vision had virtually no effect on the actual politics of his time, and his attempts to advise Dionysius II (ruled 367–344 B.C.), tyrant of Syracuse in Sicily, on how to rule as a true philosopher ended in utter failure. But political philosophy formed only one portion of Plato's interests, which ranged widely in astronomy, mathematics, and metaphysics (theoretical explanations for phenomena that cannot be understood through direct experience or scientific experiment). After Plato's death, his ideas attracted relatively little attention among philosophers for the next two centuries, until they were revived as important points for debate in the Roman era. Nevertheless, the sheer intellectual power of Plato's thought and the controversy it has engendered ever since his lifetime have won him fame as one of the world's greatest philosophers.

Plato did not compose philosophical treatises in the abstract fashion familiar from more recent times but rather composed works called dialogues from their form as conversations or reported conversations. Almost as if they were short plays, the dialogues have settings and casts of conversationalists, often including Socrates, who talk about philosophical issues. Divorcing the philosophical content of a Platonic dialogue from its literary form is no doubt an error; a dialogue of Plato demands to be understood as a whole. The form of the dialogues and their sometimes indirect approach to their philosophical subjects were intended to provoke readers into thoughtful reflection rather than to spoon-feed them a circumscribed set of doctrines.

Furthermore, Plato's views seem to have changed over time, and he nowhere presents one coherent set of doctrines. He does seem to have disagreed with Socrates' insistence that fundamental knowledge meant moral knowledge based on inner reflection. Plato concluded that knowledge meant searching for truths that are independent of the observer and could be taught to others. He acted on this latter belief by founding the Academy, a shady gathering spot just outside the walls of Athens, which was named after the local hero whose shrine was nearby. The Academy was not a school or college in the modern sense but rather an informal association of people, who were interested in studying philosophy, mathematics, and theoretical astronomy with Plato as their guide. The Academy became so famous as a gathering place for intellectuals that it continued to operate for nine hundred years after Plato's death, with periods in which it was directed by distinguished philosophers and others during which it lapsed into mediocrity under lackluster leaders.

Although it is unwise to try to summarize Plato rather than to read his dialogues as complete works, it is perhaps not too misleading to say that Plato taught that we cannot define and understand absolute virtues such as goodness, justice, beauty, or equality by the concrete evidence of these qualities in our lives. Any earthly examples will in another context display the opposite quality. For instance, always returning what one has borrowed might seem to be just. But what if a person who has borrowed a weapon from a friend is confronted by that friend who wants the weapon back to commit a murder? In this case, returning the borrowed item would be unjust. Examples of equality are also only relative. The equality of a stick two feet long, for example, is evident when it is compared with another two-foot stick. Paired with a three-foot stick, however, it displays inequality. In sum, in the world that human beings experience with their senses, every example of the virtues and every quality is relative in some aspect of its context.

Plato refused to accept the relativity of the virtues as reality, and his spirited rejection of relativism attacked the doctrines of the sophists. Plato developed the theory that the virtues cannot be discovered through experience; rather, the virtues are absolutes that can be apprehended only by thought and that somehow exist independently of human existence. The separate realities of the pure virtues Plato referred to in some of his works as Forms; among the Forms were Goodness, Justice, Beauty, and Equality. He argued that the Forms were invisible, invariable, and eternal entities located in a higher realm beyond the empirical world of human beings. The Forms are, according to Plato, true reality; what humans experience with their senses are the mere shadows of this reality. Plato's concept of Forms required the further belief that knowledge of them came through the human soul, which must be immortal. When a soul is incarnated in its current body, it brings with it knowledge of the Forms. The soul then uses reason in argument and proof, not empirical observation through the senses, to recollect its preexistent knowledge. Plato was not consistent throughout his career in his views on the nature or the significance of Forms, and his later works seem quite divorced from the theory. Nevertheless, Forms provide a good example of both the complexity and the wide range of Platonic thought.

Plato's idea that humans possessed immortal souls distinct from their bodies established the concept of dualism, positing a separation between spiritual and physical being. This notion of the separateness of soul and body would play an influential role in later philosophical and religious thought. In a dialogue written late in his life, the *Timaeus*, Plato said the preexisting knowledge possessed by the immortal human soul is in truth the knowledge known to the supreme deity. Plato called this god the Demiurge ("craftsman") because the deity used knowledge of the Forms to craft the world of living beings from raw matter. According to this doctrine of Plato, a knowing, rational god created the world, and the world therefore has order. Furthermore, its beings have goals, as evidenced by animals adapting to their environments in order to flourish. The Demiurge wanted to reproduce in the material world the perfect order of the Forms, but the world as crafted turned out not to be perfect because matter is necessarily imperfect. Plato suggested that human beings should seek perfect order and purity in their own souls by making rational desires control their irrational desires. The latter cause harm in various ways. The desire to drink wine to excess, for example, is irrational because the drinker fails to consider the hangover to come the next day. Those who are governed by irrational desires thus fail to consider the future of both body and soul. Finally, since the soul is immortal and the body is not, our present, impure existence is only one passing phase in our cosmic existence.

Plato employed his theory of Forms not only in speculating metaphysically about the original creation of the everyday world in which people live but also in showing the way human society should be constructed in an ideal world. One version of Plato's utopian vision is found in his most famous dialogue, *The Republic*. This work, whose Greek title (*Politeia*) would more accurately be rendered as *System of Government*, primarily concerns the nature of justice and the reasons that people should be just instead of unjust. Justice, Plato argues, is advantageous; it consists of subordinating the irrational to the rational in the soul. By using the truly just and therefore imaginary polis as a model for understanding this notion of proper subordination in the soul, Plato presents a vision of the ideal structure for human society as an analogy for understanding what the individual should do to have a just and moral soul. Like a just soul, the just society would have its parts in proper hierarchy, parts that Plato in the *Republic* presents as three classes of people, as distinguished by their ability to grasp the truth of Forms. The highest class constitutes the rulers, or "guardians" as Plato calls them, who are educated in mathematics, astronomy, and metaphysics. Next come the "auxiliaries," whose function it is to defend the polis. The lowest class is that of the producers, who grow the food and make the objects required by the whole population. Each part contributes to society by fulfilling its proper function.

Women as well as men qualify to be guardians because they possess the same virtues and abilities as men, except for a disparity in physical strength between the average woman and the average man. The axiom justifying the inclusion of women—that virtue is the same in women as in men—is perhaps a notion that Plato derived from Socrates. The inclusion of women in the ruling class of Plato's utopian city-state represented a startling departure from the actual practice of his times. Indeed, never before in Western history had anyone proposed—even in fantasy, which the imaginary city of the *Republic* certainly is—that work be allocated in human society without regard to gender. Moreover, to minimize distraction, guardians are to have neither private property nor nuclear families. Male and female guardians are to live in shared houses, to eat in the same mess halls, and to exercise in the same gymnasiums. Their children are to be raised as a group in a common environment by special caretakers. Although this scheme is meant to free women guardians from child-care responsibilities and enable them to rule equally with men, Plato fails to consider that women guardians would in reality have a much tougher life than the men because they would have to be pregnant frequently and undergo the strain and danger of giving birth. At the same time, he evidently does not believe that they are disqualified from ruling on this account. The guardians who achieved the highest level of knowledge in Plato's ideal society would qualify to rule over the ideally just state as philosopher-kings.

To become a guardian, a person from childhood must be educated for many years in mathematics, astronomy, and metaphysics to gain the knowledge that Plato in the *Republic* presented as necessary for the common good. Plato's specifications for the education of guardians in fact make him the first thinker to argue systematically that education should be the training of the mind and the character rather than simply the acquisition of information and practical skills. Such a state would necessarily be authoritarian because only the ruling class would possess the knowledge to determine its policies and make decisions determining who is allowed to mate with whom to produce the best children.

The severe regulation of life that Plato proposed for his ideally just state in *The Republic* was a reflection of his tight focus on the question of a rational person's true interest and his identification of morality as the key to answering this question. Furthermore, he insisted that politics and ethics are fields in which objective truths can be found by the use of reason. Despite his harsh criticism of existing governments such as Athenian democracy and his scorn for the importance of rhetoric in its functioning, Plato also recognized the practical difficulties in implementing radical changes in the way people actually lived. Indeed, his late dialogue *The Laws* shows him wrestling with the question of improving the real world in a far less radical, though still authoritarian, way than in the imagined community of *The Republic*. Plato hoped that, instead of ordinary politicians, whether democrats or oligarchs, the people who know truth and can promote the common good would rule because their rule would be in everyone's real interest. For this reason above all, he passionately believed that the study of philosophy mattered to human life.

The Science and Philosophy of Aristotle

Greece in the fourth century B.C. produced a second thinker whose intellectual legacy achieved monumental proportions. Aristotle (384–322 B.C.), Plato's most brilliant follower, earned his enduring reputation in science and philosophy from his groundbreaking work in promoting scientific investigation of the natural world and developing rigorous systems of logical argument. The enormous influence of Aristotle's works on scholars in later periods, especially the Middle Ages, has made him a central figure in the history of Western science and philosophy.

The son of a wealthy doctor from Stagira in northern Greece, Aristotle came to Athens at the age of seventeen to study in Plato's Academy. In 335 B.C., Aristotle founded his own informal philosophical school in Athens named the Lyceum, later called the Peripatetic School after the covered walkway (*peripatos*) in which its students carried on conversations while strolling out of the glare of the Mediterranean sun. Aristotle lectured on nearly every branch of learning: biology, medicine, anatomy, psychology, meteorology, physics, chemistry, mathematics, music, metaphysics, rhetoric, political science, ethics, literary criticism. He also worked out a sophisticated system of logic for precise argumentation. Creating a careful system to identify the forms of valid arguments, Aristotle established grounds for distinguishing a logically sound case from a merely persuasive one. He first gave names to contrasts, such as premise versus conclusion and the universal versus the particular, that have been commonplaces of thought and speech ever since. He also studied the process of explanation itself, formulating the influential doctrine of four causes. According to Aristotle, four different categories of explanation exist that are not reducible to a single, unified whole: form (defining characteristics), matter (constituent elements), origin of movement (similar to what we commonly mean by "cause"), and *telos* (aim or goal). This analysis exemplifies Aristotle's care never to oversimplify the complexity of reality.

Apparently an inspiring teacher, Aristotle encouraged his followers to conduct research in numerous fields of specialized knowledge. For example, he had student researchers compile reports on the systems of government of 158 Greek states. Much of Aristotle's philosophical thought reflected the influence of Plato, but he also refined and even rejected ideas that his teacher had advocated. He denied the validity of Plato's theory of Forms, for example, on the grounds that the separate existence that Plato postulated for them failed to make sense. This position typified Aristotle's general preference for explanations based on common sense rather than metaphysics. By modern standards his scientific thought paid relatively limited attention to mathematical models of explanation and quantitative reasoning, but mathematics in his time had not yet reached the level of sophistication appropriate for such work. His method also differed from that of modern scientists because it did not include controlled experimentation. Aristotle believed that investigators had a better chance of understanding objects and beings by observing them in their natural setting than under the artificial conditions of a laboratory. His coupling of detailed investigation with perceptive reasoning served especially well in such physical sciences as biology, botany, and zoology. For example, as the first scientist to try to collect all the available information on the animal species and to classify them, Aristotle recorded information about more than five hundred different kinds of animals, including insects. His human gynecology was particularly inaccurate, but many of his descriptions represented significant advances in learning. His recognition that whales and dolphins were mammals, for instance, which later writers on animals overlooked, was not rediscovered for another two thousand years.

In his zoological research Aristotle set forth his teleological view of nature—that is, he believed organisms developed as they did because they had a natural goal (telos), or what we might call an end or a function. To explain a phenomenon, Aristotle said that one must discover its goal— to understand "that for the sake of which" the phenomenon in question existed. A simple example of this kind of explanation is the duck's webbed feet. According to Aristotle's reasoning, ducks have webbed feet for the sake of swimming, an activity that supports the goal of a duck's existence, which is to find food in the water so as to stay alive. Aristotle argued that the natural goal of human beings was to live in the society of a polis and that the city-state came into existence to meet the human need to live together, since individuals living in isolation cannot be self-sufficient. Furthermore, existence in a city-state made possible an orderly life of virtue for its citizens. The means to achieve this ordered life were the rule of law and the process of citizens' ruling and being ruled in turn.

Some of Aristotle's most influential discussions concentrated on understanding qualitative concepts that human beings tend to take for granted, such as time, space, motion, and change. Through careful argumentation he probed the philosophical difficulties that lie beneath the surface of these familiar notions, and his views on the nature of things exercised an overwhelming influence on later thinkers. Aristotle was conventional for his times in regarding slavery as natural on the argument that some people were by nature bound to be slaves because their souls lacked the rational part that should rule in a human being. Individuals propounding the contrary view were rare, although one fourth-century B.C. orator, Alcidamas, asserted that "god has set all men free; nature has made no one a slave" (scholion to Aristotle, Rhetorica 1373b). Also in tune with his times was Aristotle's conclusion that women were by nature inferior to men. His view of the inferiority of women was based on faulty notions of biology. He wrongly believed, for example, that in procreation the male with his semen actively gave the fetus its form, while the female had only the passive role of providing its matter. His assertion that females were less courageous than males was justified by dubious evidence about animals, such as the report that a male squid would stand by as if to help when its mate was speared but that a female squid would swim away when the male was impaled. Although his erroneous biology led Aristotle to evaluate females as incomplete males, he believed that human communities could be successful and happy only if they included the contributions of both women and men. Aristotle argued that marriage was meant to provide mutual help and comfort, but that the husband should rule.

Aristotle sharply departed from the Socratic idea that knowledge of justice and goodness was all that was necessary for a person to behave justly. He argued that people in their souls often possess knowledge of what is right but that their irrational desires overrule this knowledge and lead them to do wrong. People who know the evils of hangovers still get drunk, for instance. Recognizing a conflict of desires in the human soul, Aristotle devoted special attention to the issue of achieving self-control by training the mind to win out over the instincts and passions. Self-control did not mean denying human desires and appetites; rather, it meant striking a balance between suppressing and heedlessly indulging physical yearnings, of finding "the mean." Aristotle claimed that the mind should rule in striking this balance because intelligence is the finest human quality and the mind is the true self, indeed the godlike part of a person.

Aristotle regarded science and philosophy not as abstract subjects isolated from the concerns of ordinary existence but rather as the disciplined search for knowledge in every aspect of life. That search epitomized the kind of rational human activity that alone could bring the good life and genuine happiness. Some modern critics have charged that Aristotle's work lacks a clear moral code, but he did the study of ethics a great service by insisting that standards of right and wrong have merit only if they are grounded in character and aligned with the good in human nature and do not simply consist of lists of abstract reasons for behaving in one way rather than another. An ethical system, that is, must be relevant to the actual moral situations that human beings continually experience in their lives. In ethics, as in all his scholarship, Aristotle distinguished himself by the insistence that the life of the mind and experience of the real world were inseparable components in the quest to define a worthwhile existence for human beings.

Aristotle believed that human happiness, which was not to be equated with the simpleminded pursuit of pleasure, stems from fulfilling human potentialities. These potentialities can be identified by rational choice, practical judgment, and recognition of the value of choosing the mean instead of extremes. The central moral problem is the nearly universal human tendency to want to "get more," to act unjustly whenever one has the power to do so. The aim of education is to dissuade people from this inclination, which has its worst effects when it is directed at acquiring money or honor. In this context Aristotle was thinking of men in public life outside the home, and he says that the dangerous disorder caused by men's desire for "getting more" occurs both in democracies and oligarchies. Like Plato, he criticized democracy because he saw it as rule by the majority and the poor, not by the educated and elite. The goal of democracy, he said, was living exactly as one likes, which could never be a valid principle for organizing the best government. True freedom, he stressed, consisted in ruling and being ruled in turn and not always insisting on fulfilling one's desires. Athens served as Aristotle's home for many years, but its democracy never won his approval.

Isocrates on Rhetoric and Society

Despite his interest in subjects relevant to politics such as the history of the constitutions of states and the theory and practice of rhetoric, Aristotle remained a theoretician in the mold of Plato. He was also inimical to the kind of democracy open to all male citizens that distinguished Athens and for which persuasive public speaking was the most valued skill. These characteristics set him apart from the major educational trend of the fourth century B.C., which emphasized practical wisdom and training with direct application to the public lives of male citizens in a democratic city-state. The most important subject in this education was rhetoric, the techniques of public speaking and argumentation. Effective rhetoric required not only oratorical expertise but also knowledge of the world and of human psychology.

Influential believers in the value of practical knowledge and rhetoric were to be found even among the followers of Socrates, himself no admirer of democracy or rhetorical techniques. Xenophon, for example, knew Socrates well enough to write extensive memoirs recreating many conversations with the great philosopher. But he also wrote a wide range of works in history, biography, estate management, horsemanship, and the public revenues of Athens. The subjects of these treatises reveal the manifold topics that Xenophon considered essential to the proper education of young men.

The works of Isocrates (436–338 B.C.) did the most to emphasize the importance of rhetoric as a practical skill. Born to a rich family, he studied both with sophists and Socrates. The Peloponnesian War destroyed his property and forced him to seek a living as a writer and teacher. Since he lacked the voice to address large gatherings and preferred quiet scholarly work to political action, Isocrates composed speeches for other men to deliver and sought to influence public opinion and political leaders at Athens and elsewhere by publishing treatises on education and politics. Regarding education as the preparation for a useful life doing good in matters of public importance, he sought to develop an educational middle ground between the theoretical study of abstract ideas and training in rhetorical techniques for influencing others to one's own private advantage. In this way Isocrates stood between the ideals of Plato and the promises of unscrupulous sophists. Isocrates on occasion criticized Athenian democracy because it allowed anyone at all to participate, but his pride in his city-state never waned. In his nineties he composed a long treatise, Panathenaicus, praising Athens for its leadership in Greece and insisting on its superiority to Sparta in the cutthroat arena of international politics.

Rhetoric was the skill that Isocrates sought to develop, but that development, he insisted, could come only with natural talent and the practical experience of worldly affairs that trained orators to understand public issues and the psychology of the people whom they had to persuade for the common good. Isocrates saw rhetoric therefore not as a device for cynical self-aggrandizement but as a powerful tool of persuasion for human betterment, if it was wielded by properly gifted and trained men with developed consciences. Women were excluded from participation because they could not take part in politics. The Isocratean emphasis on rhetoric and its application in the real world of politics won many more adherents among men in Greek and, later, Roman culture than did the Platonic vision of the philosophical life, and it would have great influence when revived in Renaissance Europe, two thousand years later.

Throughout his life Isocrates tried to recommend solutions to the most pressing problems of his era. He was particularly worried by the growing social unrest created by friction between the rich and the poor in communities throughout Greece. Athens was more fortunate than many city-states in avoiding conflict between social classes in the fourth century, perhaps because its democracy required wealthier men to spend money on benefactions to the community as a whole, especially through the liturgical system. Such men had to fulfill liturgies by paying for and sometimes also personally participating in activities that supported the city-state, such as buying the equipment for warships and serving on them or financing the costumes and training of choruses for plays produced in the public dramatic festivals. These benefactions won their sponsors gratitude (*charis*, the source of the modern word *charity*) from the public on the grounds that they were putting their wealth to use in an appropriately democratic fashion. Any rich man involved in a court case would try to win sympathy from the jury, which as a randomly selected group would include many men of moderate means, by citing all the liturgies that he and his family had performed. Indeed, in all their public speaking wealthy citizens had to signal their allegiance to democratic principles in order to win popular support. The politics of charis, then, helped to lessen tensions between rich and poor in Athens.

Elsewhere in Greece hostility between rich and poor was evidently worse. The situation was only exacerbated by the traditional fractiousness of the city-states, which could find no grounds for cooperation to solve their social problems. For Isocrates, the state of affairs in Greece had become so unstable that only a radical remedy would do: Panhellenism — political harmony among the Greek states — put into action not by Greeks but under the leadership of Philip II, king of Macedonia. Philip would unite the Greeks in a crusade against Persia, recalling the glorious success of the wars of a century and a half earlier. This alliance, as Isocrates imagined it, would end war among the city-states and also relieve the impoverished population by establishing new Greek colonies on land to be conquered and carved out of Persian-held territory in Anatolia. That a prominent and proud Athenian would openly appeal for a Macedonian king to save the Greeks from themselves reflected the startling new political and military reality that had emerged in the Greek world by the second half of the fourth century B.C.

The Macedonian Kingdom and Philip II

The rise to international power of the kingdom of Macedonia filled the power vacuum that had been created by the fruitless wars of the Greek city-states with each other in the early fourth century and that Xenophon had so acutely summed up at the end of his *Hellenica* with his bleak assessment of the consequences of the battle of Mantinea. Macedonia was a rough land of mountains and lowland valleys just to the north of Greece, and life there was harder than in Greece because the climate was colder and more dangerous and because the Macedonians' western and northern neighbors periodically launched devastating raids into Macedonian territory. The Macedonian population was especially vulnerable to such raids because they generally lived in small villages and towns without protective walls. Macedonia had more natural resources than Greece, especially in timber and precious metals, but that this formerly minor kingdom become the supreme power in Greece in the latter part of the fourth century and then conquered the vast Persian Empire must rank as one of the major surprises in ancient military and political history.

The power of the king of the Macedonian state was constrained by the tradition that he was supposed to listen to his people, who were accustomed to addressing their monarch with considerable freedom of speech. Above all, the king could govern effectively only as long as he maintained the support of the most powerful families in Macedonia, whose leaders counted as his social equals and controlled large bands of followers. Fighting, hunting, and heavy drinking were the favorite pastimes of these men. The king was expected to demonstrate his prowess in these activities to show that he was a man's man capable of heading the state. Macedonian queens and royal mothers received respect in this male-dominated society because they belonged to powerful families of the Macedonian social elite or the ruling houses of lands bordering Macedonia and bore their husbands the male heirs needed to carry on royal dynasties. In the king's absence these royal women could vie with the king's designated representative for power at court.

Macedonians had their own language related to Greek, but the members of the elite that dominated Macedonian society routinely learned to speak Greek because they thought of themselves and indeed all Macedonians as Greek by blood. At the same time, Macedonians looked down on the Greeks to the south as a soft lot unequal to the adversities of life in Macedonia. The Greeks reciprocated this scorn. The famed Athenian orator Demosthenes (384–322 B.C.) lambasted the Macedonian king Philip II (ruled 359–336) as "not only not a Greek nor related to the Greeks, but not even a barbarian from a land worth mentioning; no, he's a pestilence from Macedonia, a region where you can't even buy a slave worth his salt" (Orations 9.31). Barbed verbal attacks like this one characterized Demosthenes' speeches on foreign and domestic policy to the Athenian assembly, where he consistently tried to convince his fellow Athenians to oppose Macedonian expansionism in Greece. His exceptional rhetorical skill also made him the foremost of his time in the writing of speeches for other men to deliver in court cases.

Demosthenes spoke so forcefully against Philip II because he recognized how ambitious was this king, the person most responsible for making Macedonia into an international power and doing so against heavy odds. For one thing, strife in the royal family and disputes among the leading families had always been so common that Macedonia before Philip's reign had never been sufficiently united to mobilize its full military strength. So real was the fear of violence from their own countrymen that Macedonian kings stationed bodyguards at the door to the royal bedroom. Moreover, Macedonian princes married earlier than did most men, soon after the age of twenty, because the instability of the kingship demanded the production of male heirs as soon as possible.

The situation was therefore grave in 359 B.C., when the Macedonian king Perdiccas and four thousand Macedonian troops were slaughtered in battle with the Illyrians, hostile neighbors to the north of Macedonia. Philip was then twenty-two years old. In this moment of crisis, he persuaded the most important Macedonian leaders to recognize him as king in place of his infant nephew, for whom he was now serving as regent after the death of Perdiccas in battle. Philip soon restored the army's confidence by teaching the infantrymen an unstoppable new tactic. Macedonian troops carried thrusting spears fourteen feet long, which they had to hold with two hands. Philip drilled his men to handle these heavy weapons in a phalanx formation, whose front line bristled with outstretched spears like a lethal porcupine. With the cavalry deployed as a strike force to soften up the enemy and protect the infantry's flanks, Philip's reorganized army promptly routed Macedonia's attackers and suppressed local rivals to the young new king.

Philip next embarked on a whirlwind of diplomacy, bribery, and military action to make the states of Greece acknowledge his political superiority. He financed his ambition by prodigious spending of the gold and silver coinage he had minted from the mines of Macedonia and those that he captured in Thrace. A Greek contemporary, the historian Theopompus of Chios, labeled Philip "insatiable and extravagant; he did everything in a hurry . . . a soldier, he never spared the time to reckon up his income and expenditure" (FGrH 115 F 224). In the 350s Philip achieved a great coup by convincing the most powerful leaders in Thessaly, the prosperous region of central Greece just over the mountains south of Macedonia, to elect him hegemonial commander of their confederacy, thereby investing him with legitimacy as a leader of Greeks. The Thessalian barons apparently justified the choice of a Macedonian to lead their alliance by asserting that Philip was their kin as a descendant of the legendary Heracles and therefore perfectly qualified for the post.

In the mid-340s Philip entered a bitter dispute over alleged sacrilege by the Phocians, the Greeks just south of the Thessalians. This so-called Sacred War, a tangled affair involving the oracle of Apollo at Delphi, pitted Philip and his Greek allies against the Phocians and their allies, among whom were the Athenians. Philip and his side gained the upper hand in this conflict, and by the late 340s B.C. Philip had cajoled or forced most of northern and central Greece to follow his lead in foreign policy. His goal then became to lead a united Macedonian and Greek army against the Persian Empire. His announced reason sprang from a central theme in Greek understanding of the past: the need to avenge the Persian invasion of Macedonia and Greece of 480 B.C. Philip also feared the potentially destabilizing effect on his kingdom if his reinvigorated army were left with nothing to do. To launch his grandiose invasion, however, he needed to strengthen his alliance by adding the forces of southern Greece to it.

At Athens, Demosthenes used his stirring rhetoric to castigate the Greeks for their failure to resist Philip: they stood by, he thundered, "as if Philip were a hailstorm, praying that he would not come their way, but not trying to do anything to head him off" (*Orations* 9.33). Finally, Athens and Thebes headed a coalition of southern Greek states to try to block Philip's plans by concerted military action. In 338, however, Philip and his Greek allies trounced the coalition's forces at the battle of Chaeronea in Boeotia. The defeated Greek states retained their internal freedom, but they were compelled to join an alliance under Philip's undisputed leadership, called the League of Corinth by modern scholars after the location of its headquarters. Sparta managed to stay out of the League of Corinth, but its days as an important power in its own right were over. The battle of Chaeronea was a decisive turning point in Greek history: never again would the states of Greece make foreign policy for themselves without considering, and usually following, the wishes of outside powers. This change marked the end of the Greek city-states as independent actors in international politics, but they unquestionably retained their significance as the basic economic and social units of the Greek world. That role now had to be fulfilled, however, either as subjects or allies of Macedonia or, after the death of Alexander the Great in 323 B.C., of the kingdoms subsequently created by Alexander's former generals. The Hellenistic kingdoms, as these new monarchies are called, like the Roman provinces that eventually replaced them as political masters of the Greeks, depended on the local leaders of the Greek city-states to collect taxes for the imperial treasuries and to insure the loyalty and order of the rest of the citizens. Thus, the city-states remained important constituent elements of the political organization of the Greek world and maintained a vital public life for their citizens, but they were never again to be the sole arbiters of their own fates.

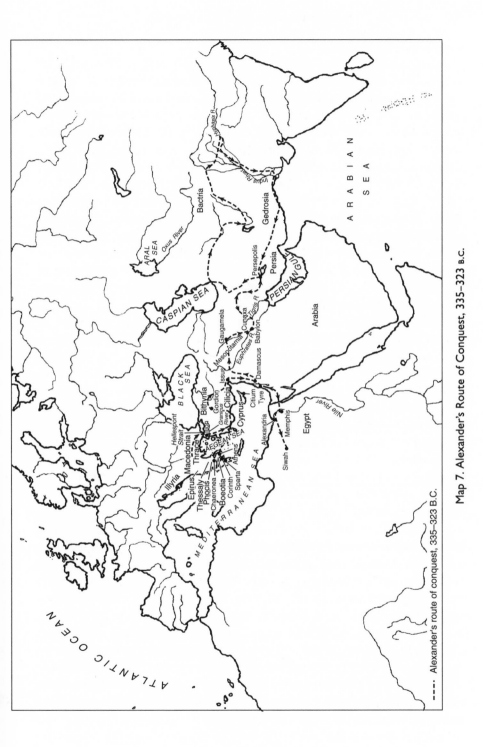

Map 7. Alexander's Route of Conquest, 335–323 B.C.

- - - - Alexander's route of conquest, 335–323 B.C.

The Conquests of Alexander the Great

A disgruntled Macedonian assassinated Philip in 336 B.C. Unconfirmed rumors circulated that the murder had been instigated by one of his several wives, Olympias, a princess from Epirus to the west of Macedonia and mother of Philip's son, Alexander (356–323 B.C.). Alexander promptly liquidated potential rivals for the throne and won recognition as king while barely twenty years old. In several lightning-fast campaigns, he subdued Macedonia's traditional enemies to the west and north. Next he compelled the city-states in southern Greece that had rebelled from the League of Corinth at the news of Philip's death to rejoin the alliance. (As in Philip's reign, Sparta remained outside the league.) To demonstrate the price of disloyalty, Alexander destroyed Thebes in 335 as punishment for its rebellion. This lesson in terror made it clear that Alexander might claim to lead the Greek city-states by their consent (the kind of leader called a hegemon in Greek) but that the reality of his power rested on his superior force and his unwavering willingness to employ it.

With Greece cowed into peaceful if grudging allegiance, Alexander in 334 led a Macedonian and Greek army into Anatolia to fulfill his father's plan to avenge Greece by attacking Persia. Alexander's astounding success in the following years in conquering the entire Persian Empire while still in his twenties earned him the title "the Great" in later ages. In his own time, his greatness consisted of his ability to inspire his men to follow him into hostile, unknown regions where they were reluctant to go, beyond the borders of civilization as they knew it. Alexander inspired his troops with his reckless disregard for his own safety, often, for example, plunging into the enemy at the head of his men and sharing the danger of the common soldier. No one could miss him in his plumed helmet, vividly colored cloak, and armor polished to reflect the sun. So intent on conquering distant lands was Alexander that he had rejected advice to delay his departure from Macedonia until he had married and fathered an heir, to forestall instability in case of his death. He had further alarmed his principal adviser, an experienced older man, by giving away virtually all his land and property in order to strengthen the army, thereby creating new landowners who would furnish troops. "What," he was asked, "do you have left for yourself?" "My hopes," Alexander replied (Plutarch, *Alexander* 15). Those hopes centered on constructing a heroic image of himself as a warrior as glorious as the incomparable Achilles of Homer's *Iliad*. Alexander always kept a copy of the *Iliad* under his pillow, along with a dagger. Alexander's aspirations and his behavior represented the ultimate expression of the Homeric vision of the glorious conquering warrior.

Alexander cast a spear into the earth of Anatolia when he crossed the

Hellespont strait from Europe to Asia, thereby claiming the Asian continent for himself in Homeric fashion as territory "won by the spear" (Diodorus, Library of History 17.17.2). The first battle of the campaign, at the River Granicus in western Anatolia, proved the worth of Alexander's Macedonian and Greek cavalry, which charged across the river and up the bank to rout the opposing Persians. Alexander visited Midas's old capital of Gordion in Phrygia, where an oracle had promised the lordship of Asia to whoever could loose a seemingly impenetrable knot of rope tying the yoke of an ancient chariot preserved in the city. The young Macedonian, so the story goes, cut the Gordion knot with his sword. In 333 B.C. the Persian king Darius finally faced Alexander in battle at Issus, near the southeastern corner of Anatolia. Alexander's army defeated its more numerous opponents with a characteristically bold strike of cavalry through the left side of the Persian lines followed by a flanking maneuver against the king's position in the center. Darius had to flee from the field to avoid capture, leaving behind his wives and daughters, who had accompanied his campaign in keeping with royal Persian tradition. Alexander's scrupulously chivalrous treatment of the Persian royal women after their capture at Issus reportedly boosted his reputation among the peoples of the king's empire.

When Tyre, a heavily fortified city on the coast of what is now Lebanon, refused to surrender to him in 332 B.C., Alexander employed the assault machines and catapults developed by his father to breach the walls of its formidable offshore fortress after a long siege. The capture of Tyre rang the death knell of the walled city-state as a settlement impregnable to siege warfare. Although successful sieges remained rare after Alexander because well-constructed city walls still presented formidable barriers to attackers, Alexander's success against Tyre increased the terror of a siege for a city's general population. No longer could the citizens of a city-state confidently assume that their defensive system could withstand the technology of their enemy's offensive weapons indefinitely. The now-present fear that a siege might actually breach a city's walls made it much harder psychologically for city-states to remain united in the face of threats from enemies like aggressive kings.

Alexander next took over Egypt, where hieroglyphic inscriptions seem to show that he probably presented himself as the successor to the Persian king as the land's ruler rather than as an Egyptian pharaoh. On the coast, to the west of the Nile river, Alexander in 331 founded a new city named Alexandria after himself, the first of the many cities he would later establish as far east as Afghanistan. During his time in Egypt, Alexander also paid a mysterious visit to the oracle of the god Ammon, whom the Greeks regarded as identical to Zeus, at the oasis of Siwah far out in the western Egyptian desert. Alexander told no one the details of his consultation of the oracle, but the news got out that he had been informed he was the son of the god and that he joyfully accepted the designation as true.

In 331 B.C., Alexander crushed the Persian king's main army at the battle of Gaugamela in northern Mesopotamia, near the border of modern Iraq and Iran. He subsequently proclaimed himself king of Asia in place of the Persian king. For the heterogeneous populations of the Persian Empire, the succession of a Macedonian to the Persian throne meant essentially no change in their lives. They continued to send the same taxes to a remote master, whom they rarely if ever saw. As in Egypt, Alexander left the local administrative system of the Persian Empire in place, even retaining some Persian governors. His long-term aim seems to have been to forge an administrative corps composed of Macedonians, Greeks, and Persians working together to rule the territory he conquered with his army.

To India and Back

Alexander next led his army farther east into territory hardly known to the Greeks. He pared his force to reduce the need for supplies, which were difficult to find in the arid country through which they were marching. Each hoplite in Greek armies customarily had a personal servant to carry his armor and pack. Alexander, imitating Philip, trained his men to carry their own equipment, thereby creating a leaner force by cutting the number of army servants dramatically. As with all ancient armies, however, a large number of noncombatants trailed after the fighting force: merchants who set up little markets at every stop, women whom soldiers had taken as mates along the way and their children, entertainers, and prostitutes. Although supplying these hangers-on was not Alexander's responsibility, their foraging for themselves made it harder for Alexander's quartermasters to find what they needed to supply the army proper.

An ancient army's demand for supplies usually left a trail of destruction and famine for local inhabitants in the wake of its march. Hostile armies simply took whatever they wanted. Friendly armies expected local people to sell or donate food to its supply officers and also to the merchants trailing along. These entrepreneurs would set up markets to resell locally obtained provisions to the soldiers. Since most farmers in antiquity had practically no surplus to sell, they found this expectation—which was in reality a requirement—a terrific hardship. The money the farmers received was of little use to them because there was nothing to buy with it in the countryside, where their neighbors had also had to participate in the forced marketing of their subsistence.

From the heartland of Persia, Alexander in 329 B.C. marched northeastward into the trackless steppes of Bactria (modern Afghanistan). When he proved unable to subdue completely the highly mobile locals, who avoided pitched battles in favor of the guerrilla tactics of attack and retreat, Alexander settled for an alliance sealed by his marriage to the Bactrian princess Roxane in 327. In this same period, Alexander completed the cold-blooded suppression of both real and imagined resistance to his plans among the leading men in his officer corps. As in past years, he used accusations of treachery or disloyalty as justification for the execution of those Macedonians he had come to distrust. These executions, like the destruction of Thebes in 335, demonstrated Alexander's appreciation of terror as a disincentive to rebellion.

From Bactria Alexander pushed on eastward to India. He probably intended to march all the way through to China in search of the edge of the farthest land on the earth, which Aristotle, once Alexander's tutor, had taught was a sphere. Seventy days of marching through monsoon rains, however, finally shattered the nerves of Alexander's soldiers. In the spring of 326 B.C. they mutinied on the banks of the Hyphasis River (the modern Beas) in western India. Alexander was forced to agree to lead them in the direction of home. When his men had balked before, Alexander had always been able to shame them back into action by sulking in his tent like Achilles in the *Iliad*. This time the soldiers were beyond shame.

Alexander thereupon proceeded south down the Indus River. Along the way he took out his frustration at being stopped in his eastward march by slaughtering the Indian tribes who resisted him and by risking his life more flamboyantly then ever before. As a climax to his frustrated rage, he flung himself over the wall of an Indian town to face the enemy alone like a Homeric hero. His horrified officers were barely able to rescue him in time; even so, he received grievous wounds. At the mouth of the Indus on the Indian Ocean, Alexander turned a portion of his army west through the fierce desert of Gedrosia. Another portion took an easier route inland, while a third group sailed westward along the coast to explore for possible sites for new settlements and harbors. Alexander himself led the contingent that braved the desert, planning to surpass earlier Persian kings by marching through territory that they had found impassable. There a flash flood wiped out most of the noncombatants following the army. Many of the soldiers also died on the march through the desert, expiring from lack of water and the heat, which has been recorded at 127 degrees in the shade in that area. Alexander, as always, shared his men's hardships. In one legendary episode from this horrible ordeal, a few men were said to have brought him a helmet containing some water they had found. Alexander spilled the water out onto the sand rather than drink when his men could not. The remains of the army finally reached safety in the heartland of Persia in 324 B.C. Alexander promptly began plans for an invasion of the Arabian peninsula and, to follow that, all of North Africa west of Egypt.

By the time Alexander returned to Persia, he had dropped all pretense of ruling over the Greeks as anything other than an absolute monarch. Despite his earlier promise to respect the internal freedom of the Greek city-states, he now impinged on their autonomy by sending a peremptory decree ordering them to restore to citizenship the large number of exiles wandering homeless in the Greek world. The previous decades of war in Greece had created many of these unfortunate wanderers, and their status as stateless persons was creating unrest. Even more striking was Alexander's communication to the city-states that he wished to receive the honors due a god. Initially dumbfounded by this request, the leaders of most Greek states soon complied by sending honorary delegations to him as if he were a god. The Spartan Damis pithily expressed the only prudent position on Alexander's deification open to the cowed Greeks: "If Alexander wishes to be a god, we agree that he be called a god" (Plutarch, *Moralia* 219e).

Scholarly debate continues over Alexander's motive for desiring the Greeks to acknowledge him as a god, but few now accept a formerly popular theory that he sought divinity because he believed the city-states would then have to obey his orders as originating from a divinity, whose authority would supersede that of all earthly regimes. Personal rather than political motives best explain his request. He almost certainly had come to believe that he was the son of Zeus; after all, Greek mythology told many stories of Zeus producing children by mating with a human female. Most of those legendary offspring were mortal, but Alexander's conquest showed that he had surpassed them. His feats must be superhuman, he could well have believed, because they exceeded the bounds of human possibility. In other words, Alexander's accomplishments demonstrated that he had achieved godlike power and therefore must be a god himself. The divinity of Alexander, in ancient terms, emerged as a natural consequence of his power.

Alexander's overall aims can best be explained as interlinked goals: the conquest and administration of the known world and the exploration and possible colonization of new territory beyond. Conquest through military action was a time-honored pursuit for ambitious Macedonian leaders such as Alexander. He included non-Macedonians in his administration and army because he needed their expertise, not because he had any dream of promoting an abstract notion of what has sometimes been called "the brotherhood of man." Alexander's explorations benefited numerous scientific fields, from geography to botany, because he took along scientifically minded writers to collect and catalogue the new knowledge that they encountered. The far-flung new cities that he founded served as loyal outposts to keep the peace in conquered territory and provide warnings to headquarters in case of local uprisings. They also created new opportunities for trade in valuable goods such as spices that were not produced in the Mediterranean region.

Alexander's plans to conquer Arabia and North Africa were extinguished by his premature death from a fever and heavy drinking on June 10, 323 B.C., in Babylon. He had already been suffering for months from depression brought on by the death of his best friend, Hephaistion. Close since their boyhoods, Alexander and Hephaistion were probably lovers. When Hephaistion died in a bout of excessive drinking, Alexander went wild with grief. The depth of his emotion was evident when he planned to build an elaborate temple to honor Hephaistion as a god. Meanwhile, Alexander threw himself into preparing for his Arabian campaign by exploring the marshy lowlands of southern Mesopotamia. Perhaps it was on one of these trips that he contracted the malaria-like fever that, exacerbated by a two-day drinking binge, killed him.

Like Pericles, Alexander had made no plans about what should happen if he should die unexpectedly. His wife Roxane was to give birth to their first child only some months after Alexander's death. When at Alexander's deathbed his commanders asked him to whom he bequeathed his kingdom, he replied, "To the most powerful [kratistos]" (Arrian, Anabasis of Alexander 7.26.3).

The Athenian orator Aeschines (c. 397–322 B.C.) well expressed the bewildered reaction of many people to the events of Alexander's lifetime: "What strange and unexpected event has not occurred in our time? The life we have lived is no ordinary human one, but we were born to be an object of wonder to posterity" (Orations 3.132). Alexander himself certainly attained legendary status in later times. Stories of fabulous exploits attributed to him became popular folk tales throughout the ancient world, even reaching distant regions where Alexander had never trod, such as deep into Africa. The popularity of the legend of Alexander as a symbol of the height of achievement for a masculine warrior-hero served as one of his most persistent legacies to later ages. That the worlds of Greece and the Near East had been brought into closer contact than ever before represented the other long-lasting effect of his astonishing career. Its immediate political and military consequences were the struggles among his generals that led to the creation of the kingdoms of the Hellenistic world.

10

The Hellenistic Age

Relocating Greek Culture

The term *Hellenistic* was invented in the nineteenth century to designate the period of Greek and Near Eastern history from the death of Alexander the Great in 323 B.C. to the death of Cleopatra VII, the last Macedonian ruler of Egypt, in 30 B.C. The early Hellenistic period saw the emergence of a new form of kingship, compounded from Macedonian and Near Eastern traditions, which became the dominant political structure in the eastern Mediterranean after Alexander's premature death. The men who founded the Hellenistic kingdoms were generals from Alexander's forces, who made themselves into monarchs although they had neither a blood relationship to any traditional royal family line nor any historical claim to a particular territory. Their military power, their prestige, and their ambition were their only justifications for transforming themselves into kings.

"Hellenistic" also conveys the idea that a mixed, cosmopolitan form of social and cultural life combining Hellenic (that is, Greek) traditions with indigenous traditions emerged in the eastern Mediterranean region in the aftermath of Alexander's conquests. The Hellenistic kings spurred this development by bringing Greeks to live in the midst of long-established indigenous communities and also by founding new cities on Greek lines. Since these imported Greeks primarily lived in cities, Greek ideas and customs had their greatest impact on the urban populations of Egypt and southwestern Asia. The great number of people farming the Near Eastern countryside, who rarely visited the cities, had much less contact with Greek ways of life. Since the kings favored Greek culture, there was never any doubt that it would be adopted by the elite of the Hellenistic kingdoms, whatever their own origins. At the same time, Greek culture could hardly remain unchanged once it was relocated to so many new places outside the Greek homeland.

Creating Hellenistic Kingdoms

After Alexander's death, his mother, Olympias, sought for several years to establish her infant grandson, Alexander's son by Roxane, as the Macedonian king under her protection. Her plan foundered because Alexander's former commanders wanted power for themselves, and within twenty years three of the most powerful of them had established new kingdoms in place of the old. Antigonus (c. 382–301 B.C.) and his son Demetrius (c. 336–283 B.C.) took over in Macedonia and Greece, Seleucus (c. 358–281 B.C.) in Syria and the old Persian Empire, and Ptolemy (c. 367–282 B.C.) in Egypt. Since these men succeeded to the largest parts of Alexander's conquests as if they had been his heirs, they were referred to as the "successor kings."

The first Hellenistic kings faced the same challenge shared by all new political regimes: to establish a tradition of legitimacy for their rule. Legitimacy was essential if they were to found a royal line that had a chance of enduring beyond their deaths. As a result, Hellenistic queens enjoyed a high social status as the representatives of distinguished families, who then became the mothers of a line of royal descendants. The successors' positions ultimately rested on their personal ability and their power. The city of Ilion in northwest Anatolia summed up the situation in conveying honors on Seleucus's son and heir, Antiochus I (ruled 281–261 B.C.), in the 270s: "He has made his kingdom prosperous and brilliant mostly through his own excellence but also with the good will of his friends and his forces" (OGIS 219). In sum, Hellenistic kingship had its origins in the personal attributes of the king instead of inherited privileges and perquisites. For this reason, it is often described as "personal monarchy."

It took decades after Alexander's death for the general territorial outlines of the new kingdoms to be settled. Antigonus tried to expand his personal monarchy into a large empire by attacking the kingdoms of the other successors, but they in response temporarily banded together to defeat and kill him at the battle of Ipsus in Anatolia in 301 B.C. His son, Demetrius, regained the Macedonian throne from about 294 to 288, but further defeats

c. **320–301 b.c.**: Macedonian generals Antigonus and his son Demetrius try to establish a large kingdom in Greece, Macedonia, and the Near East.

310 b.c.: Murder of Alexander's son, the last member of the Macedonian royal house; Zeno founds the Stoic philosophical school at Athens.

307 b.c.: Epicurus establishes his philosophical school at Athens.

306–304 b.c.: "Successors" of Alexander declare themselves kings.

303 b.c.: Seleucus cedes eastern territory of his kingdom to the Indian king Chandragupta.

301 b.c.: Antigonus defeated and killed at battle of Ipsus in Anatolia.

300 b.c.: King Ptolemy I establishes the Museum in Alexandria.

c. **284–281 b.c.**: Foundation of Achaean League in southern Greece.

279 b.c.: Gauls invade Macedonia and Greece.

263–241 b.c.: Eumenes I founds independent Attalid kingdom in Anatolia, with Pergamum as capital.

256 b.c.: Mauryan king Asoka in India proclaims his Buddhist mission to Greeks.

239–130 b.c.: Independent Greek kingdom in Bactria (modern Afghanistan).

238–227 b.c.: Attalid king Attalus I defeats the Gauls and confines them to Galatia.

214–205 b.c.: Philip V, king of Macedonia, fights the first of the wars with the Romans that will eventually involve the Romans in Macedonia, Greece, Egypt, and the Near East.

167 b.c.: Antiochus IV forcibly introduces a statue of the Syrian god Baal into the Temple of the Jews in Jerusalem.

30 b.c.: Death of Cleopatra VII, queen of Egypt, the last Macedonian monarch of the Hellenistic period.

---

forced Demetrius to spend his last years in benign captivity as a helpless guest under the power of Seleucus. Demetrius's son, Antigonus Gonatas (c. 320–239 B.C.), reestablished the Antigonid kingdom, centered in Macedonia, by about 276. The Seleucid kingdom ceded its easternmost territory early in its history to the Indian king Chandragupta (ruled 323–299 B.C.), founder of the Mauryan dynasty, and later lost most of Persia to the Parthians, a north Iranian people; nevertheless, its territory remained huge. The Ptolemaic kingdom was able to retain continuous control of the rich land of Egypt, which was easier to defend because the deserts on its borders made invasions by land difficult. By the middle of the third century B.C., the three successor kingdoms had in practice reached a balance of power that pre-

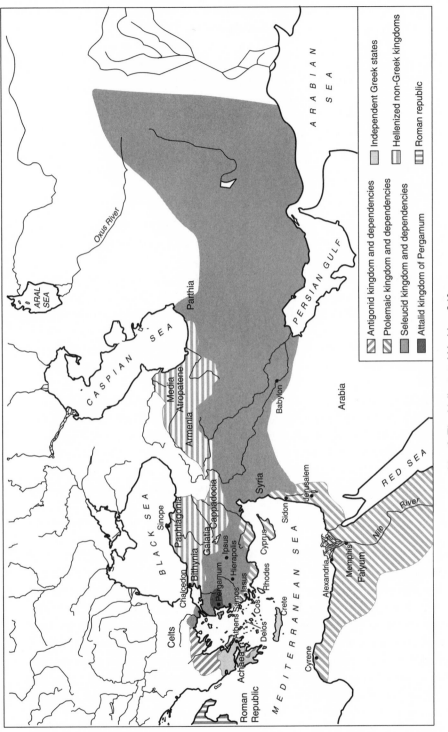

	Antigonid kingdom and dependencies		Independent Greek states
	Ptolemaic kingdom and dependencies		Hellenized non-Greek kingdoms
	Seleucid kingdom and dependencies		Roman republic
	Attalid kingdom of Pergamum		

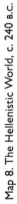

Map 8. The Hellenistic World, c. 240 B.C.

ARABIAN SEA

Oxus River

ARAL SEA

CASPIAN SEA

Parthia

PERSIAN GULF

Media Atropatene
Armenia

Babylon

Arabia

Syria

Jerusalem

BLACK SEA

Sinope

Paphlagonia

Cappadocia

Galatia
Bithynia
Ipsus
Chalcedon
Pergamum
Hierapolis
Teaus

Cyprus

Sidon

RED SEA

Nile River

Alexandria
Memphis
Faiyum

Rhodes

Cos
Samos
Delos
Crete

Athens

Achaea

Celts

Roman Republic

Cyrene

MEDITERRANEAN SEA

cluded their expanding much beyond their core territories. Nevertheless, the Hellenistic monarchs were to remain competitive, especially in conflicts over contested border areas. The Ptolemies and the Seleucids, for example, periodically engaged in a violent tug of war over Palestine and Syria.

Some smaller regional kingdoms also developed in the Hellenistic period. Most famous among them was the kingdom of the Attalids in Anatolia, with the wealthy city of Pergamum as its capital. The Attalids were strong enough to defeat a large band of Celtic people called Gauls, who invaded the Pergamene kingdom from northern Europe in the third century B.C., and confine them to an area in Anatolia thereafter known as Galatia from their name. As far away as central Asia, in what is today Afghanistan, a new kingdom formed when Diodotos I led a successful rebellion of Bactrian Greeks from the Seleucid kingdom in the mid-third century B.C. These Greeks, whose ancestors had been settled in Bactria by Alexander the Great, had flourished because their land was the crossroads for overland trade in luxury goods between India and China and the Mediterranean world. By the end of the first century B.C. the Bactrian kingdom had fallen to Asian invaders from north of the Oxus River (now the Amu Daria), but the region continued to serve as a cauldron for the interaction of the artistic, philosophical, and religious traditions of East and West.

All the Hellenistic kingdoms in the eastern Mediterranean region eventually fell to the Romans. Diplomatic and military blunders by the kings of Macedonia beginning in the third century B.C. first drew the Romans into Greece, where they became dominant by the middle of the second century. Thereafter, Greek history was part of Roman history. Smaller powers, such as the city-state of Rhodes and the Attalid kings in Pergamum, further encouraged the Romans to take a hand in affairs in the eastern Mediterranean. Despite its early losses of territory and later troubles from both internal uprisings and external enemies, the Seleucid kingdom remained a major power in the Near East for two centuries. Nevertheless, it, too, fell to the Romans in the mid-first century B.C. As for Egypt, even though Ptolemy II (ruled 282–246 B.C.) created difficulties for his successors by imposing disastrous financial measures to pay for a war in Syria, the Ptolemaic kingdom survived the longest. Eventually, however, its growing weakness forced the Egyptian kings to summon intermittent Roman support. When Queen Cleopatra chose the losing side in the Roman civil war of the late first century B.C., a Roman invasion in 30 B.C. ended her reign and the long succession of Ptolemaic rulers.

Defending and Administering Hellenistic Kingdoms

The armies and navies of Hellenistic kingdoms provided security against internal unrest as well as external enemies. Unlike the citizen militias of the city-states of Classical Greece, Hellenistic royal forces were composed of professional soldiers. The Greek city-states of the Hellenistic period also increasingly hired mercenaries instead of calling up citizens as troops. To develop their military might, the Seleucid and Ptolemaic kings vigorously promoted immigration by Greeks and Macedonians, who received grants of land in return for military service. When this source of people later dwindled, the kings had to rely more on the local populations, often employing indigenous troops to do military service. Military expenditures rose because the kings faced ongoing pressure to pay their mercenaries regularly and because technology had developed more expensive artillery, such as catapults capable of flinging a projectile weighing 170 pounds a distance of nearly two hundred yards. Hellenistic navies were expensive because warships were larger, with some dreadnoughts requiring hundreds of men as crews. War elephants, popular items in Hellenistic arsenals for their shock effect on enemy troops, also entailed large expenses.

To administer their kingdoms, Hellenistic kings initially depended for the most part on immigrant Greeks and Macedonians. The title "king's friends" identified the inner circle of advisers and courtiers. Like Alexander before them, however, the Seleucids and the Ptolemies necessarily also employed indigenous men throughout the middle and lower levels of their administrations. Even local men who made successful careers in government employ, however, only rarely were admitted to the highest ranks of royal society, such as the king's friends. Greeks and Macedonians generally saw themselves as too superior to mix with locals. The most valuable qualification local men could acquire for a governmental career was to learn to read and write Greek in addition to their native languages. They would then be able to fill positions communicating the orders of the highest-ranking officials, Greeks and Macedonians all, to the local farmers, builders, and crafts producers whose job it was to carry them out. The Greek that these administrators had learned was koine ("common Greek"), a standardized form of the language based on the Athenian dialect. For centuries, koine was the common language of commerce and culture all the way from Sicily to the border of India. It is the language in which the New Testament was written during the early Roman Empire and was the parent of Byzantine and modern Greek.

Administrators had as their principal jobs the maintenance of order and the control of the direct and indirect tax systems of the kingdoms. In many ways the goals and the structures of Hellenistic royal administrations recalled those of the earlier Assyrian, Babylonian, and Persian empires. They kept order among the kingdom's subjects by arbitrating between disputing parties whenever possible, but they could if necessary call on troops to serve police functions. Overseeing the collection of taxes could be complicated. For instance, in Ptolemaic Egypt, the most tightly organized of the

Hellenistic kingdoms, royal officials collected customs duties of 50, $33\frac{1}{3}$, 25, or 20 percent, depending on the type of goods. The central planning and control of the renowned Ptolemaic organization were inherited from much earlier periods of Egyptian history. Officials continued to administer royal monopolies, such as that on vegetable oil, intended to maximize the king's revenue. Ptolemaic administrators, in a system much like modern schemes of centralized agriculture, decided how much royal land was to be sown in oil-bearing plants, supervised production and distribution of the oil, and set all prices for every stage of the oil business. The king, through his officials, also often entered into partnerships with private investors to produce more revenue.

Cities were the economic and social centers of the Hellenistic kingdoms. In Greece, some cities tried to increase their strength to counterbalance that of the monarchies by banding together into new federal alliances, such as the Achaean League in the Peloponnese, established in the late 280s. Making decisions for the league in a shared assembly, these cities agreed on common institutions such as coinage, weights and measures, and legal protections for citizens. Many Greeks and Macedonians also now lived in new cities founded by Alexander and the successors in the Near East. Hellenistic kings also refounded existing cities to bring honor on themselves and introduce new immigrants and social patterns supportive of their policies. The new settlements had the traditional features of Classical Greek city-states, such as gymnasiums and theaters. Although these cities often also possessed such traditional political institutions of the city-state as councils and assemblies for citizen men, the limits of their independence depended strictly on the king's will. When writing to the city's council, the king might express himself in the form of a polite request, but he expected his wishes to be fulfilled as if they were commands. Moreover, the cities often had to pay taxes directly to the king.

The kings needed the good will of the wealthiest and most influential city dwellers—the Greek and Macedonian urban elites—to keep order in the cities and ensure a steady flow of tax revenues. These wealthy people had the crucial responsibility of collecting the kingdom's taxes from the surrounding countryside as well as their cities and sending them on to the royal treasury. The kings therefore honored and flattered these members of the cities' upper class to secure their good will and cooperation. Favored cities would receive benefactions from the king to pay for expensive public works like theaters and temples or restorations after such natural disasters as earthquakes. The wealthy men and women of the urban upper classes in turn helped to keep the general population tractable by providing donations and loans that would secure a reliable supply of grain to feed the city's population, subsidize teachers and doctors, and construct public works. The Greek tradition that the wealthy elite of a city-state should make benefactions for the common good was therefore continued in a new way, through the social interaction of the kings and the urban upper classes.

Well-to-do members of the indigenous populations also mattered to the kings. Since indigenous cities had long been powerful in Syria and Palestine, for example, the kings had to develop cordial relations with their leading members. Non-Greeks and non-Macedonians from eastern regions also moved westward to Hellenistic Greek cities in increasing numbers. Jews in particular moved away from Palestine into Anatolia, Greece, and Egypt. The Jewish community eventually became an influential minority in Alexandria, the most important Hellenistic city. In Egypt, the king also had to come to terms with the priests who controlled the temples of the traditional Egyptian gods because the temples owned large tracts of productive agricultural land worked by tenant farmers. The linchpin in the organization of the Hellenistic kingdoms was the system of mutual rewards by which the kings and their leading subjects—Greeks, Macedonians, and indigenous elites—became, as it were, partners in government and public finance.

The successor kingdoms nevertheless amounted to foreign rule over indigenous populations by kings and queens of Macedonian descent. Monarchs had to accommodate the urban elites and the favored immigrants in their kingdoms, but royal power pervaded the lives of the kingdoms' subjects, above all in the meting out of justice. Seleucus, for one, claimed this right as a universal truth: "It is not the customs of the Persians and other peoples that I impose upon you, but the law which is common to everyone, that what is decreed by the king is always just" (Appian, *Syriake* 61). Even Antigonus's successors, who claimed to lead the Greeks in a voluntary alliance that allegedly reestablished Philip's League of Corinth, frequently interfered in the internal affairs of the Greek city-states. Like the other kings, they regularly installed their own governors and garrisons in cities where loyalty was suspect. Never again would ancient Greeks live their lives free of the shadow of monarchy, sometimes faint in the distance, sometimes looming near.

Economy and Society in the Hellenistic Kingdoms

Hellenistic society in the eastern Mediterranean world was clearly divided into separate layers. At the top of the hierarchy came the royal family and the circle of the king's friends. The Greek and Macedonian elites of the major cities ranked next in social status. Closely following came the wealthy elites of the indigenous cities, the leaders of large minority urban populations, and the traditional lords and princes of indigenous groups maintaining their ancestral domains in more rural regions. Lowest of the free population were the masses of small merchants, crafts producers, and laborers. Slaves remained where they had always been, outside the bounds of society, although those who worked at court sometimes could live physically comfortable lives.

Poor people performed the overwhelming bulk of the labor required to support the economies of the Hellenistic kingdoms. Agriculture remained the economic base, and conditions for farmers and field workers changed little over time. Many of them worked on the huge agricultural estates belonging to the royal family, but city-states that retained their countrysides still had free peasants working small plots as well as larger farms belonging to wealthy landowners. Rural people rose early to begin work before the heat of the day, cultivating the same kinds of crops and animals as their ancestors had with the same simple hand tools and beasts of burden. The level of technology was such that perhaps as many as 80 percent of all adult men and women, free as well as slave, had to work on the land to produce enough food to sustain the population. Along certain international routes, however, trade by sea did thrive. Tens of thousands of amphoras (large ceramic jars used to transport commodities such as olive oil and wine) made on the Greek island of Rhodes, for example, have been found in Ptolemaic Egypt. Consortiums of foreign merchants turned the Aegean island of Delos into a busy transportation hub for the cross-shipping of goods, such as the ten thousand slaves a day the port could handle. In the cities, poor women and men could work as small merchants, peddlers, and artisans producing goods such as tools, pottery, clothing, and furniture. Men could sign on as deck hands on the merchant ships that sailed the Mediterranean and Indian Oceans in pursuit of profits from trade.

In the Seleucid and Ptolemaic kingdoms, a large section of the rural population existed in a state of dependency between free and slave. The "peoples," as they were called, farmed the estates belonging to the king, who was the kingdom's greatest landowner. The king theoretically claimed title to all his kingdom's land because it had been, following Alexander's terminology of conquest, "won by the spear," but in practice he ceded much territory to cities, temples, and favored individuals. The peoples were not landowners but compulsory tenants. Although they could not be sold like chattel slaves, they were not allowed to move away or abandon their tenancies. They had to pay a certain quota of produce per area of land to the king like rent to a landlord. The rent was sufficiently heavy that the "peoples" had virtually no chance to improve their economic lot in life.

Women at the pinnacle of the social pyramid in the Hellenistic world, which is to say members of the royal families, commanded riches and status unprecedented in Greek historical times. Hellenistic queens usually exercised political and military power only to the extent that they could influence their husbands' decisions, but they ruled on their own when no male heir existed. Since the Ptolemaic royal family permitted brother-sister marriage for dynastic purposes, royal daughters as well as sons were in line to rule. Arsinoë II (c. 316–270 B.C.), the daughter of Ptolemy I, for example, first married the Macedonian successor king Lysimachus, who gave her four towns as her personal domain. After Lysimachus's death, she married her brother, Ptolemy II of Egypt, and exerted at least as much influence on policy as he did. The virtues publicly praised in a queen reflected traditional Greek values for women. When the city of Hierapolis around 165 B.C. passed a decree in honor of Queen Apollonis of Pergamum, for example, she was praised for her piety toward the gods, her reverence toward her parents, her distinguished conduct toward her husband, and her harmonious relations with her "beautiful legitimate children" (*OGIS* 308).

Some queens evidently paid special attention to the condition of women. About 195 B.C., for example, the Seleucid queen Laodice gave a ten-year endowment to the city of Iasus in southwestern Anatolia to provide dowries for needy girls. Her endowing a foundation to help less fortunate women reflected the increasing concern on the part of the wealthy for the welfare of the less fortunate during the Hellenistic period. The royal families led the way in this tendency toward philanthropy as part of their cultivation of an image of generosity befitting kings and queens, in the best tradition of Greek benefaction by the social elite. That Laodice funded dowries shows that she recognized the importance to women of owning property, the surest guarantee of a certain respect and a measure of power in their households.

The lives of most women, nevertheless, were still under the influence of decisions made by men. "Who can judge better than a father what is to his daughter's interest?" remained the dominant creed of the fathers of daughters. Upper-class women remained largely separated from men not members of their families; poor women still worked in public. Greeks continued to abandon infants they could not or would not raise, and girls were abandoned more often than boys. Other peoples, such as the Egyptians and the Jews, did not practice abandonment, or exposure, as it is often called. Exposure differed from infanticide because the expectation was that someone else would find the child and bring it up, albeit usually as a slave. The third-century B.C. comic poet Posidippus overstated the case by saying, "A son, one always raises even if one is poor; a daughter, one exposes, even if one is rich" (*CAF*, fragment 11). Daughters of the wealthy were of course usually not abandoned, but as many as 10 percent of other infant girls may have been. In some limited ways, however, women did achieve greater control over their own lives in the Hellenistic period. A woman of exceptional wealth could enter public life, for example by making donations or loans to her city and being rewarded with an official post in the government of her community. Of course, such posts were now less prestigious and important than in the days of the independent city-states because real power resided in the hands of the king and his top administrators. In Egypt, women acquired greater say in the conditions of marriage because marriage contracts, a standard procedure, gradually evolved from an agreement between the groom and the bride's parents to one between the bride and groom themselves.

Even with power based in the cities, most of the population continued to live where people always had, in small villages in the countryside. There different groups of people lived side-by-side but nevertheless separately. In one region of Anatolia, for example, twenty-two different languages were spoken. Life in the new and refounded Hellenistic cities developed largely independently of indigenous rural society. Urban life acquired special vitality because the Greek and Macedonian residents of these cities, surrounded by the non-Greek countryside, tended to remain in the urban centers more than had their predecessors in the Classical city-state, whose habit it was to go back and forth frequently between city and countryside to attend to their rural property, participate in local festivals, and worship in local shrines. Now the activities of city dwellers were more and more centered on the city. Residents became attached to their cities also because the wealthy, following the tradition of the elites in the Classical city-states, increasingly gave their cities benefactions that endowed urban existence with new advantages over country life. On the island of Samos, for example, wealthy contributors endowed a foundation to finance free distribution of grain every month to all the citizens so that shortages of food would no longer trouble their city. State-sponsored schools for universal education of the young also sprang up in various Hellenistic cities, often financed by wealthy donors. In some places girls as well as boys went to school. Many cities also began ensuring the availability of doctors by sponsoring their practices. Patients still had to pay for medical attention, but at least they could count on finding a doctor when they needed one. The wealthy whose donations and loans made many of the cities' new advantages possible were paid back by the respect and honor they earned from their fellow citizens. Philanthropy even touched international relations on occasion. For example, when an earthquake devastated Rhodes, many other cities joined kings and queens in sending donations to help the Rhodians recover from the disaster. The Rhodians in turn showered honors on their benefactors.

Wealthy non-Greeks more and more adopted Greek habits of life in

the process of accommodating themselves to the new social hierarchy. Dio-
timus of Sidon, in Lebanon, for example, although not a Greek by birth,
had a Greek name and pursued the premier Greek sport, chariot racing. He
traveled to Nemea in the Peloponnese to enter his chariot in the race at the
prestigious festival of Zeus there. When he won, he put up an inscription
in Greek to announce that he was the first Sidonian to do so. He announced
his victory in Greek because, much like English in today's world, koine
Greek had become the international language of the eastern Mediterranean
coastal lands. The explosion in the use of Greek by non-Greeks is certainly
the best indication of the emergence of an international culture based on
Greek models, which was adopted by rulers and their courts, the urban
upper classes, and intellectuals during the Hellenistic period. The most
striking evidence of the spread of Greeks and Greek throughout the Hellenistic world comes from Afghanistan. There, Aśoka (ruled c. 268–232 B.C.),
third king of the Mauryan dynasty and a convert to Buddhism, used Greek
as one of the languages in his public inscriptions that announced his efforts
to introduce his subjects to Buddhist traditions of self-control such as ab-
stinence from eating meat. Even in far-off Afghanistan, non-Greeks used
Greek to communicate with Greeks with whom they were now in contact.

The Greek Literature and Art of a New Age

Even as knowledge of the Greek language was becoming more common throughout the Hellenistic world, literature in Greek was beginning
to reflect the new conditions of life. At Athens, for one, gone with the city-
state's freedom from outside interference was the focus on contemporary
affairs and the fierce attacks on political leaders that had characterized the
comedies of the fifth-century B.C. Instead, comic dramatists like Menan-
der (c. 342–289 B.C.) and Philemon (c. 360–263 B.C.) now presented timeless
plots concerning the trials and tribulations of fictional lovers, in works not
unlike modern soap operas. These comedies of manners proved so popular
that they were closely imitated in later times by Roman writers of comedy.

Poets such as Theocritus from Syracuse in Sicily (born c. 300 B.C.) and
Callimachus from Cyrene in North Africa (c. 305–240 B.C.), both of whom
came to Alexandria to be supported by the patronage of the Ptolemies,
made individual emotions a central theme in their work. Their poetry broke
new ground in demanding great intellectual effort as well as emotional en-
gagement from the audience. Only the erudite could fully appreciate the
allusions and complex references to mythology that these poets employed
in their elegant poems, which were quite short, unlike Homeric epics. Theocritus was the first Greek poet to express the cleavage between the town
and the countryside, a poetic stance corresponding to a growing reality.

His pastoral poems called the Idylls emphasized the discontinuity between the environment of the city and the bucolic life of the country dweller, although the rural people depicted in Theocritus's poetry were Greeks in idealized landscapes rather than the actual workers of the Egyptian fields. Nevertheless, his artistic pose reflected the fundamental social division of the Ptolemaic kingdom between the food consumers of the town and the food producers of the countryside.

The themes of Callimachus's prolific output underlined the division in Hellenistic society between the intellectual elite and the uneducated masses. "I hate the common crowd" could stand for Callimachus's authorial stance toward poetry and its audience. A comparison between Callimachus's work and that of his literary rival, Apollonius of Rhodes, emphasizes the Hellenistic development of intellectually demanding poetry suited only for an educated elite. Even though Apollonius wrote a long epic about Jason and the Argonauts instead of short poems like those of Callimachus, Apollonius's verses, too, displayed an erudition that only readers with a literary education could share. Like the earlier lyric poets, who in the sixth and fifth centuries B.C. had often written to please rich patrons, these Hellenistic authors necessarily had to take into account the tastes of the royal patrons who were paying the bills. In one poem expressly praising his patron, Ptolemy II, Theocritus spelled out the quid pro quo of Hellenistic literary patronage: "the spokesmen of the Muses [that is, poets] celebrate Ptolemy in return for his benefactions" (Idylls 17.115–116).

The Hellenistic kings promoted intellectual life principally by offering scholars financial support to move to the royal capitals as human proof of royal magnanimity and grandeur. The Ptolemies won this particular form of competition with their fellow monarchs by making Alexandria the leading intellectual center of the Hellenistic world. There they established the world's first scholarly research institute. Its massive library had the daunting goal of collecting all the books (that is, manuscripts) in the world; it grew to hold a half-million scrolls, an enormous number for the time. Linked to it was a building in which the hired scholars dined together and produced encyclopedias of knowledge, such as The Wonders of the World and On the Rivers of Europe by Callimachus, who wrote learned prose works in addition to poetry. The name of this building, the Museum (meaning "place of the Muses," the Greek goddesses of learning and the arts), endures to this day as a designation for institutions for the preservation and promotion of knowledge. The output of the Alexandrian scholars was prodigious. Their champion was Didymus (c. 80–10 B.C.), nicknamed "Brass Guts" for his indefatigable writing of nearly four thousand books.

None of the women poets known from the Hellenistic period seems to have enjoyed royal patronage. But women excelled in writing epigrams, a style of short poems originally used for funerary epitaphs, for which Callimachus was famed. In this era the epigram was transformed into a vehicle for the expression of a wide variety of personal feelings, love above all. Elegantly worded epigrams survive from the pens of women from diverse regions of the Hellenistic world: Anyte of Tegea in the Peloponnese, Nossis of Locri in southern Italy, Moero of Byzantium at the mouth of the Black Sea. Women, from courtesans to respectable matrons, figured as frequent subjects in their poems. No Hellenistic literature better conveyed the depth of human emotion than their epigrams, such as Nossis's poem on the power of Eros (Love, regarded as a divinity): "Nothing is sweeter than Eros. All other delights are second to it—from my mouth I spit out even honey. And this Nossis says: whoever Aphrodite has not kissed knows not what sort of flowers are her roses" (*Palatine Anthology* 5.170).

Like their literary contemporaries, Hellenistic sculptors and painters brought the emotions of the individual to the forefront in their art. Artists of the Classical period had usually imbued the faces of their subjects with a serene calm that represented an ideal rather than human reality. Hellenistic sculptors, by contrast, strove for a more naturalistic depiction of emotion in a variety of artistic genres. In portrait sculpture, Lysippus's famous bust of Alexander the Great captured the passionate dreaminess of the young commander. A sculpture from Pergamum by an unknown artist commemorated the third-century Attalid victory over the plundering Gauls by showing a defeated Gallic warrior stabbing himself after having killed his wife to prevent her enslavement by the victors. This tableau dramatically represented the pain that the Gallic code of suicide instead of surrender imposed on its adherents. A large-scale painting of Alexander in battle against the Persian king Darius similarly portrayed Alexander's intense concentration and Darius's horrified expression. The artist, who was probably either Philoxenus of Eretria or a Greek woman from Egypt named Helena (one of the first female artists known), used foreshortening and strong contrasts between shadows and highlights to accentuate the emotional impact of the picture.

To appreciate fully the appeal of Hellenistic sculpture, we must remember that, like earlier Greek sculpture, it was painted in bright colors. The fourth-century sculptor Praxiteles, in fact, reportedly remarked that his best statues were "the ones colored by Nicias," a leading painter of the time (Pliny, *Natural History* 35.133). Hellenistic art differed from Classical art, however, in its social context. Works of Classical art had been commissioned by the city-states as a whole for public display, or by wealthy individuals to present to their city-state. Now sculptors and painters created their works more and more as commissions from royalty and from the urban elites who wanted to demonstrate that they had artistic taste aligned with that of their social superiors in the royal family. To be successful, the artists had to please their rich patrons, and so the increasing diversity of subjects that emerged in Hellenistic art presumably represented a trend approved by kings, queens, and the elites. Sculpture best reveals this new preference for depictions of human beings in a wide variety of poses, many from private life, again in contrast with Classical art. Hellenistic sculptors portrayed subjects unknown in that earlier period: foreigners (such as the dying Gaul), drunkards, battered athletes, wrinkled old people. The female nude became a particular favorite. A naked Aphrodite, which Praxiteles sculpted for the city of Cnidos, became so renowned that Nicomedes, king of Bithynia in Anatolia, later offered to pay off Cnidos's entire public debt if he could have the statue. The Cnidians refused.

A lasting innovation of Hellenistic art was the depiction of abstract ideas as sculptural types. Such statues were made to represent ideas as diverse as Peace and Insanity. Modern sculptures such as the Statue of Liberty in New York harbor belong in this same artistic tradition. So, too, modern neoclassical architecture imitates the imaginative public architecture of the Hellenistic period, whose architects often boldly combined the Doric and Ionic orders on the same building and energized the Corinthian order with florid decoration.

New Ideas in Philosophy and Science

Greek philosophy in the Hellenistic period reached a wider audience than ever before. Although the mass of the working poor as usual had neither the leisure nor the resources to attend the lectures of the philosophers, the more affluent members of the population studied philosophy in growing numbers. Theophrastus (c. 370–285 B.C.), Aristotle's most accomplished pupil, lectured to crowds of two thousand in Athens. Most of the students of philosophy continued to be men, but now women could also become members of the groups attached to certain philosophers. Kings competed to attract famous thinkers to their courts, and Greek settlers brought their interest in philosophy with them even to the most remote of the new Hellenistic cities. Archaeological excavation of a city located thousands of miles from Greece on the Oxus River in Afghanistan, for example, has turned up a Greek philosophical text as well as inscriptions of moral advice imputed to Apollo's oracle at Delphi.

Fewer thinkers now concentrated on metaphysics. Instead, philosophers concerned themselves with philosophical materialism, denying the immaterial soul described by Plato and ignoring any other such entity. The goal of much philosophical inquiry was now centered on securing human independence from the effects of chance or other worldly events. Scientific investigation of the physical world also tended to become a specialty separate from philosophy. Hellenistic philosophy itself was regularly divided into three related areas: logic (the process for discovering truth), physics (the fundamental truth about the nature of existence), and ethics (the way human beings should achieve happiness and well-being as a consequence of logic and physics). The most significant new philosophical schools of thought to arise were Epicureanism and Stoicism, and Epicurean and Stoic doctrines later proved exceptionally popular among upper-class Romans. The various philosophies of the Hellenistic period were in many ways focused on the same question: What is the best way for human beings to live? Different philosophies recommended different paths to the same answer: Individual human beings must attain personal tranquillity to achieve freedom from the turbulence of outside forces. This philosophic goal had special poignancy for Greeks experiencing the changes in political and social life that accompanied the rise to dominance of the Macedonian and later Hellenistic kingdoms. Outside forces in the persons of aggressive kings had robbed the city-states of their previous freedom of action internationally, and the fates and fortunes of city-states as well as individuals now often resided in the hands of distant, sometimes fickle monarchs. More than ever before, human life and opportunities for free choice seemed poised to careen out of the control of individuals. It therefore made sense, at least for those people wealthy enough to spend time philosophizing, to look for personal, private solutions to the unsettling new conditions of life in the Hellenistic era.

Epicureanism took its name from its founder, Epicurus (341–271 B.C.), who settled his followers in Athens in a house set amid a verdant garden (hence the Garden as the name of his informal school). Under Epicurus the study of philosophy represented a new social form in opposition to previous traditions because he admitted women and slaves as regular members of his group. His lover, Leontion, became notorious for her treatise criticizing the views of Theophrastus. Epicurus believed that human beings should pursue pleasure, by which he did not mean what other people might expect. He insisted that true pleasure consisted of an "absence of disturbance" from pain and the everyday turbulence, passions, and desires of an ordinary human existence. A sober life lived in the society of friends apart from the cares of the common world could best provide this essential peace of mind. This teaching represented a serious challenge to the ideal of Greek citizenship, which required men of means to participate in the politics of the city-state and for women of the same class to participate in public religious cults.

Human beings should above all be free of worry about death, Epicurus taught. Since all matter consisted of microscopic atoms in random movement, as Democritus and Leucippus had earlier theorized, death was nothing more than the painless disassociation of the body's atoms. Moreover, all human knowledge must be empirical, that is, derived from experience and perception. Phenomena that most people perceive as the work of the gods, such as thunder, do not result from divine intervention in the world. The gods live far away in perfect tranquility, taking no notice of human affairs. Human beings therefore have nothing to fear from gods, in life or in death.

The Stoics recommended a different, less isolationist path for individuals. Their name derived from the Painted Stoa in Athens, where they discussed their doctrines. Zeno of Citium on Cyprus (c. 333–262 B.C.) founded stoicism, but Chrysippus from Cilicia in Anatolia (c. 280–206 B.C.) did the most to make it a comprehensive guide to life. Stoics believed that human beings should make their goal the pursuit of virtue. Virtue, they said, consisted of putting oneself in harmony with universal Nature, the rational force of divine providence that directed all existence under the guise of Fate. Reason as well as experience should be used to discover the way to that harmony, which required the "perfect" virtues of good sense, justice, courage, and temperance. According to the Stoics, the doctrines of Zeno and Chrysippus applied to women as well as men. In his controversial work *Politeia*, Zeno even proposed that in an ideal, philosophically governed society, unisex clothing should be worn as a way to obliterate unnecessary distinctions between women and men.

The Stoics' belief that fate was responsible for everything that happened gave rise to the question of whether human beings truly have free will. Employing some of the subtlest reasoning ever brought to bear on this fundamental issue, Stoic philosophers concluded that purposeful human actions did have significance. A Stoic should therefore take action against evil, for example, by participating in politics. Nature, itself good, did not prevent vice from occurring because otherwise virtue would have no meaning. What mattered in life, indeed, was the striving for good, not the result. To be a Stoic furthermore meant to shun desire and anger while enduring pain and sorrow calmly, an attitude that informs the meaning of the word "stoic" today. Through endurance and self-control, a Stoic attained tranquility. Death was not to be feared because, Stoics believed, we will all live our lives over and over again an infinite number of times in a fashion identical with our present lives. This repetition will occur as the world is periodically destroyed by fire and then reformed after the conflagration.

Other schools of thought carried on the work of earlier philosophical leaders such as Plato and Pythagoras. Still others like the Sceptics and the Cynics struck out in idiosyncratic directions. Sceptics aimed at the same state of personal imperturbability as did Epicureans, but from a completely different premise. Following the doctrines of Pyrrho of Elis in the Peloponnese (c. 360–270 B.C.), they believed that secure knowledge about anything was impossible because the human senses yield contradictory information about the world. All we can do, they insisted, is to depend on appearances of things while suspending judgment about their reality. Pyrrho's thought had been influenced by the Indian ascetic wise men (the magi) he met as a member of Alexander the Great's entourage. The basic premise of scepticism inevitably precluded any unity of doctrine.

Cynics ostentatiously rejected every convention of ordinary life, especially wealth and material comfort. Human beings should instead aim at a life of complete self-sufficiency. Whatever was natural was good and could be done without shame before anyone; even public defecation and fornication, for example, were acceptable, according to this idea. Women and men alike were free to follow their sexual inclinations. Above all, Cynics should disdain the comforts and luxuries of a comfortable life. The name Cynic, which meant "like a dog," reflected the common evaluation of this ascetic and unconventional way of life. The most famous early Cynic, Diogenes of Sinope on the Black Sea (c. 400–c. 325 B.C.), was reputed to go around wearing borrowed clothing and to sleep in a big storage jar. Almost as notorious was Hipparchia, a female Cynic of the late fourth century B.C. She once bested an obnoxious philosophical opponent named Theodorus the Atheist with the following argument, which recalled the climactic episode between father and son in Aristophanes' *Clouds*: "That which would not be considered wrong if done by Theodorus would also not be considered wrong if done by Hipparchia. Now if Theodorus strikes himself, he does no wrong. Therefore, if Hipparchia strikes Theodorus, she does no wrong" (Diogenes Laertius, *The Lives and Doctrines of Famous Philosophers* 6.97).

Science benefited from its widening divorce from philosophy during the Hellenistic period. Indeed, historians have called this era the Golden Age of ancient science. Various factors contributed to this flourishing of thought and discovery: the expeditions of Alexander had encouraged curiosity and increased knowledge about the extent and differing features of the world; royal patronage provided scientists with financial support; and the gathering together of scientists in Alexandria promoted a fertile exchange of ideas that could not otherwise take place because travel and communication were so difficult. The greatest advances came in geometry and mathematics. Euclid, who taught at Alexandria around 300 B.C., made revolutionary progress in the analysis of two- and three-dimensional space. The fame and utility of Euclidean geometry endures to this day. Archimedes of Syracuse (287–212 B.C.) was an arithmetical polymath, who calculated the approximate value of pi and devised a way to manipulate very large numbers. He also invented hydrostatics (the science of the equilibrium of a fluid system) and mechanical devices such as a screw for lifting water to a higher elevation. The modern expression "Eureka!" immortalizes Archimedes' shout of delight "I have found it" (*heureka* in Greek) when the solution to a problem came to him as he immersed himself into a bathing pool (Vitruvius, *On Architecture 9*, preface 10).

The sophistication of Hellenistic mathematics yielded benefits in other fields that required complex computations. Aristarchus of Samos early in the third century B.C. first proposed the correct model of the solar system by theorizing that the earth revolved around the sun, which he also identified as being far larger and far more distant than it appeared. Later astronomers rejected Aristarchus's heliocentric model in favor of the traditional geocentric one because calculations based on the orbit he postulated for the earth failed to correspond to the observed positions of celestial objects. Aristarchus had made a simple mistake: he had postulated a circular orbit instead of an ellipse. It was to be another eighteen hundred years before the correctness of the heliocentric system would be recognized by the Polish astronomer Copernicus (A.D. 1473–1543), the founder of modern astronomy. Eratosthenes of Cyrene (c. 275–194 B.C.) pioneered mathematical geography. He calculated the circumference of the earth with astonishing accuracy by having measurements made of the length of the shadows of widely separated but identically tall structures at the same moment. Ancient scientists in later periods, especially the astronomer and geographer Ptolemy, who worked in Alexandria in the second century A.D., would improve and refine the image of the natural world elaborated by Hellenistic researchers, but the basic ideas remained dominant in scientific thought until the advent of modern science.

Greek science was as quantitative as it could be, given the technological limitations of measurement imposed by ancient technology. Precise scientific experimentation was not possible because no technology existed in ancient times for the precise measurement of very short intervals of time. Measuring tiny quantities of matter was also almost impossible. But the spirit of invention prevailed in spite of these difficulties. Ctesibius of Alexandria, a contemporary of Aristarchus, devised machines operated by air pressure. In addition to this invention of pneumatics, he built a working water pump, an organ powered by water, and the first accurate water clock. His fellow Alexandrian of the first century A.D., Hero, continued the Hellenistic tradition of mechanical ingenuity by building a rotating sphere powered by steam. This invention did not lead to viable steam engines, perhaps because the metallurgical technology to produce metal pipes, fittings, and screws was not yet developed. Much of the engineering prowess of the Hellenistic period was applied to military technology, as in the modern world. The kings hired engineers to design powerful catapults and wheeled siege towers many stories high, which were capable of battering down the defenses of walled cities. The most famous large-scale application of technology for nonmilitary purposes was the construction of a lighthouse three hundred feet tall (the Pharos) for the harbor at Alexandria. Using polished metal mirrors to reflect the light from a large fire fueled by wood, it shone many miles out over the sea. Awestruck sailors regarded it as one of the wonders of the world.

Medicine also shared in the spirit of progress that inspired developments in Hellenistic science. The increased contact between Greeks and people of the Near East in this period made the medical knowledge of the ancient civilizations of Mesopotamia and Egypt better known in the West and gave an impetus to further understanding of human health and illness. Around 325 B.C. Praxagoras of Cos discovered the value of measuring the human pulse in diagnosing illness. A bit later Herophilus of Chalcedon, working in Alexandria, became the first scientist in the West to study anatomy by dissecting human cadavers. Anatomical terms that Herophilus coined are still in modern use, such as "duodenum," a section of the small intestine. Other Hellenistic advances in understanding anatomy included the discovery of the nerves and nervous system. Anatomical knowledge, however, outstripped knowledge of human physiology. The earlier idea that human health depended on the balance in the body of four humors or fluids remained the dominant theory in physiology. A person was healthy—in "good humor"—so long as the correct proportions of the four humors were maintained. Since illness was thought to be the result of an imbalance of the humors, doctors prescribed various regimens of drugs, diet, and exercise to restore balance. Physicians also believed that drawing blood from patients could help rebalance the humors, a practice that endured in medicine until the nineteenth century A.D. Many illnesses in women were diagnosed as caused by displacements of the womb, which was wrongly believed to be able to move around in the body.

Hellenistic Religions

The expansion and diversification of knowledge that characterized Hellenistic intellectual life found a parallel in the growing diversity of religious practice. The traditional cults of Greek religion remained very popular, but new cults, such as the ones deifying ruling kings, also responded to new political and social conditions. Preexisting cults with previously local significance, such as that of the Greek healing deity Asclepius or the mystery cult of the Egyptian goddess Isis, grew to prominence all over the Hellenistic world. In many cases, Greek cults and indigenous cults from the eastern Mediterranean came to be identified with each other and shared cultic practices in a process of mutual influence. This mixing of traditions came about because originally diverse cults were found to share assumptions about the remedies for the troubles of human life. In other instances, local and Greek cults simply existed side by side. The inhabitants of villages in the Faiyum district of Egypt, for example, went on worshipping their traditional crocodile god and mummifying their dead in the old way while also paying homage to Greek deities. Following the tradition of polytheistic religion, the same people could worship in both old and new cults.

To the extent that diverse new Hellenistic cults encompassed a shared concern, they recalled a prominent theme of Hellenistic philosophy: the relationship between the individual and what seemed the controlling, unpredictable power of Luck or Chance. Greek religion had always addressed this concern at some level, but the chaotic course of Greek history since the Peloponnesian War had made the unpredictable aspects of human existence appear more prominent than ever. Yet advances in astronomical knowledge revealed the mathematical precision of the celestial sphere of the universe. Religious experience now had to address the apparent disconnection between that heavenly uniformity and the shapeless chaos of life on earth. One increasingly popular approach to bridging that gap was to rely on astrology for advice deduced from the movement of the stars and planets, thought of as divinities.

In another approach offering devotees protection from the cruel tricks of Chance or Luck, the gods of popular Hellenistic cults promised salvation of various kinds. One form was that expected from powerful rulers, who enjoyed divine status in what are now known as ruler cults. These cults were established in recognition of great benefactions. The Athenians, for example, deified the living Macedonians Antigonus and his son Demetrius as savior gods in 307 B.C., when they bestowed magnificent gifts on the city and restored the democracy (which had been abolished fifteen years before by another Macedonian commander). Like most ruler cults, this one expressed both spontaneous gratitude and a desire to flatter the rulers in the hope of obtaining additional favors. As a rule the Antigonid kings had no divine cult in their honor in Macedonia, but many cities in the Ptolemaic and Seleucid kingdoms instituted ruler cults for their kings and queens. (The Ptolemaic king and queen were also regarded as gods, in keeping with traditions of ancient Egyptian religion.) An inscription put up by Egyptian priests in 238 B.C. concretely described the qualities appropriate for a divine king and queen: "King Ptolemy III and Queen Berenice, his sister and wife, the Benefactor Gods . . . have provided good government . . . and [after a drought] sacrificed a large amount of their revenues for the salvation of the population, and by importing grain . . . they saved the inhabitants of Egypt" (*OGIS* 56).

Healing divinities offered another form of protection to anxious individuals. Scientific Greek medicine had rejected the notion of supernatural causes and cures for disease ever since Hippocrates had established his medical school on the Aegean island of Cos in the late fifth century B.C. Nevertheless, popular support grew in the Hellenistic period for the cult of Asclepius, son of Apollo, who offered cures for illness and injury at his many shrines. There suppliants seeking his help would sleep in special dormitories to await dreams from the god in which he prescribed healing treatments. These prescriptions mainly emphasized diet and exercise, but numerous inscriptions set up by grateful patients also testified to miraculous cures and surgery performed by the god while the sufferer slept. The following example is typical: "Ambrosia of Athens was blind in one eye . . . . She . . . ridiculed some of the cures [described in inscriptions in the sanctuary] as being incredible and impossible . . . . But when she went to sleep, she saw a vision; she thought the god was standing next to her . . . he split open the diseased eye and poured in a medicine. When day came she left cured" (*IG* 4, 2d ed., 1, no. 121.IV).

Other cults proffered secret knowledge as a key to worldly and physical salvation. Protection from physical dangers was more a concern than the care of the soul or the afterlife. The Mysteries of Demeter at Eleusis, however, did continue to address these concerns. The mystery cults of the Greek god Dionysus and, in particular, the Egyptian goddess Isis gained popularity in this period. Isis, like the goddesses Atargatis from Syria and Cybele (the Great Mother) from Phrygia and Lydia in Anatolia, was a female divinity whose cult achieved near universal distribution in the Hellenistic world. The popularity of Isis received a boost from the patronage of King Ptolemy I, who established an official seat for her cult in Alexandria. He also refashioned the Egyptian deity Osiris in a Greek mold as the new god Sarapis, whose job was to serve as Isis's consort. Sarapis reportedly performed miracles of rescue from shipwreck and illness. The cult of Isis, who became the most popular female divinity in the Mediterranean, involved extensive rituals and festivals incorporating features of Egyptian religion mixed with Greek elements. Followers of Isis apparently hoped to achieve personal purification as well as the aid of the goddess in overcoming the demonic influence on human life of Chance and Luck.

That an originally Egyptian deity like Isis could achieve enormous popularity among Greeks (and Romans in later times) alongside the traditional deities of Greek religion, who remained popular themselves, is the best evidence of the cultural cross-fertilization of the Hellenistic world. Equally striking was the adoption of the Greek language and many aspects of Greek culture by many Jews, especially those living in the large Jewish communities that had grown up in Hellenistic cities outside Palestine, such as Alexandria. The Hebrew Bible was even translated into Greek in Alexandria in the early third century B.C., reportedly at the request of King Ptolemy II. Hellenized Jews largely retained the ritual practices and habits of life that defined traditional Judaism, and they refused to worship Greek gods. Hellenistic politics and culture also affected the Jewish community in Palestine. The region, caught between the great kingdom of the Ptolemies in Egypt and that of the Seleucids in Syria, was controlled militarily and politically by the Ptolemies in the third century B.C. and by the Seleucids in the second B.C. Both dynasties allowed the Jews to continue to live their lives according to ancestral tradition under the political leadership of a high priest in Jerusalem. Internal dissension erupted among Jews in second-century Palestine over the amount of Greek influence that was compatible with traditional Judaism. The Seleucid king Antiochus IV (ruled 175–163 B.C.) intervened in the conflict in support of an extreme Hellenizing faction of Jews in Jerusalem, who had taken over the high priesthood. In 167, Antiochus converted the main Jewish sanctuary there into a temple to the Syrian god Baal Shamen, whom he worshiped, and outlawed the practice of Jewish religious rites such as the observation of the Sabbath and circumcision. A revolt led by Judah the Maccabee eventually won Jewish independence from the Seleucids after twenty-five years of war. The most famous episode of the Maccabean Revolt was the retaking of the temple in Jerusalem and its rededication to the worship of the Jewish god, a triumphant moment commemorated by Jews ever since on the holiday of Hanukkah. That Greek culture attracted Jews, whose strong traditions reached far into antiquity, provides a striking example of the transformations that affected many—though far from all—people of the Hellenistic world.

The diversity of the Hellenistic world encompassed much that was new. The creation of kingdoms reconfigured the political map and dynamics of the Greek world. The queens of its kingdoms commanded greater wealth and status than any women of the city-states of Classical Greece. Its philosophers sought modes of thought and action through which individuals could work to create personal tranquility for themselves despite the turbulence and troubles of the outside world. Its scientists and doctors made new discoveries about the natural world and in mathematics that contributed more often to abstract knowledge than to applied technology. The rituals and beliefs of new religious cults were meant to protect worshippers from the dangers of Chance and provide more personal contact with the divine. In the midst of these new developments in the expanded world into which

Greek culture had been relocated, the basic characteristics of everyday life for the majority remained the same as they had been throughout the historical period—the physical labor, the poverty, and the limited opportunities for material and social self-improvement. Like their ancestors, most people spent most of their time toiling in the fields, vineyards, pastures, craft shops, and markets. This was the most abiding continuity in ancient Greek history.

Suggested Readings

To serve this book's intended audience, who will not ordinarily have access to professional journals in research libraries, this list contains only books in English or articles collected in books. It therefore omits much pertinent material; the bibliographies of the books listed include many items of additional interest. Some ancient sources in translation are included, in the hope that they will be interesting and accessible in libraries and bookstores.

Chapter One

Barber, Elizabeth Wayland. *Women's Work: The First 20,000 Years: Women, Cloth, and Society in Early Times* (New York, 1994). A discussion of the significance of women's designing and producing textiles from prehistoric times.

Burkert, Walter. *Homo Necans: The Anthropology of Ancient Greek Sacrificial Ritual and Myth*, trans. Peter Bing (Berkeley and Los Angeles, 1983). A study identifying the origins of the ritual slaughter of animals in Greek religion in the experience of prehistoric hunters.

Cambridge Ancient History, 3d ed., vol. 1, part 1, *Prolegomena and Prehistory*, ed. I. E. S. Edwards et al. (Cambridge, 1970). A standard scholarly survey, now somewhat out of date.

Carrington, Dorothy. *The Dream-Hunters of Corsica* (London, 1994). A study of Corsican sorcery arguing that its preoccupation with death has its roots in the religious beliefs of prehistoric hunter-gatherers.

Childe, V. Gordon. *The Dawn of European Civilization*, 6th ed. (New York, 1958). An influential work by the most famous exponent of the theory that diffusion of technology from the Near East underlay the development of civilization in Europe.

Cunliffe, Barry, ed. *The Oxford Illustrated Prehistory of Europe* (Oxford, 1994). A survey including information on prehistoric Greece from the Paleolithic period through the Bronze Age.

Ehrenberg, Margaret. *Women in Prehistory* (Norman, Okla., 1989). A study of women's contributions to the development of agriculture and of their social status in Europe from the Paleolithic Age to the Iron Age.

Fagan, Brian M. *People of the Earth: An Introduction to World Prehistory*, 6th ed. (Glenview, Ill., 1989). An introduction to prehistoric anthropology.

———. *The Journey from Eden: The Peopling of our World* (London, 1990). A survey of the archaeological and fossil evidence for the spread of human populations from Africa to the rest of the world.

Gimbutas, Marija. *The Goddesses and Gods of Old Europe, 6500–3500 B.C.: Myths and Cult Images*, rev. ed. (Berkeley and Los Angeles, 1984). An updated presentation of the author's theory on the matrifocal nature of the indigenous culture of Neolithic Europe.

Knapp, A. Bernard. *The History and Culture of Ancient Western Asia and Egypt.* (Belmont, Calif., 1988). A concise introduction from prehistoric times to the fourth century B.C.

Lerner, Gerda. *The Creation of Patriarchy* (Oxford, 1986). A discussion of possible origins of patriarchal ancient civilizations.

Piggott, Stuart. *The Earliest Wheeled Transport from the Atlantic Coast to the Caspian Sea* (Ithaca, 1983). A full treatment of the "technological explosion" that brought to Europe the invention of the wheel and the domestication of the horse.

Renfrew, Colin. *Before Civilization: The Radiocarbon Revolution and Prehistoric Europe* (Cambridge, 1979). An introduction to this dating technique, arguing against diffusion from the Near East as the primary explanation of change in prehistoric Europe.

Tringham, Ruth. *Hunters, Fishers and Farmers of Eastern Europe, 6000–3000 B.C.* (London, 1971). An investigation of the causes of cultural change that considers both diffusion of technology from outside and independent local invention.

Chapter Two

Bernal, Martin. *Black Athena: The Afroasiatic Roots of Classical Civilization*, vol. 1, *The Fabrication of Ancient Greece, 1785–1985*, and vol. 2, *The Archaeological and Documentary Evidence* (New Brunswick, N.J., 1987 and 1991). The opening volumes of a study arguing that the Near Eastern contribution to Greek civilization has been much underestimated and suggesting that Greece was colonized from Egypt in the second millennium B.C.

Cambridge Ancient History, 3d ed., vol. 2, part 1, *The Middle East and the Aegean Region, c. 1800–1380 B.C.*, ed. I. E. S. Edwards et al., and part 2, *The Middle East and the Aegean Region, c. 1380–1000 B.C.*, ed. I. E. S. Edwards et al. (Cambridge, 1973 and 1975). A standard scholarly survey.

Chadwick, John. *The Mycenaean World* (Cambridge, 1976). An introduction to Bronze Age Greece.

———. *Linear B and Related Scripts* (London, 1987). The story of the discovery and decipherment of Mycenaean writing as well as the puzzle of undeciphered scripts of the Bronze Age Aegean.

Dickinson, Oliver. *The Aegean Bronze Age* (Cambridge, 1994). A topically arranged survey of the evidence for the Aegean in the period c. 3000–1000 B.C.

Drews, Robert. *The Coming of the Greeks: Indo-European Conquests in the Aegean and the Near East* (Princeton, 1988). An analysis of the evidence for Indo-European penetration of these regions, concluding that the movement occurred later than is commonly assumed and that Indo-European power depended on chariot warfare.

———. *The End of the Bronze Age: Changes in Warfare and the Catastrophe ca. 1200 B.C.* (Princeton, N.J., 1993). An argument that mercenary infantry overthrew the kingdoms of the Bronze Age, which had relied on chariot forces for military strength.

Fitton, J. Lesley. *The Discovery of the Greek Bronze Age* (Cambridge, 1995). A survey of the colorful personalities and controversial excavations of the archaeological investigation of Bronze Age Greece.

Mallory, J. P. *In Search of the Indo-Europeans: Language, Archaeology, and Myth* (London, 1989). A survey and analysis of the various competing theories on the Indo-Europeans.

Pedley, John Griffiths. *Greek Art and Archaeology* (Englewood Cliffs, N.J., 1993). A well-illustrated survey from c. 3000 to 31 B.C.

Renfrew, Colin. *Archaeology and Language: The Puzzle of Indo-European Origins* (New York, 1988). An attack on the usual assumptions about the earliest Indo-Europeans as mobile and warlike invaders.

Saggs, H. W. F. *Civilization before Greece and Rome* (New Haven, 1989). A topically arranged introduction to the ancient civilizations of the Near East and Egypt.

Sanders, N. K. *The Sea Peoples: Warriors of the Ancient Mediterranean, 1250–1150 B.C.*, rev. ed. (London, 1985). A comprehensive review of the different areas affected by these disparate groups of raiders.

Taylour, William. *The Mycenaeans*, rev. ed. (London, 1983). A general account of the archaeology of the Mycenaeans.

Vermeule, Emily. *Greece in the Bronze Age* (Chicago, 1972). A comprehensive treatment ranging from the Stone Age to the Mycenaeans.

Ward, William, and Martha Joukowsky, eds. *The Crisis Years: The Twelfth Century B.C.* (Dubuque, Iowa, 1992). Essays on the end of the Bronze Age.

Willetts, R. F. *The Civilization of Ancient Crete* (Berkeley and Los Angeles, 1977). A survey of Cretan history from earliest times until the eve of the Classical period.

Wood, Michael. *In Search of the Trojan War* (New York, 1985). An illustrated popular survey of the evidence for the story of the Greek war against Troy.

Chapter Three

Boardman, John, et al. *The Oxford History of the Classical World* (Oxford, 1986). A collection of articles on central historical topics as well as Homer, myth, and Hesiod.

Cambridge Ancient History, 2d ed., vol. 3, part 1, *The Prehistory of the Balkans; the Middle East and the Aegean World, Tenth to Eighth Centuries* B.C., ed. John Boardman et al. (Cambridge, 1982). A standard scholarly survey.

Coldstream, J. N. *Geometric Greece* (New York, 1977). A detailed treatment of Greece in the ninth and eighth centuries B.C., with much discussion of artifacts.

Donlan, Walter. *The Aristocratic Ideal in Ancient Greece: Attitudes of Superiority from Homer to the End of the Fifth Century* B.C. (Lawrence, Kan., 1980). An interpretation of the functioning of concepts such as honor, excellence, and justice in Greek society.

Finley, M. I. *The World of Odysseus*, 2d ed. (Harmondsworth, England, 1965). A standard work on the vexed question of how much history is to be found in Homeric poetry.

————. *Early Greece: The Bronze and Archaic Ages*, rev. ed. (New York, 1981). A brief introduction to Greek history to the dawn of the Classical Age, with emphasis on the difficulties of clear interpretation.

Finley, M. I., and H. W. Pleket. *The Olympic Games: The First Thousand Years* (London, 1976). An introduction to the history of the games throughout antiquity.

Gibson, J. C. L. *Canaanite Myths and Legends*, 2d ed. (Edinburgh, 1978). A study of the myths of the Levant.

Hart, George. *Egyptian Myths* (Austin, 1990). A concise introduction to the myths of ancient Egypt.

Hesiod. *Theogony, Works and Days, Shield*, trans. Apostolos N. Athanassakis (Baltimore, 1983). A translation, with introduction and notes, of the works of the eighth-century poet.

Homer. *The Iliad*, trans. Robert Fagles (New York, 1990). A translation with extensive introduction by Bernard Knox.

Homer. *The Odyssey*, trans. Allen Mandelbaum (Berkeley and Los Angeles, 1990). A translation with index.

Hurwitt, Jeffrey M. *The Art and Culture of Early Greece, 1100–480* B.C. (Ithaca, N.Y., 1985). A detailed treatment of the cultural significance of Greek art before the Classical Age.

McCall, Henrietta. *Mesopotamian Myths* (Austin, 1990). A concise introduction to the myths of Mesopotamia.

Morford, Mark P. O., and Robert J. Lenardon. *Classical Mythology*, 2d ed. (New York, 1977). A topically arranged general introduction with frequent quotation of translated ancient sources.

Morris, Sarah. *Daidalos and the Origins of Greek Art* (Princeton, N.J., 1992). A discussion of the importance for Greek art, poetry, and politics of the continuing contacts between Dark Age Greece and the Near East.

Sallares, Robert. *The Ecology of the Ancient Greek World* (Ithaca, N.Y., 1991). An investigation of the fundamental processes of ancient Greek life through historical population biology.

Snodgrass, A. M. *The Dark Age of Greece* (Edinburgh, 1971). An extensive treatment making the most of the limited evidence available for this period.

Swaddling, Judith. *The Ancient Olympic Games* (Austin, 1980). A brief illustrated history of the games.

Chapter Four

Aubet, Maria E. *The Phoenicians and the West: Politics, Colonies, and Trade*, trans. Mary Turton (Cambridge, 1993). A study of Phoenician exploration and colonization.

Boardman, John. *The Greeks Overseas: Their Early Colonies and Trade*, rev. ed. (London, 1980). A survey of Greek colonization and overseas commerce.

Burkert, Walter. *The Orientalizing Revolution: Near Eastern Influence on Greek Culture in the Early Archaic Age*, trans. Margaret E. Pinder and Walter Burkert (Cambridge, Mass., 1992). An analysis of the influence of the civilizations of the Near East on Greece in the period 750–650 B.C.

Cambridge Ancient History, 2d ed., vol. 3, part 3, *The Expansion of the Greek World, Eighth to Sixth Centuries B.C.*, ed. John Boardman and N. G. L. Hammond (Cambridge, 1982). A standard scholarly survey.

Finley, M. I. *Ancient Slavery and Modern Ideology* (New York, 1980). A discussion of the nature of ancient slavery as compared to more modern systems of slavery.

Garlan, Yvon. *Slavery in Ancient Greece*, rev. ed., trans. Janet Lloyd (Ithaca, N.Y., 1988). A discussion of the various categories of Greek slavery.

Hanson, Victor Davis. *The Western Way of War: Infantry Battle in Classical Greece* (New York, 1989). A graphic study of the violence of hoplite combat.

Harden, Donald. *The Phoenicians*, 2d ed. (Harmondsworth, England, 1980). An introduction to the history of the Phoenicians.

Jameson, Michael. "Private Space and the Greek City," in Oswyn Murray and Simon Price, eds. *The Greek City from Homer to Alexander* (Oxford, 1990), pp. 171–195. An examination of the way private space—houses and land—was integrated into the city-state.

Jeffrey, L. H. *Archaic Greece: The City-States, c. 700–500 B.C.* (London, 1976). A comprehensive political history of the Greek world in the Archaic Age, presented geographically.

Morris, Ian. *Burial and Ancient Society: The Rise of the Greek City-State* (Cambridge, 1987). A discussion of the archaeological evidence for the social conflicts that provided the context for the rise of the city-state.

Nixon, Lucia, and Simon Price, "The Size and Resources of Greek Cities," in Oswyn Murray and Simon Price, eds. *The Greek City from Homer to Alexander* (Oxford, 1990), pp. 137–170. An analysis of the data based on the so-called Tribute Lists of the fifth-century Athenian empire.

Snodgrass, Anthony. *Archaic Greece: The Age of Experiment* (Berkeley and Los Angeles, 1980). An analysis of the innovative character of the Greek Archaic Age.

Starr, Chester G. *The Economic and Social Growth of Early Greece, 800–500 B.C.* (Oxford, 1977). A brief account of the interdependency of economic and social changes in the Archaic Age.

————. *Individual and Community: The Rise of the Polis, 800–500 B.C.* (Oxford, 1986). A concise survey of the balancing of communal interests and the emerging concept of individual freedom in the Archaic Age.

Chapter Five

Barnes, Jonathan. *Early Greek Philosophy* (Harmondsworth, England, 1987). A brief introduction to the Ionian thinkers, followed by excerpts in context from them and other early Greek philosophers.

Cartledge, Paul. *Sparta and Lakonia: A Regional History, 1300–362 B.C.* (London, 1979). A survey beginning in the late Bronze Age, with emphasis on geography and the material conditions affecting Spartan history.

Crawford, Michael, and David Whitehead. *Archaic and Classical Greece: A Selection of Ancient Sources in Translation* (Cambridge, 1983). A collection of excerpts from literature and historical documents with introductions and annotations.

Emlyn-Jones, C. J. *The Ionians and Hellenism: A Study of the Cultural Achievements of Early Greek Inhabitants of Asia Minor* (London, 1980). An assessment of the art, literature, and philosophy of the Ionians from the eighth to the sixth century B.C.

Fantham, Elaine, et al. *Women in the Classical World: Image and Text* (Oxford, 1994). A collection of essays including pieces on women in the Archaic period, at Sparta, and in Classical Athens.

Ferguson, John. *Among the Gods: An Archaeological Exploration of Ancient Greek Religion* (London, 1989). An account of Greek religious activity based on physical evidence such as cult-statues and inscriptions.

Fitzhardinge, L. F. *The Spartans* (London, 1980). An illustrated, topical survey of Spartan history and society.

Forrest, W. G. *The Emergence of Greek Democracy, 800–400 B.C.* (New York, 1966). A classic, arguing that developments at Sparta set the stage for the rise of democracy.

Guthrie, W. K. C. *A History of Greek Philosophy,* vol. 1, *The Earlier Presocratics and the Pythagoreans* (Cambridge, 1962). A standard introduction to the Ionian thinkers and other early Greek philosophers.

McGlew, James F. *Tyranny and Political Culture in Ancient Greece* (Ithaca, N.Y., 1993). An examination of Greek political vocabulary as affected by tyranny.

Murray, Oswyn. *Early Greece,* 2d ed. (Cambridge, Mass., 1993). A survey placing Archaic Greece in the context of Mediterranean civilization of the time, especially the Near East.

Rhodes, P. J. *The Greek City States: A Source Book* (Norman, Okla., 1986). A collection of translated sources arranged in sections of explanatory narrative.

Ward, Anne G., et al. *The Quest for Theseus* (New York, 1970). An illustrated introduction to the myths of the founder of Athens.

West, M. L., ed. *Greek Lyric Poetry* (Oxford, 1993). A translation, with introduction and notes, of Greek lyric poetry down to 450 B.C. (excluding Pindar and Bacchylides).

Wilbur, J. B., and H. J. Allen. *The Worlds of the Early Greek Philosophers* (Buffalo, 1979). A discussion of the philosophers of early Greece in their historical contexts.

Chapter Six

Brommer, Frank. *The Sculptures of the Parthenon* (London, 1979). A photographic record and description of the sculptural decoration of the Parthenon.

Cambridge Ancient History, 2d ed., vol. 4, *Persia, Greece and the Western Mediterranean, c. 525 to 479 B.C.,* ed. John Boardman et al. (Cambridge, 1988). A standard scholarly survey.

Camp, John M. *The Athenian Agora: Excavations in the Heart of Classical Athens* (London, 1986). An illustrated survey of the buildings and monuments of Athens's civic center and their functions.

Cook, J. M. *The Persian Empire* (New York, 1983). A general survey complementing Olmstead.

Davies, J. K. *Democracy and Classical Greece,* 2d ed. (Cambridge, Mass., 1993). A survey of classical Greek history, with frequent discussion of documents.

Ehrenberg, Victor. *From Solon to Socrates,* 2d ed. (London, 1973). A survey of Greek history and civilization in the sixth and fifth centuries B.C.

Farrar, Cynthia. *The Origins of Democratic Thinking: The Invention of Politics in Classical Athens* (Cambridge, 1988). An analysis of democratic political theory in the writings of Protagoras, Thucydides, and Democritus.

Finley, M. I. *Democracy Ancient and Modern,* rev. ed. (New Brunswick, N.J., 1973). A collection of lectures advocating the application to modern democracies of the principles of Athenian participatory democracy.

Fornara, Charles W., and Loren J. Samons II. *Athens from Cleisthenes to Pericles* (Berkeley and Los Angeles, 1991). A thematic study of Athenian democracy, with close attention to the ancient evidence.

Guthrie, W. K. C. *A History of Greek Philosophy,* vol. 2, *The Presocratic Tradition from Parmenides to Democritus* (Cambridge, 1965). A detailed introduction to Greek philosophy in the fifth century B.C.

Harris, William V. *Ancient Literacy* (Cambridge, Mass., 1989). An analysis arguing against the idea that literacy was common in the ancient Greek world.

MacDowell, Douglas M. *The Law in Classical Athens* (Ithaca, N.Y., 1978). A discussion of the operation of law in Athenian society.

Morrison, J. S., and J. F. Coates. *The Athenian Trireme: The History and Reconstruction of an Ancient Greek Warship* (Cambridge, 1986). A description of the reconstruction of a working model of a trireme.

Olmstead, A. T. *History of the Persian Empire* (Chicago, 1948). A still useful comprehensive introduction to the subject.

Osborne, Robin. *Classical Landscape with Figures: The Ancient Greek City and Its Countryside* (London, 1987). A reevaluation of the significance of the countryside in the life of the Greek city-state.

Pollitt, J. J. *Art and Experience in Classical Greece* (Cambridge, 1972). An interpretation of the messages conveyed by Greek art in the Classical period.

Rhodes, Robin Francis. *Architecture and Meaning on the Athenian Acropolis* (Cambridge, 1995). An illustrated interpretation of the iconography of the buildings and monuments of the Periclean acropolis.

Robertson, D. S. *Greek and Roman Architecture*, 2d ed. (Cambridge, 1971). A detailed survey of the techniques of Greek architecture.

Stewart, Andrew. *Greek Sculpture: An Exploration*, vol. 1, *Text*, and vol. 2, *Plates* (New Haven, 1990). A comprehensive study of Greek sculpture and the ancient sources referring to it.

Todd, S. C. *The Shape of Athenian Law* (Oxford, 1993). A description of the law of Athens and an interpretation of its function in Athenian democracy.

Woodford, Susan. *Cambridge Introduction to the History of Art: Greece and Rome* (Cambridge, 1982). A concise introduction to the development of Greek art, especially sculpture.

Wycherly, R. E. *How the Greeks Built Cities*, 2d ed. (New York, 1976). An examination of the relationship of architecture and town planning to ancient Greek life.

Chapter Seven

Aeschylus. *The Oresteia* (*Agamemnon, The Libation Bearers, Eumenides*), trans. Robert Fagles (London, 1979). A translation, with extensive introduction, of the only surviving tragic trilogy.

Bremmer, Jan. N. *Greek Religion* (Oxford, 1994). A short, critical survey of developments in scholarship on Greek religion since Burkert's *Greek Religion*.

Burkert, Walter. *Greek Religion*, trans. John Raffan (Cambridge, Mass., 1985). An interpretative catalogue of data on Greek religious practice.

Cambridge Ancient History, 2d. ed., vol. 5, *The Fifth Century* B.C., ed. D. M. Lewis et al. (Cambridge 1992). A standard scholarly survey.

Cohen, David. *Law, Sexuality, and Society: The Enforcement of Morals in Classical Athens* (Cambridge, 1991). An examination of the social and legal contexts of adultery, homosexuality, impiety, and the dichotomy between private behavior and public coercion.

De Romilly, Jacqueline. *A Short History of Greek Literature* (Chicago, 1985). A concise survey including discussions of poetry, philosophy, history, rhetoric, and medical writings.

Dodds, E. R. *The Greeks and the Irrational* (Berkeley and Los Angeles, 1951). A classic and provocative treatment of Greek religion.

Dover, K. J. *Greek Homosexuality* (Cambridge, Mass., 1978). A ground-breaking work on the practice of and attitudes toward homosexuality in Classical Greece.

Easterling, P. E., and J. V. Muir, eds. *Greek Religion and Society* (Cambridge, 1985). A collection of introductory essays on topics including views of life after death, temples, festivals, oracles, and divination.

Euripides. *Medea and Other Plays*, trans. Philip Vellacott (Harmondsworth, England, 1963). A translation with brief introduction of *Medea, Hecabe, Electra*, and *Heracles*.

Golden, Mark. *Children and Childhood in Classical Athens* (Baltimore, 1990). A study of Athenian attitudes toward children and of the lives of the children themselves.

Guthrie, W. K. C. *The Sophists* (Cambridge, 1971)[*A History of Greek Philosophy*, vol. 4, part 1]. A presentation of the evidence for the views of the Sophists.

Herodotus. *The History*, trans. David Grene (Chicago, 1987). A translation with introduction to the work of, in Cicero's words, "the father of history."

Kerferd, G. B. *The Sophistic Movement* (Cambridge, 1981). An introduction to the thought and the impact of the fifth-century B.C. Sophists.

Lacey, W. K. *The Family in Classical Greece*, rev. ed. (Auckland, New Zealand, 1980). An introductory survey.

Lefkowitz, Mary R., and Maureen B. Fant. *Women's Life in Greece and Rome: A Source Book in Translation* (Baltimore, 1982). A collection of excerpts from documents and literature on many aspects of women's lives.

Loraux, Nicole. *The Invention of Athens: The Funeral Oration in the Classical City* (Cambridge, Mass., 1986). A study of how orations for the war dead helped shape civic ideology in Athens.

————. *The Great Sophists in Periclean Athens* (Oxford, 1992). A treatment of the impact of the sophistic movement in the Golden Age.

Mikalson, Jon D. *Athenian Popular Religion* (Chapel Hill, N.C., 1983). A concise survey of the religious beliefs and practices of the people of Athens.

Parke, H. W. *Festivals of the Athenians* (Ithaca, N.Y., 1977). A description of the chief ceremonial occasions of Athens.

Mylonas, George E. *Eleusis and the Eleusinian Mysteries* (Princeton, N.J., 1961). An extensive presentation of the archaeological and documentary evidence by one of the excavators of the sanctuary.

Parker, Robert. *Miasma: Pollution and Purification in Early Greek Religion* (Oxford, 1983). A wide-ranging treatment of these central themes in Greek life, attributing their importance to a desire for order.

Powell, Anton. *Athens and Sparta: Constructing Greek Political and Social History from 478*

B.C. (London, 1988). A survey of main topics of Greek history in the Classical period, including an extensive section on the citizen women of Athens.

Schaps, David M. *Economic Rights of Women in Ancient Greece* (Edinburgh, 1979). An exploration of the rights and disabilities of women with regard to property, inheritance, dowry, and commerce.

Sealey, Raphael. *Women and Law in Classical Greece* (Chapel Hill, N.C., 1990). An analysis of women's rights in marriage, the ownership of property, and questions of inheritance.

Sophocles. *The Three Theban Plays: Antigone, Oedipus the King, Oedipus at Colonus*, trans. Robert Fagles (Harmondsworth, England, 1982). Translations of the Oedipus plays in chronological order, with an introduction by Bernard Knox.

Stockton, David. *The Classical Athenian Democracy* (Oxford, 1990). An explanation of the institutions, practices, and assumptions of Athenian democracy in the fifth and fourth centuries B.C.

Chapter Eight

Aristophanes. *The Acharnians, The Clouds, Lysistrata*, trans. Alan H. Sommerstein (Harmondsworth, England, 1973). Lively versions of three comedies, with introduction.

Dover, K. J. *Aristophanic Comedy* (Berkeley and Los Angeles, 1972). An introduction to Athenian Old Comedy in general and to the eleven surviving plays of Aristophanes in particular.

Fornara, Charles W., ed. *Translated Documents of Greece and Rome*, 2d ed., vol. 1, *Archaic Times to the End of the Peloponnesian War* (Cambridge, 1983). A briefly annotated collection of inscriptions, documents, and historical sources.

Goldhill, Simon. *Reading Greek Tragedy* (Cambridge, 1986). An introduction to different approaches taken by modern critics in interpreting Greek tragedy.

Kagan, Donald. *The Outbreak of the Peloponnesian War, The Archidamian War, The Peace of Nicias and the Sicilian Expedition*, and *The Fall of the Athenian Empire* (Ithaca, N.Y., 1969, 1974, 1981, and 1987). A thorough examination of the ancient evidence for and modern opinion on the Peloponnesian War.

Henderson, Jeffrey. "The Demos and the Comic Competition," in J. Winkler and F. Zeitlin, eds. *Nothing to Do with Dionysus? Athenian Drama in Its Social Context* (Princeton, N.J., 1990), pp. 271–313. A discussion of the place of comedy in Athenian society.

Knox, Bernard, ed. *The Norton Book of Classical Literature* (New York, 1993). An anthology across the chronological range of Greek literature, with an extensive introduction to its special characteristics.

Kraut, Richard. *Socrates and the State* (Princeton, N.J., 1984). A critical examination of the reasons for the Platonic Socrates' refusal to escape in the Crito and his attitudes toward democracy.

McLeish, Kenneth. *The Theatre of Aristophanes* (London, 1980). An examination of how the comedies of Aristophanes might have worked on stage as humor and as social commentary.

Richter, G. M. A. *Portraits of the Greeks*, rev. R. R. R. Smith (Ithaca, N.Y., 1984). A collection of ancient portraits of Aristophanes, Socrates, Plato, Aristotle, Alexander, Hellenistic kings and queens, and many others.

Thucydides, *History of the Peloponnesian War*, trans. Richard Crawley (London, 1993). A reedition of Crawley's classic translation, with a new introduction by W. Robert Connor.

Woozley, A. D. *Law and Obedience: The Arguments of Plato's "Crito"* (Chapel Hill, N.C., 1979). A critical study that finds the Platonic Socrates' arguments in the *Crito* "interestingly bad."

Chapter Nine

Adcock, F. E. *The Greek and Macedonian Art of War* (Berkeley and Los Angeles, 1957). A classic introduction to the martial strategy and technology of this era.

Aristotle. *The Complete Works*, ed. Jonathan Barnes, 2 vols. (Princeton, N.J., 1984). A revised version of the Oxford translations.

Barnes, Jonathan. *Aristotle* (Oxford, 1982). A succinct but comprehensive introduction to the thought of Aristotle.

Borza, Eugene N. *In the Shadow of Olympus: The Emergence of Macedon* (Princeton, N.J., 1990). A survey of the history of Macedonia through the reign of King Philip II.

Bosworth, A. B. *Conquest and Empire: The Reign of Alexander the Great* (Cambridge, 1988). A comprehensive survey of the career of Alexander.

Connor, W. Robert, ed. *Greek Orations: Fourth Century* B.C. (Waveland Heights, Ill., 1987). A reissue of the 1966 translations of selected orations of Lysias, Isocrates, Demosthenes, Aeschines, and Hyperides, with introduction and brief annotations.

Gosling, J. C. B. *Plato* (London, 1973). An introductory discussion of some of Plato's central ideas.

Green, Peter. *Alexander of Macedon, 356–323* B.C.: *A Historical Biography* (Berkeley and Los Angeles, 1991). A reprint of Green's 1974 narrative history of the career of Alexander the Great.

Hamilton, J. R. *Alexander the Great* (Pittsburgh, 1973). A brief introduction to the Macedonian background and career of Alexander.

Hammond, N. G. L., and G. T. Griffith. *A History of Macedonia*, vol. 2, 550–336 B.C. (Oxford, 1979). A detailed scholarly survey through the reign of King Philip II.

Hansen, Mogens Herman. *The Athenian Democracy in the Age of Demosthenes* (Oxford, 1991). A detailed study of the institutions of fourth-century Athenian democracy.

Harding, Phillip, ed. *Translated Documents of Greece and Rome*, vol. 2, From the End of the Peloponnesian War to the Battle of Ipsus (Cambridge, 1985). A collection of translated documents and excerpts from primary sources covering the period 403–301 B.C.

Hornblower, Simon. *The Greek World, 479–323 B.C.*, rev. ed. (London, 1991). A survey covering the areas of the Mediterranean world in which Greek culture flourished in the fifth and fourth centuries.

Mossé, Claude. *Athens in Decline, 404–86 B.C.*, trans. J. Stewart (London, 1973). An interpretation of the loss of Athenian dominance in the Greek world.

Ober, Josiah. *Mass and Elite in Democratic Athens: Rhetoric, Ideology, and the Power of the People* (Princeton, N.J., 1989). An analysis of the dynamics of political and legal rhetoric in Athenian democracy.

Plato. *The Collected Dialogues, Including the Letters*, ed. Edith Hamilton and Huntington Cairns (Princeton, N.J., 1961). All the works of Plato translated by various hands.

Sinclair, R. K. *Democracy and Participation in Athens* (Cambridge, 1988). A study of the level of citizen participation covering the period c. 450–322 B.C.

Stone, I. F. *The Trial of Socrates* (Boston, 1988). An argument that Socrates rejected Athenian democracy.

Stoneman, Richard, trans. *The Greek Alexander Romance* (London, 1991). A translation with introduction of an influential and entertaining legendary history of Alexander.

———. *Legends of Alexander the Great* (London, 1994). A collection of fourteen translated medieval retellings of legends of Alexander.

Strauss, Barry S. *Athens after the Peloponnesian War: Class, Faction, and Policy, 403–386 B.C.* (Ithaca, N.Y., 1986). A treatment of the economic and political restoration of Athens after the devastation of the war.

Chapter Ten

Austin, M. M., ed. *The Hellenistic World from Alexander to the Roman Conquest: A Selection of Ancient Sources in Translation* (Cambridge, 1981). A collection of excerpts from documents, inscriptions, and literature, with introduction and annotation.

Burstein, Stanley M., ed. *Translated Documents of Greece and Rome*, vol. 3, The Hellenistic Age from the Battle of Ipsos to the Death of Kleopatra VII (Cambridge, 1985). A collection of excerpts from documents and inscriptions, with brief annotations.

Canfora, Luciano. *The Vanished Library: A Wonder of the Ancient World* (Berkeley and Los Angeles, 1989). A scholarly evocation of the history of the Ptolemaic library in Alexandria written as a mystery story.

Clayton, Peter and Martin Price. *The Seven Wonders of the Ancient World* (London, 1988). An illustrated introduction including a section on the lighthouse at Alexandria.

Cambridge Ancient History, 2d ed., vol. 7, part 1, *The Hellenistic World,* ed. F. W. Walbank et al. (Cambridge, 1984). A standard scholarly survey.

Grant, Michael. *From Alexander to Cleopatra: The Hellenistic World* (New York, 1982). An introductory survey of political and intellectual history.

Green, Peter. *Alexander to Actium: The Historical Evolution of the Hellenistic Age* (Berkeley and Los Angeles, 1990). A massive interpretative study of the entire Hellenistic period as a continuum.

Kuhrt, Amélie, and Susan Sherwin-White, eds. *Hellenism in the East: The Interaction of Greek and Non-Greek civilizations from Syria to Central Asia after Alexander* (Berkeley and Los Angeles, 1987). A collection of essays on Hellenistic subjects ranging from Seleucid Babylonia to the interaction of Greek and non-Greek art and architecture.

Lewis, Naphtali. *Greeks in Ptolemaic Egypt: Case Studies in the Social History of the Hellenistic World* (Oxford, 1986). A collection of vivid stories of everyday life from papyrus documents.

Long, A. A. *Hellenistic Philosophy: Stoics, Epicureans, Sceptics,* 2d ed. (Berkeley and Los Angeles, 1986). An analysis of these three major movements, with a brief treatment of later Hellenistic developments.

Martin, Luther. *Hellenistic Religions: An Introduction* (Oxford, 1987). A brief survey of the many religious traditions of the Greco-Roman and Near Eastern world from the fourth century B.C. to the fourth century A.D.

Nussbaum, Martha C. *The Fragility of Goodness: Luck and Ethics in Greek Tragedy and Philosophy* (Cambridge, 1986). An investigation of Greek views on the significance of events in life beyond human control.

Onians, John. *Art and Thought in the Hellenistic Age: The Greek World View, 350–50 B.C* (London, 1979). An illustrated survey of intellectual trends in the Hellenistic period and possible reflections of them in art.

Pollitt, J. J. *Art in the Hellenistic Age* (Cambridge, 1986). An illustrated, topically arranged interpretation of Hellenistic art.

Sherwin-White, Susan, and Amélie Kuhrt. *From Samarkand to Sardis: A New Approach to the Seleucid Empire* (Berkeley and Los Angeles, 1993). A treatment of the Seleucid kingdom seen as the heir of the Persian empire and as part of the Near Eastern world.

Tcherikover, Victor. *Hellenistic Civilization and the Jews* (New York, 1975). A classic work examining contacts between Jewish and Greek civilization.

Walbank, F. W. *The Hellenistic World* (Cambridge, Mass., 1993). A concise survey of the military, political, and cultural history of the Hellenistic period.

Index

slaves and slavery (*continued*)
  Age, 64–65; debts resulting in, 84–85;
  education of, 213; freed, 67, 75, 76; of
  Hellenistic kingdoms, 206; labor of, 66,
  75–77, 167, 168; opposition to, 184; and
  Peloponnesian War, 157, 159–160; population of, 66, 75, 168; religion and, 67, 76,
  127; sexual relations and, 66, 69, 139; of
  Sparta, 75–77, 79, 106, 109–110, 153. See also
  labor; mines; revolt
social differentiation: Dark Age, 39, 40–
  46; early agricultural, 12–13; and equality
  as concept, 53; of Hellenistic kingdoms,
  205–207; hunter-gatherer, 7; metallurgy
  and, 22–23. See also class; democracy;
  gender roles; social elite
social elite: achieving status as, 42–43;
  antidemocratic elements of, 109, 160,
  161, 162, 185; Dark Age, 42–46; gender-
  divided society of, 137–138, 139, 207; of
  Hellenistic period, 204–206, 207–209;
  labor, attitude toward, 66; Peloponnesian
  War, effect on, 163; playwrights as, 131;
  political cohesion weakened, 64, 82–84,
  87, 88; the poor, attitudes toward, 63, 66;
  and upward mobility, 60; wealth, necessity of, 42, 46, 60; women of, 45, 67,
  125, 137–138, 139, 163, 207. See also public
  works; values; wealth
social structure: Bronze Age, 22–23; Dark
  Age, 39, 42–50; early agricultural, 10–
  13, 19–20, 23; of Hellenistic kingdoms,
  205–209; hunter-gatherer, 6–9, 20; Indo-
  European, 19; Macedonian, 188–189;
  Minoan, 24–26; Persian, 97; Spartan,
  75–79, 105, 106; undesirables, disposing
  of, 58. See also Athens; city-states; marriage; patriarchy; politics; punishment;
  religion; women
Socrates, 168–173; economic advice to
  friend, 166–167; Plato and, 169, 171, 172,
  177, 178, 181; trial of, 166, 171–173
Solon, 84–86, 90, 126, 130
sophists, 141–142, 143–145; Isocrates and,
  186; and Plato, 179; and Socrates, 169, 170,
  173
Sophocles, 131–133, 134

soul: Aristotle on, 184; denial of, 212; Plato
  on, 179–180
Spain, 55–56
Sparta: Athena as protector deity of, 52;
  colonization by, 58; aggression in fourth
  century, 175–177; geographical influences
  on, 71; military of, see Spartan military;
  and Persian Wars, 99–100, 103–104, 105–
  106; political form of, 73–74; sexual
  policies of, 69, 79; slavery of helots in, 73,
  75–77, 106, 109–110, 153; social structure,
  69, 75–79, 105, 106, 136; unification of, 71–
  73; women of, 68, 78–79, 136, 156. See also
  Athens/Sparta relations; Peloponnesian
  League
Spartan military: organization of, 73–74,
  75–77; in Peloponnesian War, 152–153,
  155–156, 159–160, 161–162, 164, 167; in
  Persian Wars, 103–104, 105–106
speech, persuasive. See rationalism; rhetoric
Sphacteria, 155
sports: as competitive value, 46–47; marathons, origin of, 101; music praising, 89;
  women and, 46, 47, 68, 78
Statue of Liberty, 212
status. See social differentiation
stoas, 117, 214
Stoics, 213, 214–215
Stone Age, 4–15
Stonehenge, 14
subjectivism, 142
successor kings, 199
sussition, 78
symposium, 140–141, 169
synoecism, 71–73, 82
Syracuse, 80, 103, 158, 159
Syria, 199, 202

Tanagra, battle of, 114
taxes: and Alexander's conquests, 194;
  city-states and, 85, 86, 117, 167, 190; of
  Hellenistic kingdoms, 190, 203–205
technology: diffusion vs. local innovation
  of, 13–15; Near East influence on, 13–15,
  23, 37, 40, 43
Tecmessa, 132
teleological view of nature, 183–184